D1556554

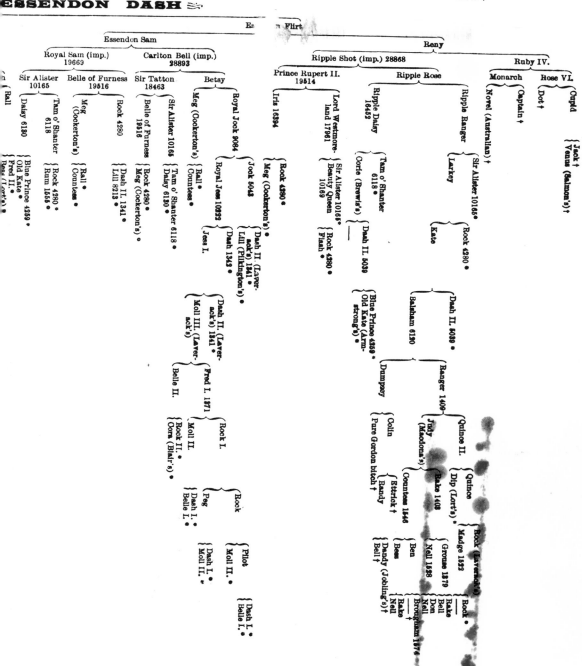

THE TRUTH
ABOUT
SPORTING DOGS

"It's been a great day!"—Photo study of Labrador Retrievers
by *Dr. Marlowe Dittebrandt,* Portland, Oregon.

The 18th century Newfoundlands as reproduced in Sydenham Edwards' classic, *Cynographia Brittanica*, London, 1800. The original presentation in color clearly depicts that the transAtlantic breed as introduced to England strongly possessed the yellow factor. Undoubtedly as black became fashionable, the yellow became masked, cropping up occasionally as a recessive, even after dog folk had forgotten that Newfoundlands could also carry yellow. Also to note is the curl in the coat. The cut ear of the standing dog is to the exact pattern of the ears of the boar-and-bear fighting hounds of medieval European tapestries, and may represent French fashion carried over to the New World.

THE TRUTH ABOUT SPORTING DOGS

by
C. BEDE MAXWELL

PELHAM BOOKS

HERTFORDSHIRE
COUNTY LIBRARY

636.452

6005015

First published in Great Britain by
Pelham Books Ltd
52 Bedford Square
London, W.C.1
1972

© 1972 by Howell Book House Inc.

All Rights Reserved. No part of this publication may be reproduced,
stored in a retrieval system, or transmitted, in any form or by any
means, electronic, mechanical, photocopying, recording or otherwise,
without the prior permission of the Copyright owner.

7207 0500 2

Printed in Great Britain by
Fletcher & Son Ltd, Norwich
and bound by Richard Clay (The Chaucer Press) Ltd.,
Bungay, Suffolk

To the memory of
Frank A. Longmore,
my good friend
and tireless instructor in
the important fundamentals of dog construction.

The Gallery at a Derby in Austria, 1968.—*C. Bede Maxwell.*

Contents

On the inside cover:

This fantastically-extended pedigree is from *The Dog in Australasia,* a large tome published in 1897 by George Robertson and Co., Australia. The author, Walter Beilby, provided pedigrees of this kind in respect of many breeds in and out of the Sporting Group. Those familiar with Setter historical names and associations will readily identify the three varieties. Laverack documentation carries back to the basics, Ponto and Old Moll. There are interweavings of Gordons, of the Irish of Mr. McDona, and about the middle of the page will be found the famous "Flame" that founded Mallwyd English Setters, and brought there the red that has survived right down the line of this famous strain, and doubtless influences the very red ones we may still occasionally find in English. The dam of Flam was Llewellin's famous show Irish Setter, Carrie, but her parents Prince and Cora were Laveracks brought in by Llewellin, and one notices that Prince's pedigree is non-existent. Too much to analyze here, but for a student the weldings are of a tremendous fascination. My publisher, Mr. Elsworth Howell, agrees with me that this compilation, likely alone of its kind in the world, should be preserved in a modern work.—*Republished by permission, Angus & Robertson, Ltd., Sydney, Australia.*

Introduction

A LONG time ago Mrs. Bede Maxwell and I agreed that a scrap of dog lore was not necessarily true because it had appeared in print ten times as we both realized that many dog authors, particularly in the past, had plagiarized each other's works. There are cases of representatives of several different breeds claiming the same ancient picture as proof of the long existence of their breeds. Dog history really began with the formation of the Kennel Club in 1873, and of developments prior to that there is little certainty. The few authors who have done original research have provided the basis of the true history of dogs and I have the greatest respect for them.

Mrs. Bede Maxwell has taken her place among the few. The result of her labors in the British Museum and at the Kennel Club alone will place this book among the classics of dog lore. No possible source of information has been neglected and I feel some personal satisfaction in the small contribution I made in guiding the author through the maze of the Kennel Club's archives. The result is a standard work on the Gundog.

—C. A. BINNEY

(Mr. Binney, former secretary of The Kennel Club, England, died in 1971. The author is honored to have had this testament for her manuscript from so honored a figure of dogdom.)

Wirehaired Pointing Griffon, Snow Bird Vantage Home ("Maudie"). Her leaps take her from high banks 20 feet out! Owner, Mike Nelson, Montana.—*Photo, Tomie La Fon.*

Foreword

IT is with humility as well as pride that I present *The Truth About Sporting Dogs* by C. Bede Maxwell.

My humility comes in the realization that it was good fortune that placed the author in my path nearly twenty years ago. Mrs. Maxwell is a person with tremendous talent and stupendous drive. She is a dedicated and masterful researcher, as an earlier work of hers, *The New German Shorthaired Pointer,* amply attests. She dares to question the statements of earlier writers on dogs and she digs deeply for the truth, often with such success as to destroy the errors committed by other scholars and to give consternation to those who treasure these errors as pet shibboleths.

At risk of being deemed sentimental, I attribute the excellence of Mrs. Maxwell as a scholar and author to love, her love of *all* Sporting dogs—each and every breed in the Group. I once watched her judge over 300 Sporting dogs at a show in Maidstone, Kent, England. With characteristic verve, she judged from 11 A.M. to 8 P.M., completing the assignment within the remarkable span of only nine hours. What's more, she was as fresh and enthusiastic after the event as when she had started, and recounted the reasons for her decisions in the same thorough detail with which she composes her texts.

My pride comes in the recognition of the great contribution to the lore of the sporting dog world that this book constitutes. To a full, enriched lifetime of study as a fancier, breeder and judge, "Maxie"—as her friends know her—added a crash post-graduate course of more than a year in the United Kingdom and Europe to earn her "doctorate in dog knowledge." Hundreds of hours of research yielded fascinating rewards in that vast repository of art, artifacts and literature known as the British Museum. In her trusty minicar she drove herself far and wide throughout the British Isles and over European lands to search for the past and present facts one can acquire only through personal, physical contact at the source.

You will find the harvest of her search in the sprightly, sometimes shocking, but always stirring pages of *The Truth About Sporting Dogs.* You will read material and see pictures that probably never before have been placed in the light of public view on such a scale. "Maxie" is an educational experience for any dog fancier. She has increased my knowledge of dogs immensely, and I think she will increase yours, too, as you read this book.

—ELSWORTH S. HOWELL
Publisher

Preface

UNDENIABLY, the facts of dog-breed origin are for the most part swamped in the flood wave of Time. Searchers may only guess at what lies beyond the brief evidence Literature and Art afford. All else is legend, conjecture, piecings-together, as in building dinosaur skeletons from second-toe joints.

"No certain account of dogs in Great Britain can be traced further than back to the reign of Elizabeth . . . Caius counted 16 breeds, or rather varieties of dogs, for all the different breeds, it is to be imagined, are merely varieties from one original stock . . . Old breeds become extinct, new are formed by fashion and caprice."—*Cynographia Britannica,* 1800.

"The innumerable varieties of dogs now seen in Great Britain as well as in France, Germany, Holland, are due to the great intercourse of foreigners from all parts of the world. Various intercourses and consequent mixtures were crossed in endless ramifications."—*Biographical Sketches and Authentic Anecdotes of Dogs,* 1829.

Such distinguished authors, centuries closer in time than are we to the formative periods of breeds modernly recognized, would have told more if they had known more. Translations preserve classic dog descriptions from ancient Greece and Rome. Mosaics from Carthage and vases from Athens depict dogs working and fighting. Corinth's Museum of antiquities includes many dog figurines, ancient thank-offerings to the gods for cures of physical ills. These foreshadow breeds we now recognize. The Devonshire Tapestries present 15th century hunting dogs in a glitter of color and pageantry. Credulous, pedantic old Caius listened to yarn-spinners and set down what he heard.

Turberville, the Elizabethan diplomat, questioned "Pylottes and Mariners home from Farre Countries." Gervase Markham, my love, my delight, set down the manner of training a 17th century Setting Spaniel. From such we pick up bright threads to weave into a fabric that may never become whole.

This present work could not have gone forward without the practical help of many. For the most part, credit is given spontaneously in the text. Special thanks must however be given to the directorate of the British Museum. The pleasant North Library, the room where special rarities may be inspected, and blessed with most pleasant attendants, became as my second home in London. The Museum photographic department worked miracles with ancient illustrations. Credit goes also to the British taxpayers who picked up the tab of Dutch restorers who spent years to revive the 500-year old Devonshire Tapestries, and to the directorate of the Victoria & Albert Museum that so suitably houses and displays these treasures.

Mr. C. A. Binney, at that time secretary of the Kennel Club (England) was patient in coping with questions, generous in providing access to Kennel Club records, catalogs, documentations, and developed further the generous habit of unearthing unexpected goodies and inviting me to come to see these. He became a friend.

So, too, did Dennis McCarthy, of Nottingham, so fired with rich enthusiasm, and so knowing of things to see in dog-interest in England—things I would not otherwise have known existed. In a spirit of good-humored, kind companionship he took me to see such, including that fantastic collection of historically important dogs, preserved as from the late 19th century in the storage basement of the British Natural History Museum at Tring, outside London.

Memberships of breed clubs sponsoring the rarer British Spaniels that are poorly represented in the United States were generous in teaching me Fields, Clumbers, Sussex, Welsh Springers. Later in my year-long stay, they supported me with entries to judge. In this bracketing I am indebted to Dr. Esther Rickards, OBE; to Mr. R. E. Hood, of the Welsh Springer Spaniel Club; to Mrs. Manley-Cooper and Mr. E. J. Orton, of the Sussex Spaniel Club; to Mrs. A. M. Jones, MBE, and her family in respect of the Field Spaniel interest. Mr. & Mrs. B. Stanley delved patiently for me in Clumbers.

The most difficult British breed to contact in the Club sense was the Flat-coated Retriever, but here the lack was eventually made good by the interest of Mr. and Mrs. D. Izzard who extended the necessary and friendly help.

In the United States, assistance was extensive, and in photographs built up to an embarrassment of riches. Special thanks first to my publisher, Mr. Elsworth S. Howell, who proposed originally that such a book be compiled and personally edited the first draft, as well as supplying the shoulder to cry upon when the going became rough. This has not been an easy book to write.

xiv

Special thanks, too, to the American Kennel Club for their cooperation toward solving the jigsaw.

My indebtedness to Richard S. Johns, of Benton, Pennsylvania, is large. Dick is a mine of information for field trial and hunting lore, especially of dead-and-gone Llewellin Setters and, of course, his Shorthairs. He permitted me to browse through his library, and even to borrow many of his treasures for the extensive periods necessary. Additionally, he tramped out with me day after day, taking different breeds of dogs in training and showing me their versatile work. It was antidote for the despair that one feels in considering the ruin continually imposed by those who have always and historically run sporting breed strains down as water into sand. Dick showed me, as the Europeans had been showing me, that his dogs do actually hunt as well as run.

In Europe, where recurrent, profitable months were happily spent, the roll call of thanks centers mainly around those in the Shorthair interest. First, posthumously, to my much loved and dearly missed friend, Frau Maria Seydel. Thanks, too, to Dr. Julius Duy of Austria, and importantly, the Kurzhaar Klub breed-master and vice-president, Herr Richard Kölbl.

A fitting conclusion may be in terms of a quote from Mrs. Marcia Schlehr's excellent monograph on the Golden Retriever, an American publication: "Most sporting dog books are either single-breed books, or are written from the basic 'huntin' dog' approach, omitting all of the aspects of the sporting dog outside the simple one of plain field work . . . It should be possible to do better." (1969)

That, as a matter of fact, has been the aim toward which my efforts have been directed.

—C. BEDE MAXWELL

The Setting Spaniel of Europe, working with the Falcon. From the Devonshire Hunting Tapestry in the Victoria & Albert Museum, London, England, *circa 1400s A.D.* Woven at Turnai. Setter shape is clearly identifiable, as is the "leaf-shaped" ear that spaniels with French and/or Celtic associations carried on into our own time. The muzzle so lightly tapered, the stop so modest, the coat pattern and the feathering all provide interest for the historians.—*C. Bede Maxwell.*

The Spaniels

"Of Spanels first I meane to speake, for they begin the glee,
Who being once uncoupled, when they feel their collars free,
In roystering wise about they range, with cheerful chappes to ground,
To see wherein the champaign may some lurking Fowle be found.
A sport to see them stir their Sternes in hunting to and fro,
And to behold how Nature doth their power in Spanels show,
Who course the fields with wondrous skill, and deal in cunning fort
As though indeed they had conspired to make their master sport;
What merrier music can you crave, what note but half so good,
As when the Spanels crosse the Ronne of Feasants in the Wood?
Or light upon the little Poutes where they have lately been?
Assuredly no better glee is either heard or seane."

GEORGE TURBERVILLE:
The Noble Art of Venerie or Hunting, London, 1575.

IN the beginning was the Spaniel. He appears always to have been—changing shape, size, or color, hunting with voice or hunting mute as fashion seemed to require, but always in a manner become traditional, and always merry. We know he was, from ancient times, valued. We know how he was used. We know also, by available documentation from British archives, that by channels of diplomacy he moved between countries and courts, as gifts between Kings and Princes, Lords and Ladies. Those same archives establish that Elizabethan-age Spaniels moved from England into Spain, which was then the premier world power. No one seems as yet to have provided any record of Spaniels brought into England from Spain.

1

The archives preserve records of swapping British dogs for Spanish horses, and more British dogs in return for favors from the French courts. Thus, the British Ambassador, writing from Aragon, Spain, informs Robert Dudley, Earl of Leicester, Queen Elizabeth's Master of Horse, that "something better might come of the request for the horse if the Spanish were offered some British Dogges " (Ref. *H. M. Correspondence,* Pepys). The French Ambassador wrote (again to Dudley) that "he was glad to know of Lord Robert's affection for the King and the Queen Mother of France, and would tell them of your wish to give them a Spaniel, a Mastiff, some Cobs, and I thank you for those you sent me" (Ref. *Throckmorton Correspondence, H. M. Correspondence,* Pepys).

Perhaps too much has been made in the past of references cribbed from Caius and de Foix, seeming to support Spanish origin, though both writers qualify their references. Thus Caius: "Plenty of the same sort were engendered (also) in England . . . the common sort of people call them by one general word, namely Spaniells, as though these kind of Dogges came originally and first of all out of Spain." That "engendering" was an ancient thing in Britain is established in the work of the writer Oppian (*Cynegeticus* 3rd century, A.D.) who recorded that the Roman legions invading Britain found there "an excellent kind of scenting dog, small, worthy of attention, fed by the fierce nation of painted Britons. They are crooked, lean, coarse-haired, heavy-eyed, armed with powerful claws, deadly teeth, and a good nose." A third century writer, Strabo, provides a reference to a traffic in "clever hunting dogs out of Britain to Europe" (Ref. Richmond, *Roman Britain, The Pelican History of England,* Penguin, 1966, p. 12).

De Foix, who held Spaniels "noisy and troublesome, with many bad qualities like the country they come from," also qualifies his statement that Spaniels came from Spain: "notwithstanding that there are many in other countries." He thought a Spaniel was "good for a man that hath a noble Goshawk or Tiercel or a Sparrowhawk for Partridge . . . also when they are taught to be *Couchers* (Setters) they be good to take Partridges and Quail with the Net (and) they be good when they are taught to swim and be good in the river, and for Fowle when they have dived." This mention of work as a *Coucher* verifies the opinion of Edward Laverack who, centuries later, described his Setter as "merely an improved Spaniel."

The Devonshire Tapestries woven in Tournai (Flanders) in the 1400s (a century after de Foix), in the spread that is the most beautiful of the four—"Falconry," preserve the representation of the Setting Spaniel working for the falconer. The quarry flying high is duck. What is this Spaniel but a recognizable little Setter, shape, make and feathering, apart from a hound head and ears lacking feather. The frontispiece of the Turberville book (1575) also depicts a falconer using a brace with like body qualities and

2

feather, but with heads that had by then become remarkably like a Brittany Spaniel's, light-muzzled and with high short ears.

Clearly, the Spaniel of medieval times was not a specialist, as de Foix establishes with his resume of their abilities which includes waterwork. However, land or water, their principal employment was originally with the falconers. Turberville, who translated much from earlier French and Italian works which may long since have crumbled to dust, quotes Master Francesco Sforzino Vicentino, Gentleman Falconer of Italy:

> How necessary a thing is a Spanel to the Falconer, and for those that use that pastime, keeping Hawkes for their Pleasure and Recreation. No Man doeth so well to spring and retrieve for a Fowle being flown to the Marke, as also divers other Wayes to assiste and ayde Falcons and Goshawks . . . Without Spanels the Sporte would be but cold, and the Toyle far more than is good for the Man. For a good Spanel is a great Jewel, and a good Spanel maketh a good Hawke.

Vincentino's advice includes direction to "breed them first and then (to) make them goode," and to:

> . . . cutte off a little of the Spanel's Tayle when it is a Whelpe. By doing so you shall deliver him so that no Kynde of Wound or other Mischief shall greatly offend that part of your Spanel. The benefit of it besides, the Dogge becomes more beautiful by cutting the tip of his Sterne for it will bush out gallantly.

Such "gallant bushing-out" became fashionable in Europe, but it is interesting to see that the earlier-age Spaniel in the Devonshire Tapestry has a full and feathered tail such as a modern Setter would carry. The Dutch genre paintings carry the bushed-tip fashion forward, as do the Louis XIV of France dogs in the famous paintings in the Louvre in which the bushings-out have been groomed to look like lion tufts.

Cutting Spaniel tails, then, is as ancient an institution as trimming Water-Dogges' coats to patterns such as modern Poodles still carry. So—what else is new in dogges? Well, perhaps veterinary science. Master Vicentino diagnoses strange maladies and proposes cures: ". . . the Humour (that) droppeth down from their Braynes, so that their Throats and Neckes do swell unreasonably" for which he advises dosing with "Oyle of Camomil for the distillation of these ill Humours (to make them) fall from out your Spanel's head," is but one.

Most medieval art and tapestry depict hunting dogs as white, but here and there one occasionally glimpses color. Then we have, of course, the Turberville division of French hunting dogs by color. Caius, writing at about the same time as Turberville, wrote of British Spaniels that "for the most part their Skynnes are white, and if they be marked with any Spottes they are commonly Red, and somewhat great withal." Sizeable red-and-white patching remains modernly the endowment of the Welsh Springer Spaniel, a dog of ancient Celtic associations. "Othersome of them (Spaniels) be Reddishe and Blackishe," Caius continued, "but of that Sort there be but few." Separately, he describes the novelty "newe come from France," a Spaniel with black-and-white stitched hairs that gave the effect of "marble-blewe."

Variation of Spaniel size, ranging as from the Alpine Spaniel (now St. Bernard) to the "small Comforter Dogges" of the sort Caius scorned: "such as lick their Lady's Lippes when travelling with them in their Wagons," has always been considerable. As to the "Lippe-licking," in this our own time my thought is always, seeing such, to wonder what the dog may have been licking immediately before giving attention to his Lady. "Comforter Dogges" were of course the Toys, which reminds me that a modern American hunting-breed book includes a bracketing of the Caius-Comforters with Sussex and Field Spaniels in modern descent. My vision conjured is of my substantial-sized friend, "Charles" (Eng. Show Ch. Chesara Chervil of Sedora), the Sussex Spaniel who has been Best of Breed at Crufts three of the last four years. Never mind hefty size, Sussex Spaniels are of such composure in the main that one quails at the thought of one involved in any "lippe-licking." The particular dignity of "Charles" is such that he even refrains from paying customary doggy respects to trees when out strolling with his humans.

Sussex and Field Spaniels may owe to the "reddishe and blackishe" that Caius described as comparatively rare. The golden liver of the Sussex is unique to the breed and in our time, as in the time of Caius, these are "but few."

Frankly, we will never unravel the background of the various Spaniel breeds. It is folly to think in terms of purebreds. Dog breeding until modern times was always a casual thing, and the dog always a sexual adventurer. A great lady of my acquaintance, Dame Mary Gilmore, D.B.E., once remarked that the dog, having lived untold time so close to man, shared many of man's vices. My favorite dog writer, Gervase Markham (*Hunger's Prevention or the Whole Art of Fowling*, London, 1621) explodes all basis for belief in purebreedings:

> It is reasonable that people should cross Land Spaniels and Water Spaniels, and the Mungrells between these, and the Mungrells of either with the Shallow-Flewed Hound, the Tumbler, the Lurcher, and the small bastard Mastiff . . . all of which are yet inferior to the truebred Land Spaniel—if one could still find one of those.

The reference to the Shallow-Flewed Hound is one that historians might examine. Markham names it a breed. Maybe the characteristic flews, neat

Ch. Rockatello (1927)

Ch. Lucknow Creme de la Creme (1927)

Ch. Obo Fascinator (1927)

English Cocker, Ch. Lymas Master Key

Ch. Nonquitt Notable (BIS, 1940s)

Ch. Biggs Believe It or Not (1960s)

Montage of modern breed development of the Cocker Spaniel as documented by pictures of AKC champions from 1927 on. From such as the champion in 1927, much resembling Sussex Spaniel outline, to the highly individual outline of a magnificent show specimen of the 1960s, the change was not merely in terms of the spectacular but also was achieved with surprising speed.

and tidy, of the Irish Setter and the Welsh Springer Spaniel (especially) owe to some such forgotten influence of centuries past.

Probably no dog-writer has been quoted more than Markham, but only in respect of a paragraph or two that earlier (19th century) writers had already used. There seems no evidence to suggest that those reusing these same paragraphs have read the complete work. It is within my view a most fascinating book, more than meriting a full modern reprint. My access has been to the copy in the British Museum.

If early British writers had so much to say of British Spaniels, how come the belief that all such originated in Spain? Might it be that when Spain was a premier nation in the world, all wealth, all crafts and accomplishments, even all extant breeds of hunting dogs, were attracted to there, just as such various goodies are in our time attracted to America? Maybe, breeds engendered in other countries passed through Spanish ownerships as, in the 19th century, British sporting breeds of various kinds were passed, country to country, through Europe. Thus, Gordon Setters from the famous kennels of Prinz zu Solms-Brauenfels went from Germany to Scandinavia—but even if such were actually bred in Germany, they were by no more than courtesy *German* dogs. As a breed they were British! With Spanish art and documentation so unhelpful, we may be long in countering the tenaciously-held belief that the sporting breeds, Spaniels and Pointers especially, originated in the Iberian land.

The Germans have their Spaniel-type, their brown Wachtelhund, rich in voice—a characteristic that the British do not value, preferring their Spaniels to hunt mute. The French have long sponsored not only the light-muzzled *Epagneul Bretagne* (the Brittany Spaniel) but also a heavier *Epagneul Francais* (French Spaniel). As seen in European shows in 1967/68, this one appeared to me easiest described as a scaled-down St. Bernard. Which makes sense enough, in that the Saint was originally classified as a Spaniel, and that modern opinion believes all drop-eared breeds in the Sporting Group are most heavily indebted to Mastiff origin (Ref. *Fiennes*, 1970).

Way out, in Spaniel classification, is the Irish Water. By all reasonable assessment he belongs with the retrieving breeds, but of course no one visualizes any change in his classification. Nothing is more static than the filing and compartmentalization of modern dog breeds.

Spaniel classification, for that matter, always had been a mess . . . an unholy mess! From the first, the governing interests for promotion of dog shows grappled with the intricacies of Spaniel classification. The Spaniel in all his varied types and sizes has been as a river flowing, seeming constant but ever changing.

Earliest classification fell back despairingly on weight and color. Thus a Land Spaniel over a certain weight was a Field. Under, he was a Cocker.

Many the Cocker pup that in maturity had to be named a Field. The Sussex Spaniel was one of the first—followed by the Irish Water and the Clumber— to be given separate classes at early dog shows. The organizers felt secure with these, all so individual. Thus the Sussex could be identified by his golden liver coat, and if he was unlucky enough to be marked with white the judges just threw him out. Clumbers, white, were always recognized as carrying some form of yellow, light or dark. There were Norfolks, since probably absorbed into the modern English Springer Spaniel. There was no separate recognition of an English Springer Spaniel breed until the turn of the present century when it was split off, by type, from the Welsh. Toy Spaniels, of which there were several, classified principally by color patterning and head type, were something else again, and eventually became classified, as was proper, in the Toy Group. The American Cocker Spaniel, latest come of all, is essentially a 20th century product, with surprisingly few years of confirmed type safely behind him.

The Lillian Cheviot painting of 1907 usefully illustrates Field Spaniel type and presentation. The body proportioning, distinct from that of all other Spaniel breeds, the color range that includes roans, and the proper disposition of head and tail when displaying the dog for show, are all in conformity with the accepted Standards, British and American.

The Field Spaniel

THOUGH his shape and size was subject to happenstance and fashion down the centuries, the Field Spaniel is likeliest the true basic for all our modern work Spaniels. He was the jack-of-all-trades Spaniel, the very embodiment of true Spaniel working characteristics. Yet he was not a setting, but a flushing Spaniel, and remained so down the years. At any reasonable guess he is the heir to the British—as opposed to the French (European) — type of Spaniel, sturdy, compact, likely for long quite small, and always a font of useful energy. His influence was imposed on most working Spaniels and, of course, the historical spin-off was the Cocking, or Cocker Spaniel, built up from those of the Fields that tended to the diminutive. We have already noted that in the dog show classifications of the mid-19th century the rule of thumb that divided Field and Cocker Spaniels was pressured in terms of weight, and that a Cocker of this year could be a Field of next. Originally, plenty of Field Spaniels came to America. Quite possibly these imports and their produce escaped the pressure of the hideous 19th century British fashion imposed by the show fanciers. They turned a useful, sensibly-proportioned working Spaniel into a laughable caricature that was useless to boot. As the 19th century Spaniel in America was a dog much used, one cannot see anyone burdening himself with a lumbering cumbersome non-sense, any more than one could see anyone burdening himself within the sphere of practical use with a Spaniel coated as the American Cocker's sponsors modernly present it.

There exist no lack of pictures to remind us of the lengths to which un-checked fanciers' preoccupations can take them in exaggerated breedings to the fashions of the moment. Thus, the Field Spaniel that resulted from the examples bred by Phineas Bullock in England threatened for a time to influence Spaniel type in all British breeds. Undoubtedly, all that saved the day was eventual recognition of the uselessness of such a dog—short on leg, senselessly long in body, and so heavy and awkward as to be hindered in movement. But in the course of that sensible recognition, the Field Spaniel became so irrevocably damned as to virtually disappear as a breed. It was decades before the remnants that survived in shape of a more practical dog appeared before the public to any extent.

What first turned them in the right direction was probably the common sense of the buying public that had no interest in fanciers' points and didn't admire the caricatures. Within the next few decades, and well into the 20th century, the Field Spaniel interests struggled and in part succeeded in turning their breed back to the Spaniel it best deserved to be. The Bullock type was eliminated. The Field became plain Spaniel, no exaggerations, with legs that served functionally, sparse utility jacketing that was yet very attractive, and heads that have been described even as noble. The nobility is most reasonably to be found in terms of good construction, balance, and the grace of expression.

However, the sad part is that even when the mending had been achieved, and the Field Spaniel became again the dog that he could best be, his popularity remained virtually at zero. In the earliest decades of the present century, the breed was to be found almost entirely in the hands of owners uninterested in competition, field trial or show. The public had turned to other loves; the Cocker had become king in the world of the Spaniels. But the Field Spaniel's intrinsic worth did not escape the eyes of the real dog men. By 1923, in the English periodical, *Our Dogs,* the then famous Theo Marples wrote of the Field that "it is a most beautiful example of the Spaniel family, whose architecture, head (beaming with intelligence) substance, coat and contour, all spell UTILITY."

With sparse numerical support the breed weathered the two World War periods only by the skin of its teeth. Here and there an owner held onto his stock of one or two Spaniels, gracefully aging. By the 1950s, when the Field Spaniel had fallen so low numerically as to be denied even the chance to make champions, the Kennel Club having withdrawn the privilege of competing for Challenge Certificates, the breeding stock was virtually non-existent. How narrowed the breed base had become was no secret. Mr. G. R. Escott Cox, of Birmingham then had two males available for stud, Ronanyne Royalist, whelped 1957, and his son, Ronanyne Regal, whelped 1962. These can with truth be regarded as the male font of modern Field Spaniel restoration in Britain. In Staffordshire, Mrs. A. J. Everton, breed club secretary, helped to stave off extinction with her Ridware contribution.

In Malvern, Worcs., Mrs. A. M. Jones, M.B.E., drew her husband and son Roger into the interest to breed Field Spaniels. She owns a most usefully prepotent bitch in Elmbury Morwena of Rhiwlas, whelped 1962. Give or take an odd one here and there in the land, these were the basis of a restoration of the breed that was so successful that in 1969 the Kennel Club restored the privilege of Challenge Certificates.

Morwena's litter by Ridware Emperor, he by Ronanyne Regal, provided the first Field Spaniels to be introduced to the United States in quite sometime. Three imports of this breeding were the first Fields registered by the American Kennel Club for many years. When they appeared in the rings— one in the East, two in the Midwest—many American judges saw Fields in the flesh for the first time. However, a considerable hindrance to the enthusiasm for ownership was that British breeders could not promise anything for mating that was not over-close. Mrs. Jones discussed this with me in England. At the Birmingham Championship show of 1967 she took me along the benching where, on the day, every Field Spaniel alive in Britain with the exception of a couple of very old ones, was on show. It did not need two men's hands to count them, and blood relationships were closely banded.

Field color modernly is in terms of solids; blacks, and a warm rich liver described as mahogany, predominate. This liver, by the way, is of a slightly crimson cast, and different to that carried by any other breed of dog known to me. In an issue of *The Field,* England, October 1965, Frank Warner Hill, so well-qualified to express opinions in respect of all Sporting breeds, wrote: "Between the wars we still had a multiplicity of color in Field Spaniels, but during WWII something happened. When they reappeared on the show bench they were practically all self-colored."

The explanation may well be in terms of the reduction of stock.

The Field Spaniel Society advises that this should be "a self-colored dog, viz., a black (as it was originally some 60 years ago) or a 'sport' from black, i.e., liver, golden-liver, mahogany-red, roans, or any of these colors with tan over the eyes, on the cheeks, feet, pasterns. Other color, such as black and white, red or orange and white, etc., while not disqualifying a dog (provided the architecture is right) , will not be considered desirable, since the aim of the Society is to make a clear distinction between the Field and Springer Spaniel."

At Birmingham benching of 1967, and also at the subsequent Crufts' competition, there appeared only one blue-roan, appropriately named Roana. She is from the same breeding as the American imports, and as these will of necessity be in turn closely-inbred, the same color may again crop up in litters here. The American Standard as approved defines color as above, but it may as well be noted that "roan" can, and reasonably may, include blue roan.

The judges will not go far wrong if they regard the Field as "basic Spaniel," and shy from exaggerations. The 1959-approved American Kennel Club Standard asks for *"a body of moderate length, well-ribbed up to a good strong loin, straight or slightly-arched, never slack."* The "never slack" represents revulsion from the hammock-slung backlines of the 19th century caricatures.

For those judges who read pictures rather than text of Standards, one warns against accepting the photograph in the 1968-revised edition of *The Complete Dog Book*, the official publication of the American Kennel Club. This is a very misleading pose of what is intrinsically a very good dog that is well-known to me, and a member of the family above-referred, one of those first three exports to the United States. First, a Field Spaniel is not properly subject to being stretched out like a lizard. His correct outline presupposes a muzzle pointed down, not up. Such positioning is completely foreign to any breed of British Spaniel, as the other breeds pictured on the same (101) and facing page serve to demonstrate. Additionally, he is presented with a tail high-pegged and bare as a bone, hideously ugly and wholly out of breed character and requirement. And as if this wasn't bad enough, this dog in the flesh does not have such a characteristic. The pegged, bare tail has blatantly been painted on by retouching. One may only suppose that the photographer thought the dog looked better that way.

The approved Standard for the Field Spaniel reads in respect to Stern: *"Well set on and carried low, if possible below the level of the back, and in action always kept low, nicely fringed with wavy feather of a silky texture."* There is no legitimate excuse for what amounts to serious misdirection, particularly unfortunate when one reflects how reading, as such, has gone out of fashion and how picture-oriented our times have become.

Granted, we are *only* talking of tail-carriage here. A somewhat ruffled judge once told me that if he had to go to the tail of a dog to find something wrong with it, he sure wasn't going to bother about that! My view is that neither the judge, the photographer-retoucher, nor even the editorial staff of the official publication enjoys the privilege of deciding which parts of a Standard are to be honored, and which neglected. In Spaniel breeds—all of them!—tail and its carriage are fundamental characteristics. Historically, a Spaniel carries his tail below or, at highest, in line with his back, and he wags it! A pegged tail, oftenest, is not a wagging tail and conveys an erroneous impression in terms of character as well as type. To the best of my knowledge, only the parent English Springer Spaniel club of America has challenged the judges in terms of this issue, sending a letter to every judge licensed for their breed in which, among other directives, is included the reminder that a Spaniel tail be NOT pegged!

The Field Spaniel will never make a field trial star. Ancient type or modern representation, he is a worker rather than a performer. He does not have, and unless subject to some drastic out-crossing never will have, the flash and speed of trial-bred Spaniels in America or elsewhere. So, he will likely never become subject to the risks implicit in adoption by purely field trial sponsorship. Currently, the main concern of breeders is to keep the Field alive as a breed. If they can succeed in doing that, his ancient virtues, still shackled to the blood and bone of him, will make new friends to support him as the years roll by.

Field Spaniels, Elmbury Morwenne of Rhiwlas (wh. 1962) and her daughter, Sh. Ch. Mittina Ridware Samantha (1966). Samantha earned her Sh. Ch. title soon after the restoration of Challenge Certificate privileges to this still numerically-small breed. Owner, Mrs. A. M. Jones, MBE, Malvern, England.—*C. Bede Maxwell.*

Sussex Spaniels, from a painting by Cheviot, 1904.

The classic Sussex Spaniel type—long, low, with characteristic head properties and the gravely sensible countenance, the heavy fleshy tail, the solid unbroken color which so bravely, for more than two centuries, has defied loss to cross-breeding.

The question continually presents itself to my mind: had the so-fashionable 19th century Sussex, or some earlier unidentified basic that formed the Sussex, any part in the formation of the mysterious "Tweed Spaniel" that in association with the yellow Flat-Coated Retriever brought about the establishment of the Golden Retriever? This, of course, is wholly without proof in our time, but many are the tantalizing suggestions that creep into background research. (*See Golden Retriever chapter.*)

The Sussex Spaniel

ONE has to be in England to see Sussex Spaniels, and no one with interest in Sporting Breeds should be in England and not budget to see the Sussex. The best specimens still conform to the summing-up of Vero Shaw in his *Illustrated Book of the Dog*, 1890: "Sussex have earned a place of honor in any book on dogs; never common, but always held in great esteem, with a beauty of outline and the golden color that is so exceptional and of such value in covert shooting."

Color is, of course, the identification characteristic of the Sussex Spaniel, but not his entire story. His characteristic outline is properly as the best 19th century authorities described him, "of immense bone, legs short and straight in front, and behind with an ability to provide propelling power to a heavy low dog." Recurrently, there have been attempts to bring the Sussex up higher on his legs, and in some modern stock the results of this may at times be seen. Thus, at a championship show at Birmingham, in 1967, an exhibitor went past me, a brace of Sussex Spaniels on leads, one of which was long and low, the other high and short. My thought in watching them pass was whether they would ever be bred together. And indeed, such incompatible types are currently bred together in England, mainly of course because the breed base is, as in the case of the Field Spaniels, so narrow. One breeder described this to have become a matter of three pedigrees only, and those cross-linked, to serve the entire production of Sussex. One deplores the use of some studs of off-type, high and short rather than low and long, but thoroughly understands the problems involved. Trust must repose in the centuries-proved skill of British breeders to cling to the good and eliminate the undesirable.

There are many reasons for the numerical sparsity. If the breed teeters, like the Field, on the brink of extinction, that has been its situation ever since when, as the saying goes. Sussex Spaniels have survived innumerable hazards that have obliterated other strains, from 19th century rabies and distemper epidemics up to and including the ebb and flow of fashion and foible. They were somewhat caught up in the Bullock-caricature craze that destroyed the Fields, but survived that too. The breed may not specifically share the privilege reserved to Deity that "always was and always will be," but it has been around a long, long time and is still with us. *Sportsman's Cabinet* (1803) was already praising "the golden Spaniel of Sussex, the largest and strongest of the Spaniels," which brings to mind that reference, already referred to, by the American sporting-breeds writer who included Sussex in linkage with the Caius' "Comforter Dogges," the Toys.

Another explanation for Sussex scarcity may rest with mechanical breeding difficulties. The short legs and heavy bodies do not facilitate what most dogs do so naturally, the "funny toil" as Robert Burns proclaimed it in his verse. Sussex breeders have much the same difficulties as those which can plague Basset Hound breeders. There seems also to operate in some dog breeds, as in many other forms of life, a decreasing urge to reproduce, consequent on factors not always understood.

Yet, the predominant Sussex Spaniel characteristics, especially the unique and beautiful color which is shared with no other breed, possess a tenacity in inheritance, a will to live that may be matched only by the willow buds boring out each season from the bitter bark of a tree one thought doomed. It is strange that a breed numerically always so small has been able to cling to its identifying characteristics so firmly. Perhaps this originally had to do with the circumstance that, few as they have always been, the Sussex have had the fortune to be oftenest in knowledgeable ownerships. Mr. Fuller, of Rosehill, Hastings, Sussex, who stabilized the breed about the turn of the 19th century, described it frankly as "a hunting dog kept exclusively for the use of Gentlemen." "Idstone" (*The Dog*, 1872) could still record that "the Sussex has never been produced in great numbers, nor ever been common, but kept in the hands of a few families." Among such "few families," by the way, count the Dukes of Norfolk, who have sadly disappointed researchers who hoped to find that the Norfolk Spaniel, eventually absorbed into the English Springer Spaniel, was fostered by this family. No, they always kept Sussex, a spokesman explained.

Crosses have been introduced from time to time, always of necessity when extinction threatened. A century ago it was Field Spaniel, and though no black ever managed to rout the gold, some breedings did impose a brownish cast. There are such dull-brown specimens to find in Sussex today, with indications that they are being bred. One hopes the unique, tenacious gold will re-triumph in a generation or so.

Clumber cross was made in the 1960s, when the narrowness of the breed base had become desperate. The produce is now down to about the third generation, bred back to Sussex. This was no furtive procedure, nor needed to be. Frank Warner Hill wrote it up in *The Field,* with photographs of sire, dam, produce. The cross was registered with the Kennel Club in the then still-operative Crossbreeds Register. This facility, long maintained in England, is—one hears—to be discontinued. That may be a pity, as it has long provided for recording procedures openly that here in the United States in various breeds when necessity or aspiration have urged, were always done furtively, usually to the tune of false information on registration forms. The Germans also have machinery to deal openly with cross-breedings when such help is needed in a breed (see Pudelpointer chapter.) America has never had such a facility, though it has at times been discussed, but that is not to say that this country has therefore lacked "selective breedings," that familiar euphemism that has historically cloaked practices that might better have been aired and registered.

The Clumber-cross favored the Sussex color, though some pups carried a little white Clumber patching. Maybe this is how those Sussex rejected by 19th century judges came by their color (*Show Report,* Birmingham, 1867).

Sussex color is the badge, the glory, and should always be *golden.* It is not exactly the gold of a "freshly-minted sovereign" that Warner Hill prefers to find on a Golden Retriever, but rather that of an *old*-minted sovereign, with patina to suit. Whence does it stem? No one knows, though one may reasonably suspect some reddish type of hound, who knows how far back? Whatever Mr. Fuller used to form and stabilize the Gentleman's Hunting Dog was a secret he took to the grave (1847). Hound influence is further suggested by the characteristic head, the heavy thick ear, thick fleshy tail, the sleek jacketing, the sedate character. There are those who believe that the color appears most characteristically in Spaniels actually engendered in Sussex itself, a linkage with the soil or whatever. True enough, one sees different colors in different parts of the United Kingdom, but hesitates to believe it is merely a matter of geographical location.

Many authorities have discussed the Sussex character and temperament while praising its manner of work. "Idstone" notes "extreme intelligence and entire freedom from any indication of frivolity." The famous 19th century judge, William Lort, wrote: "Sussex has a weird look, and even when young is a steady sober sort of dog." This can be modernly supported, and one notes with surprise that along with such sobriety whirrs the most active tail in dogdom! It has always been so. Even Baron v. Bylandt, in his famous European compilation of all dog breeds (1905) notes the Sussex Spaniel

My friend, "Charles"—Sussex Spaniel, Sh. Ch. Chesara Chervil of Sedora, BOB at Crufts in 1967 and 1969. Owner, Miss Eileen Adams, Lincolnshire, England.

Sussex Spaniel, Sh. Ch. Sunreef Harvest Glow. "Meg," a gal who enjoys shows, danced her way into all hearts (and the last five in the Group) at Crufts 1968, at age of nine years. Owners, Messrs. Scarr and Harris, Hampshire.— *C. Bede Maxwell.*

18

Sussex Spaniel, Bury of Mountcarvey, still around in 1968 and retaining the type so clearly established in pictures of the breed historically preserved. Compare, especially the true "signature tunes" (any breed) of head and tail. Owner, Mrs. Manley-Cooper of Sussex, England, then president of the Sussex Spaniel Club, England.—*Fall*.

possessed of *beau Mouvement de la queue*. He also notes the free sound movement which is another breed characteristic. Who could forget, having seen, that 9-year-old Sussex bitch, Show Ch. Sunreef Harvest Glow, fighting her way to the top five in her Group at the 1968 Crufts! In movement and showmanship all gaiety, in her private capacity she too conforms to sober breed character.

My privilege having been to follow my friend "Charles" (Show Ch. Chesara Chervil of Sedora) on walks down the lane and later across the Lincolnshire fields where his youngsters rushed all over, splashing down the creeks, it was possible personally to assess the metronome regularity and exactness of his gait, the beat of those short, sound hocks, and the whirring of his tail. At home, "Charles" has the dignity of a Judge of the High Court, and his owner's postscript to a recent letter was undoubtedly expressing exactly what "Charles" extended to me, "a languid paw in greeting!" He doesn't care so much for shows, three Bests of Breed at Crufts notwithstanding. He doesn't care so much for "funny toil," either, but has some excellent get. In this, as in all things, he is the "Gentleman's Dog" doing with dignity activities that are required of him.

The breed was never favored in Britain for use on driven game, but rather as a dog to beat out game where pace is less important. This could be valid explanation why the breed has never caught on in America. Yet it is possible that in our shrinking, urbanized world, such qualities as this most British of all Spaniels possesses may yet come to be in demand.

To my view, it is important that identifying qualities be retained in this breed. It should never be permitted to lapse into "just another Spaniel." Who, after all, *needs* just another Spaniel? It must be permitted to retain such a separate identity, so as to fend away the chance of some tyro judge committing a faux pas such as was made by one in England recently when he described a quite good Sussex in his entry as: "an overweight Spaniel of an unfortunate color!" One could imagine the occasional judge in America, never having seen a live Sussex Spaniel, looking hard at one that might chance to appear in his Group.

One hopes that judge's experience will not be in tune with that of one who saw his first, an import, come into a Pacific Northwest show ring in 1970 with about every fault in the book. By coincidence, in 1968, in England, I had judged a half-brother to this same dog and had thrown the Sussex fanciers into a spin by publishing in my critique that within my view the dog should be denied stud privileges, being "off-type, unsound both ends, and with a bad mouth." That an English breeder would send a dog of like breeding, burdened with like faults, to an unsuspecting novice who had aim to establish the Sussex as a breed in the United States shocks me beyond expression. First the judge on the day, and then I, in looking it over, advised the novice not to breed it. But, as novices tend to do, the chances are that he will. After all, is his dog not an *import?* That sad, sad, magic word! Applicable is a wonderful quote from the late famous British judge, little John Willie Marples. Told by an exhibitor in an Australian showring that the dog he was examining was "imported," John Willie stepped back and in his harsh voice said loudly: "I'm imported too—and I'm no good either!"

Unique in this breed—well, if not unique then say less than usual—is head carriage. That big head is carried just slightly above the backline on a rather thick neck. It should be physically impossible to haul up a Sussex on a tight gallows' lead. The attempt would be against his build and also his nature.

In my various delvings into the hinterland of the separate Sporting breeds there has popped up occasionally a dog, vaguely identified, called a Tweed Water Spaniel. It was a curl-coat breed, with a head described as round, "and suggestive of a dash of the bloodhound, with heavy flews and bloodhound set to the ears" (Skidmore, quoted in *The Sporting Spaniel* of Phillips & Cane.) The coat was further described as "so close-curled as to give the idea that they belonged to some smooth." The color was given as "light liver." That this sparsely-documented Tweed Spaniel, mated to the yellow Flat-coated Retriever, provides the historical base on which the Golden Retriever breed was formed, tantalizes me sorely. Could the Tweed have shared some earlier ancestor with the Sussex Spaniel, or could even some early Sussex (for it is a very old breed indeed) have tightened the curl and lightened the color of some old Water Spaniel type? The gleam of gold in the truebred Sussex, being so tenacious, the body coat flat or slightly waved as the Standard requires, all raise the question for which one has, of course, no answer.

The Sussex Spaniel in those few *good* specimens still to see, immensely pleased me. May he continue to triumph over the difficulties of the future, as he has over those of the past.

The Clumber Spaniel

THE present-day Clumber Spaniel, keeping mostly a demo-
cratic company, earlier enjoyed very aristocratic associations in England.
Even in modern times he had the fostering interest of royal princes, even of
British kings. His origin is poorly clarified, much guessed-at, but may be
traceable, if but documentation offered, to those heavier, lower-stationed,
medieval white hounds galumphing across many tapestries. We know from
the work of George Turberville (1575) that the French princes did much
cross-breeding among their hunting hounds, and that they had long-coateds
among the packs of smooths that were commonly classified by color (as in
our Irish Setter chapter where we note the Fallow Hounds include "some
with Tayles shagged like Ears of Corn").

Turberville also tells of the Whyte Hounds surviving best in specimens
that carried a trace of color, often needing to be sought for in the longer
coats, behind the ears, and so on. Specifically he mentions yellow. Pure
Whyte Hounds became extinct, perhaps because they became spent in
battling boar and bear, for these were the Fighting Hounds. But Turberville
reported that "spotted Whelpes in Whyte Hound litters were of Small Valor"
so may have been spared slaughter.

It seems the most reasonable guess that to secure the long coats on their
smooth hounds, the French princes used Spaniel blood, which would also
have provided gentler temperament while preserving hunting skills. The
name by which the breed became commonly known in the world of British
dog ownership, and from there to the rest of the world, was provenly bestowed in England where the Spaniels of a French duke had come in the

21

Clumber Spaniel, Sh. Ch. Eastway Lion, England. Pictured at Birmingham Ch. Show in 1967, where young Lion won his first Challenge Certificate. He soon secured the other two to make up his title. Note desirable carriage of tail. Owners, Mr. and Mrs. C. Foreman-Brown, Berkshire.—*C. Bede Maxwell.*

18th century, refugees from the revolutionary Terror that engulfed aristocratic ownerships.

Those first introductions brought to Clumber Park, the seat of the Duke of Newcastle who provided the refuge, frisky little French-breds (later painted by Francis Wheatley in a well-known canvas) reported to weigh about 35 pounds. No one has ever properly explained how it came about that by the time the famous William Arkwright was exhibiting his winning Clumber, Lapis, about the turn of the 20th century, this Clumber was acceptable, not only at weight of about 60 lbs, but with the shape of a Sussex and identical Sussex head carriage, almost level with its back. From the Spaniels Wheatley painted to the Spaniel Arkwright exhibited, the type change was radical.

At least, by Arkwright's time, Clumbers, though fashionable, were no rarity. "Idstone" (*The Dog,* 1872, p. 144) reported Clumbers as "available in any quantity here . . . but Clumbers in this kingdom are all sprung from one family, one place, therefore there can be no change of blood. Interchange of puppies from a few scattered kennels cannot refresh the constitution like a new strain." So, maybe, it was *after* "Idstone's" time that the heavier dog appeared. What was used is not provable. There's that "Saint Bernard head" which may actually have owed to Pyrenees, as likely. All speculation, really.

Experimental breeding was undoubtedly indulged, and there was a period when longer legs were sought. The breed seems however to have escaped the caricature imposition of the 19th century "long and low" and in defiance of whatever cross-breeding may have been done, held its own recognizably as a Clumber. "Idstone" noted that "in cross-breeding the Clumber propagates his form but seldom his color," an observation verified also in the 1960s Clumber-Sussex cross, where the Sussex color-tenacity and the Clumber form-tenacity collided.

The high tide of Clumber fashion was in flood when British royalty hunted over the Spaniels, and these were fostered in the Sandringham Kennels that were the pride of King Edward VII. His father, Prince Albert, the Consort of Queen Victoria, had been first to introduce the Spaniels, and in turn his son, King George V, a dedicated sportsman and superb shot, used them too. King George's Clumbers were not permitted to retrieve: for this service only Labradors were used. It may also be that as this King hunted into extreme old age, the royal Clumbers helped perpetuate the myth that this breed of Spaniel was only for "old men on shooting sticks."

Despite the misinformation to this respect that is further fostered in the United States, especially in the works of bird-dog-oriented Sporting breed writers who do their "research" mainly in the pages of *The Complete Dog Book* (the official publication of the American Kennel Club), the Clumber Spaniel is not merely an Old Man's dog. He will serve an Old Man if taught

A line-up of Clumber Spaniels, England, 1969.
—*photo, courtesy of Mr. and Mrs. B. Stanley.*

The Clumber is in its inclinations rather less than "sedate." Cuerden Zona, pictured ringside at the Birmingham Championship Show, 1967. Owner, Mrs. Jenny Rostron.—*C. Bede Maxwell.*

24

—often per methods described by one British writer in reference to "those louts called gamekeepers, working the Spaniels each with a leg tied up in front to slow it down." But his inclinations are of another sort.

The misinformation is compounded in the United States by the omission of a most important word from the American Standard for the breed. That word is "active."

The present Standard was approved in 1960, replacing an earlier version. It is loaded with wordage, taking, for example, 5½ lines to describe *General Appearance* which the English Standard spells out in 1½. And it still omits the most important word of all——*active!*

The English Standard reads: *"Should be that of a heavy, massive but active dog, with a thoughtful expression."*

The American reads: *"General appearance, a long, low, heavy-looking dog of a very thoughtful expression, betokening great intelligence. Should have the appearance of great power. Sedate in all movements, but not clumsy. Weight of dogs averaging 55–65 pounds, bitches 35–50 lbs."*

If the American version wouldn't "put off" anyone with inclination towards, and not actually acquainted with, the Clumber Spaniel, it would be difficult to imagine any wordage that would.

Active!

An official of the American Kennel Club was kind enough to send me copies of the pre-1960-revised Standard, and the same omission is therein apparent. So, the American dog world has been for a long time denied the knowledge that the Clumber Spaniel is an active dog, and not a heavy slug.

Sedate in all movements? Who said?

In March, 1968, at the Leicestershire Gundog Society's show in England, it was my privilege to judge a grand Clumber entry including all ages, pups through Crufts-winning champions. Best to recall was a long line in Novice Class, mixed sexes, ages from 8 to 18 months. They leaped like spring lambs, bucked like mustangs, gaited in kangaroo hops, often airborne. The whole ring seethed with energy, liveliness, the promptings of devilment. Their expressions were such that my subsequently-published critique in English dog papers conceded that "likely the only thoughtful expression inside that ring was my own!" They were beautiful.

My fortune also includes having been out to follow Clumbers, as well as Sussex, across fields in Lincolnshire. The Clumbers included a brace of distinguished Crufts' winners, Show Champions Eastway Cherub and Voice of Fatpastures. When these took off for a distant spinney their rate of progress was such as would have had that Old Gentleman on his Shooting Stick praying for the aid of a witch's broom.

Also apt is the story of Mr. and Mrs. Stanley (Frastan Clumbers), who on vacation in Cornwall took their Clumbers into the "local" where the Cornish-men gathered in the evenings, each man with his perky little Jack Russell terrier. These owners were not admiring the big white Spaniels, though one was Show Champion Frastan Anchorfield Bardolph, who in 1968 went forward to reserve best Gundog in the Group at Crufts. But the next evening, after having during the day watched the Clumbers work, never missing a bird, going at a good pace, the Cornishmen turned on the hospitality and toasted the performances that had astonished them. "Sedate in all movements"—my eye!

At the turn of this present century, when the English Springer Spaniel first received separate breed recognition from the Kennel Club (England), the Clumber was always the dog to beat in the Spaniel trials. Modernly, owners in California, Mr. and Mrs. Wilton Meyer, tell me they have 16 mm movies that show their Clumbers working pheasant on equal terms with Springers. These owners, with a good library dealing with their breed that includes publications from England, France, as well as America, have much material concerning the use of Clumbers in field competition in America before the Common Denominator devaluation of all hunting-dog qualities other than pace. Interestingly, they have references to the fashionable status of the breed in 19th century Halifax, Nova Scotia, where British Naval officers based there mitigated the boredom of the Labrador Fisheries Patrol by hunting with the Clumbers they had brought over with them from home.

The American breed Standard is also completely at variance with the English in regard to the rear end of these Spaniels. Taking into consideration the fact that the English have fostered this breed for centuries and have currently such excellent quality in reasonable numerical strength, and that here in America the numbers have teetered for decades on the verge of extinction, one reasonably prefers to take the opinion of the practical breeders rather than the theoretical. For those unaware of how sparse the representation of this breed is in America, the relevant registration figures may prove interesting: 1965—10; 1966—13; 1967—9; 1968—10; 1969—21. The highest place reached in the table of AKC registrations over that period was 111th of 115 breeds. Practical breeder experience here, then, is virtually at zero. The few dedicated enthusiasts work mainly with imported English stock.

So, if the numerically-tiny representation of Clumber Spaniels in America is as figures establish it to be, no mandate would seem to exist here that justifies complete reversal of physical characteristics being required officially of stock bred from English imports. Let us look at the wording of the requirements in regard to that always important feature of Spaniel identification, the tail and its carriage.

English: *"Tail set low, well-feathered, carried level with the back."*
American: *"Stern set on level and carried low."*

26

Head study of a Clumber
Spaniel from "Raycroft." Owner,
Mrs. C. Furness, Chesterfield,
England.

Clumber Spaniel, Eng. and Am. Ch. Thornville Silver, bitch.
Owners, Mr. and Mrs. R. Wilton Meyer, California. —*Ludwig*.

No wonder distinguished international judges continually press for internationally-operative dog standards.

A Spaniel, any breed, with its tail clamped as though in fear of violation is a disgrace to the traditions of that species. And in this—and other!—respects, once again one feels compelled to challenge a picture used (p. 99) in *The Complete Dog Book*. A Clumber? This is wholly unsuitable to represent such a good breed——swampy-backed, high-rumped, and with that clamped and craven tail! A contemporary American breeder has written: "Judges that use that picture as a criterion could (also) be looking for a more 'Settery' type of head, and not even expect a Clumber to *have* a tail, since the painting reproduced gives no hint of one."

The AKC official has also been kind enough to send me, from the files, a copy of the Clumber that illustrated the qualities of the breed in a 1935 edition of *The Complete Dog Book*. How infinitely better—a proud, upstanding dog with a strong back and correct topline extended by his proudly-held, straight-out, short feathered tail. Such a dog, presented to the interested, could attract prospective owners, as certainly as the 1968-presented could repel all but those looking for a lazy slug—which is the overwhelming impression conveyed. Repeat, repeat! The Clumber Spaniel is NOT a slug! By nature. . . .

For sure, someone is going to tell me that the painted dog was a champion. So . . .? He was still something less than admirable as a visual directive to judges and to breeders. For many years, human vanity and the availability of a couple of hundred dollars or so have in commercial dog publications permitted the promotion as "representative breed specimens" of many dogs of less than representative type and quality. Well, that's okay; business is business, and the system provides ego-boost and pleasure to those who have that kind of money to spend. However, there should be no place in the *official* publication for anything other than type-true, properly-presented specimens by which the judges and the breeders can tailor their assessments. Perhaps selection for this official gallery should be made by expert, objective judges rather than by proud owners or an editorial staff not reasonably required to be expert also in terms of dog type and its presentation.

If it be considered that my preoccupation is too much with the after-end of Sporting breeds, at least I am in company beyond reproach. Long ago, the famous William Arkwright wrote of the Pointer: "The head is the seat of character, but for the certificate of pure blood, apply at the opposite end" (*The Pointer and his Predecessors, 1902*). The like applies to all the Sporting breeds, which in all cases yield the carriage and placement of their tails most readily to cross-breeding, especially into hound. The tail of the Spaniel breeds has been clearly defined since antiquity, that "wanton Tayle" of Elizabethan-era definition. With the correct tail is linked indivisibly the

28

correct breed character. This is proved truth to ignore at breeder peril. Therefore, judges too should carry this truth in mind.

Modernly, the Clumber Spaniel market everywhere is a sellers'. Many requests reached me in England from would-be American buyers. When passed by me to the breeders, the reply most often was that no stock was at the moment available. Litters are not large as a rule, and rate of maturing is slow. A Clumber is scarcely assessable till about age two, and may not be mature before age four. Then, if it shows exceptional quality, the breeder wants to keep it. If it does not, he hesitates to export it lest it do him no credit. However, exports are made from time to time, and dogs of good quality at that, but more go to Europe than to America. Europeans pay good prices for good Clumbers, which reminds me of English dog folk telling me, in respect of many breeds, that while Americans will pay a great deal of money to *campaign* a dog, many will back off from paying a fair price for a first-class one. Japanese buyers far outbid most buyers from other countries nowadays.

The slight upsurge in registrations here during 1969 may reflect an increase of interest, or merely be in tune with the general increase in all breeds. However, those American breeders with occasional stock to sell tell me they have waiting lists *that* long! It is not easy, then, to get started in this breed. The Wilton Meyers tell me that when they first shopped around for Clumbers only the du Ponts, of Wilmington, Delaware, appeared to have stock, and they would not sell any. In 1965, having eventually acquired stock out of England, they finished their Raycroft Sam, who broke a long dry spell in Clumber Spaniel champions here. This import, from the well-known kennels of Mrs. E. Furness of Chesterfield, has done well for his American owners. Mrs. Furness campaigns her Clumbers (and her Irish Setters) with considerable success, and Raycroft Solo, that posed for my camera at home when he was only six weeks old, appears currently to do well in the English shows. But he is "Solo" because he was the singleton produce of his dam—and one-pup litters don't add up to a glut of Clumbers to sell.

America could warmly welcome this delightful breed, and the interest is there. First of course, there is need to "catch your Clumber" as was also necessary in respect of the hare in Mrs. Beeton's famous cook book. And then, too, there is need to give attention to the matter of promotion, and to iron out the portions of the presently-approved AKC Standard that are not in accord with exact truth, remembering on behalf of Clumbers that they too can generally protect themselves against their enemies, but Heaven preserve them from their friends.

The Springer is a versatile dog, land or water.
—*photos, Dr. Marlowe Dittebrandt, Oregon.*

Springer at work in California rice field.—*Dr. Marlowe Dittebrandt.*

The English Springer Spaniel

UNCOUNTED generations of Spanieldom rest behind the useful and attractive dog modernly recognized as the English Springer Spaniel. His Spaniel heritage is proclaimed by his "pendulous ears, soft gentle expression, sturdy build, and friendly wagging tail" (*AKC-approved Standard, 1956*). His background, including crossbreeding over centuries, is not documented, but his type is distinct as from the Spaniels we have been discussing in earlier chapters. He lacks the hound signature of the heavier head of the Sussex and the Clumber. If all spring from a common Spaniel taproot, the roads taken must have become divergent very early.

The English Standard as approved, under the heading of *Characteristics* makes the brave claim that he is *"the taproot from which all our Sporting Spaniels (Clumbers excepted) have been evolved . . . breed of ancient and pure origin, and should be kept as such."*

These are claims that cannot be substantiated. There is *no* Spaniel of "ancient and pure origin," though doubtless all share some incredibly ancient linkage, perhaps even as far back as the Mastiff source modernly identified by Richard and Alice Fiennes in the Natural History Press publication, *The Natural History of Dogs*, 1970.

If there is belief in linkage with the Land Spaniel of the Elizabethans, Gervase Markham blew the whistle on that one (1621) a few decades later. The quote is repeated, lest the reader have no interest to turn back a few pages to general Spaniel discussion: "It is reasonable that people should cross Land Spaniels and Water Spaniels, and the Mungrells between these, and the Mungrells of either with the Shallow-Flewed Hound, the Tumbler, the Lurcher, and the small bastard Mastiff . . . all of which are yet inferior to the true-bred Land Spaniel—if one could still find one of those."

If "ancient status" can be claimed for a Land Spaniel working the "springing" or flushing pattern, it might possibly be more accurately for the Welsh rather than the English Springer. Caius (1550) recorded that most of the Land Spaniels of his time were patterned in red and white patchings, and the association of the white and red (or red and white) Spaniels with the ancient Celtic migratory peoples has been historically long established. To this day, the Welshie breeds one hundred percent true to his color inheritance, and is acceptable in no other. The English Springer Spaniel, though richly endowed with several colors and patternings, including tricolors, has no red-white. The Welsh, of course, was centuries immured in his valleys of the Principality. The English had island-wide distribution.

Markham described his ideal Land Spaniel: "strong, lusty, a nimble raunger, of active Foote, wanton Tayle and busie Nostril . . . his Toyle without weariness, his search without changeableness, and yet no delight nor desire transport him beyond Feare and Obedience."

If we skip the centuries from Markham to "Idstone" (1872) we find that in the comprehensive survey of all dog breeds of his time, the latter author recognizes no Springer Spaniel as of a separate breed. Dogs that work the pattern in terms of "springing," yes, but his separate breed chapters in Spaniels restrict themselves to "Sussex—Clumber—Norfolk—Irish and Other Spaniels—Smaller Field Spaniels and Cockers."

Of Norfolk Spaniels he wrote (*The Dog*, pp. 147–9) :

> Almost any liver-colored-and-white moderately large dog is called a Norfolk, more Norfolk Spaniels being used than any other . . . Most gamekeepers keep a liver-and-white one, and it goes by the name of a Norfolk dog. Some specimens are of a very great beauty, silky-coated, short, compact, moderate ears, not only useful but ornamental. Others look like Sussex Spaniels (and) only the best judges could determine the correct breeding of a Norfolk, as the breed has been very mixed for years, nor do I believe that their origin is known.

While reporting that with Clumber Spaniels so greatly the vogue he held little hope for the resuscitation of the Norfolk breed, he mentions their good use in water retrieving, though charging some with an inclination to mouth game. Weight is given at 30–35 pounds. He also mentions those painted by Reinagle, so profusely curled, while those of his own time had coats smooth as those of the Sussex. Perhaps, as Sussex were in fashion, crossings had been made that smoothed the later jacketings.

Because Reinagle's work is no passion with me, it was nice to find "Idstone" like-minded (p. 149) : "His dogs are always of the heraldic type, his Spaniels for the most part chasing after their game, open-mouthed, as he probably saw them rushing after the cats in his garden." This refers of course to such as that over-used John Scott engraving of the 1804 Reinagle which nearly every breed writer delights to use. Many better sporting artists have done better by working Spaniels—Stubbs and Marshall, of the same era, especially. They painted leggy Spaniels for the most part, tapered of muzzle, and usually with bravely bushed tails such as one sees in the Dutch genre paintings too. The Stubbs is a smooth-coated Spaniel, patterned as a modern English Springer would be, and may have been prelude to the type of game-keeper's dog that "Idstone" described as being of great beauty. However, a couple of decades after "Idstone," Vero Shaw (*The Illustrated Book of the Dog*) was still picturing Norfolks with curled coats.

Many 19th century dog writers are generous with the names of owners, "Idstone" especially. No one seems to have preserved the names of Norfolk Spaniel sponsorships, and enquiry has also established that the Dukes of Norfolk kept Sussex—which, of course, may account for the circumstance that some Norfolk Spaniels looked like Sussex. My thought is that the name could be purely geographical.

In the earliest 19th century, Norfolk was virtually the preserve of a remarkable man who preferred to be known as "Mister" Thomas Coke (pronounced Cook) rather than as the Earl of Leicester he was pressured to accept in his old age, fathering sons in his eighties! He lived in a Stately Home still standing, Holkham Hall. There he entertained royalty or snubbed royalty as best pleased him. Thus when the Prince Regent (later George IV) had offended him, and later invited himself for the shooting, Coke advised that "Holkham Hall is open to all visitors every Tuesday from two till four." There were no repercussions!

Coke pioneered agricultural science in the modern sense. He turned sandy Norfolk acres into productive fields, and scrubby Norfolk sheep into wool-producers so magnificent that most of Britain's aristocracy went to Holkham each year for the "sheep-shearing." He hunted a great deal, and that he had an interest in sporting dogs is established by the information that "Mr. Coke and the Duke (of Gordon) bred from the same stock"—Gordon Setters, in this instance. (This is one more goodie coaxed out from "Idstone"—what one would have done without him it is impossible to guess. The reference is on page 95.)

A man who bred Gordon Setters to shoot over would also have had use for a flushing (springing) breed, and the eye of Mr. Coke would not have been satisfied with scrubby nondescript stock of any sort. The beautiful dogs of the gamekeepers, those liver-and-whites, may have owed to his breeding skill—Spaniels *out of Norfolk*. That they were workers can be taken for granted. No gamekeeper ever kept a useless dog, however beautiful.

33

Fast on the water retrieve.

We may yet somewhere come upon a reference associating Mister Coke with Spaniels working a "springing" pattern. The best clues do seem to come from other than dog books, per se, too many of which merely spade over the same tired ground, making little fresh contribution to knowledge. Biography, letters, and such publications oftenest provide the pay-streak clues.

If, in those first decades of the 19th century, Coke did sponsor such a breed, as it became widely dispersed it would inevitably have become subject to crossbreedings—for it was still the time of no control. The beautiful liver-and-whites, the gamekeepers' dogs, may on the other hand have represented purer breeding from original stock, and have siphoned their qualities on and down, becoming eventually absorbed into the breed we now recognize as English Springer Spaniels. Identification rests not only on appearance but on work pattern that was described even as far back as old Caius: "the Spaniel that springeth the Byrde and betrayeth flight by pursuit."

When the Springers, English and Welsh, were first given recognition as separate breeds by The Kennel Club (England) in 1902, there operated what an Australian would call "an open go." Registration was on the basis of appearance. Many were registered with doubtful, some with no, pedigrees. If it was red-and-white, generally, it was Welsh; if liver-and-white, English, though of course, bodily characteristics varied considerably as well.

My good friend, Mary Scott, in her *The English Springer Spaniel*, 1960, p. 7, tells of the Welsh Springer, Corrin of Gerwin, first registered as a Welsh Cocker, KCSB I,13931F, being re-registered as a Welsh Springer, Corrin of Gerwin, KCSB 894G, and his son, Guy of Gerwin, being registered as an English Springer. This could interest Americans in that an earlier import to the Chevier strain of Canada, which based much American breeding subsequently, was Don Juan of Gerwin. Mrs. Scott also mentions Beechgrove Will, the first English Springer champion, siring a daughter that was registered as a Field Spaniel. These shufflings were not made in any underhand manner, and merely highlight the continuing state of Spaniel breed confusion right into modern times, and the hopelessness of trying to establish "ancient purity" claims.

Frank Warner Hill (Beauchief Springers) in the course of an hilarious lecture in London, 1968, told of competing against a certain dog one week-end in the English Springer ring and seeing it the next week-end competing as a Field!

Mention of Beechgrove Will (*above*) reminds us that at this time of new breed recognition, the Clumber Spaniel was in Trials the dog to beat. Thus, Will's owner was also the owner of the Clumber, Beechgrove Bess, the reigning star of Open Stake competition. This is one more item of evidence to establish the *activity* of the Clumber. That the heavier whites eventually dropped out of competition with the longer-legged liver-and-whites, may have had as much to do with Clumber rate of reproduction as anything else.

Spaniel Clubs, formed around the 20th century's turn, at first had the strong support of William Arkwright, but he presently resigned from the interest and abandoned show and trial judging for inability to enforce linkage of breed type within the two activities. So, *that's* an old story, too!

Some dual champions, actually three, were made in the early days in England in Springers. Warner Hill sighs about that: "It was comparatively easy in the old days." However, the breed is modernly rich in practical shooting dogs, and many double also as top-quality show dogs. Mary and Joe Scott have owned many great English Springers, Mary showing them, Joe shooting over them, right back to the famous prepotent, Boxer of Bramhope, and to the dog of the present, Show Champion Lochardils Ghillie of Bramhope. Ghillie poses a pretty picture on Joe's shooting preserve on a Yorkshire moor across from that owned by the late Princess Royal.

Modernly, the English Springers have been far forward in English show competition, taking Bests in Show at major championship events. Notably among these are the Moorcliffs, of Mr. E. Froggatt. Hard work in practical work interests is furthered also profitably there by Dr. H. F. Ferrer and, until recently, by Mr. F. O. Till (Stubham).

Nowadays, everywhere, the show English Springer has become stabilized into one of the world's most attractive dog breeds, type-fixed and breeding true. The field trial types in America are far more variant, which can be expected in that the average field trial enthusiast breeds with an aim rigidly narrowed, and is not generally concerned with appearance. Many such dogs lapse, generation by generation, away from breed type, so far even as to become unrecognizable as Springer Spaniels. The lack of rule to govern type explains such misfortune. The Europeans are wiser. Thus Germany will not permit an off-type or unsound dog to even compete in a trial. The Scandinavians will not permit a dog to be shown if it has not first qualified in the field. The English walk the median way and deny "full" championship status to a Sporting dog that cannot satisfy approved field trial judges that he possesses working instincts strong enough to gain the Qualifier.

It all adds up to the obvious fact that field trial and hunting men in America have always stubbornly refused to accept that there must be *rule.* The wisest woman I ever knew, the late Mary Gilmore, Dame of the British Empire, has defined best the function of *rule:* "Take away the banks and the stream becomes a morass."

There was a time when my belief was that "split" in Sporting breeds should be prevented, or at least mended. That was before doing research for this present book! Now the belief has gone the way of Santa Claus and the Tooth Fairy. Show or field, owners *will have* the dog they want, as per the

Joe Scott, dedicated to practical work with a dog, has a good day on the Yorkshire moors (England) with his Springer, Show Ch. Lochardils Ghillie of Bramhope.

Mary Scott, international judge, author, respected breeder of good English Springers, checks the show record of Sh. Ch. Lochardils Ghillie of Bramhope, in his alternative capacity of fine show dog.

The lasting qualities of a Springer can be impressive. National Fld. Ch. Stubblefield Ace High, pictured winning his title in 1952, was still in top competition in 1958. Handled by Stanley Head.

reminder my friend, Herm David, passes along. The man who buys, feeds, cleans up, pays for the training or for a show handler, is entitled to have the dog he pays for. If such an owner has closed his eyes and his ears to the accumulated breeding knowledge available to him, that's his entitlement too.

It has to be conceded, however, that in either sphere a dog is not merely a vehicle for some single part or quality. *He is the sum of all his parts, all his qualities.* A chain is not some single link or two. A dog whose sole connection with breed status is in terms of "papers"—and those quite often reasonably subject to suspicion—has little wherewith to endow progeny. His qualities drain out and are lost. This is the continuing story of field trial strains, what Max Riddle has so well described as the "tragedies occurring (in competitive Sporting breeds) because ownerships in general have never possessed themselves of even the sketchiest knowledge of what has gone before."

My philosophy has become that of the father in the classic movie, "It Happened One Night." Told that "the walls of Jericho are about to fall," he merely replied: "Let 'em fall!" If the Sporting breeds in the U.S.A. promise a continuing breed-split—Let 'em Split! Not to worry. . . . At least we can rely on the *show people* to keep breeds separately recognizable and breeding type-true. And provably, the working instincts, the properly defined *hunting instincts,* are retained in breeds and when the time is right will surface.

The separation of English from Welsh Springers is no mere happenstance of color. Body type and head type are as distinctively different. There was confusion at the time of early separation, but British breeding skills soon put that right. There is no *official* interbreeding now, though one inclines to wonder just how the Welshie came by his darkened pigmentation these days. Asking Mary Scott, in view of that reference to Norfolks that resembled Sussex, what she would think of an English Springer in her ring carrying a golden liver patch pattern, she said she would possibly accept a light liver *if* the type was thoroughly English, though of course preferring a dark. At no time, however, would she accept a red and white, no matter the look-like. Blue roan? The Standard permits it, she noted, but added that she would need to be sure there was no English Setter in back. Black-and-whites? She first gained a liking for those after coming to America in 1956, going home to rave about the beautiful American Springers in this color patterning. Am. Ch. Dr. Primrose of Wakefield, brought into England, stamped a more clear-cut black-and-white there, she believed. But English dogs still incline to carry more roaning.

In America, many black-and-whites, for several years, were of different body type compared with the liver-whites. These have, in the main, since become absorbed in stock of more acceptable proportioning, the length in relation to height which provides the desirable **English Springer** outline.

38

It was never a blatant thing, merely a suggestion of shorter mid-piece as related to leg length, perhaps rather a matter for the eye than for the tape-measure. But it did—and still does when it is seen—detract from the classic conception of type. Nowadays, one may expect to see a majority of the very desirable in black-and-whites. Discussing body proportioning it is also important to remember that the outlines of the English Springer and the Welsh Springer differ to a considerable degree, so important that though already referred to in passing (*above*), it is worth mentioning again. As in the three Setters, identification between the two Springers is much more than just a variance of color and patterning.

This breed appears to be blessed with a most admirable Parent Club organization that takes good care of its own. Little in dogs has impressed me more than the letter that the Parent Club sent out in 1968 to all American judges licensed for English Springer Spaniels. It included advice that tricolor is an acceptable color, not to be penalized; that the English Springer tail, like all Spaniel tails, is an index of character, which cannot be properly presented when a dog is shown with a tail pegged high by a handler; and advised that closer attention be paid to movement.

The AKC-approved Standard (1956) is extremely detailed. It runs to $5\frac{1}{2}$ pages. The English-approved, blue-printing the same dog, gets by in $1\frac{1}{2}$. The extra wordage is in part the result of patient intention to clarify everything, including terms that one takes for granted are commonly known. One does hope such explanations as: "Skull means Upper Head" and "Foreface means Head in Front of the Eyes" are not considered necessary for judges!

The *head* of the English Springer Spaniel is decisively his own, neither Cocker nor Setter, and as widely divergent as possible from that of a Welshie. It is modestly-rounded, somewhat flattened on top, stop not too pronounced, with a slight trough between the eyes. Earset is at eye-level, leather fine, feathering reasonable, not cap-string long. The wordage re eyes is all in negatives—not small, not full and prominent, not bold and hard in expression. *Muzzle* is asked to convey the impression of ability to carry game—which reminds me of how many field trial Springers tend to the snipey!

Necks are, as in many Standards of other breeds, described in terms of aid to the picking-up of game. This could stand clarification in terms of lay of shoulder which actually governs *apparent* length of neck. All dogs in all breeds have the same number of neck vertebrae. Front-end flexibility, which calls for correct engineering, facilitates the picking up of game. "Length" of neck, as the eye discerns this, has as much use as length of tail for practical purposes.

Bodies, required to be strong and compact, should never be overshort, a condition that hinders freedom of movement. One does see (and in some major winners) English Springers with short mid-sections (as opposed to compact, which is another matter again). Sometimes this undesirability is associated with a steep shoulder, and one is faced with a sharply sloped topline on a dog that looks tall, even if it is not. Length of back, of course, is provided by assessment, withers to loin. This area *must* be strong. A weak-backed dog is useless. In my judging, I look also for hard condition, flesh and muscling, and take particular notice of *feet*. It is my practice to examine the feet of all my entrants, all breeds, a procedure that absorbs no more than a split second of time. Many otherwise good looking dogs in many breeds have gone down under me for lack of muscle and/or poor feet. *Feet carry the load!*

Beautiful jacketing and furnishings are indivisibly part of the show Springer. But the Springer, whether he is in competition or not, represents a breed to be held desirably workmanlike, and so while a beautiful show coat is also wholly desirable, over-exaggeration of feather especially is not. One West Coaster under me recently, an important winner by his record, had leg feather so long it literally folded under his front feet. This within my view constitutes absurdity, and while the dog, on his quality, went on to my Best of Breed, it was impossible to withhold the gesture of distaste in pulling the feather back from under the feet. The handler saw, shrugged: "We're taking him East, that's the way they like them over there!" In relating this, my purpose is merely reportage, not comment!

The American Standard tolerates waviness in the coat, the English opts for *"close, straight, and weather-resisting without being coarse."* The measure for an American judge might be the *degree* of waviness. Waviness is not curl. Many Springers are visibly barbered, and the Standard penalizes *"over-trimming, especially of the body coat . . . and any chopped, barbered, or artificial effect."*

This is a most important section for novices (their handlers, too) to consider, because in this, as in many other breeds, cutting the body coat represents robbery that cannot be compensated.

The sleek beauty of topcoat does not regenerate after cutting. What replaces it is soft woolliness from beneath, undercoat, entirely different in character, easily recognizable, and not to be judicially approved. A Spaniel (or a Setter) may be cut down the thighs, the shoulders, under the jawline (not neck!) but topcoat should be kept from the blade. For cosmetic smoothing of body coat, continued use of rough sandpaper does wonders, makes no marks, and does no harm.

Famous breeder, Mrs. Julie Gasow (Salilyn) permits me to round out this discussion in terms of a great Springer of her breeding, Ch. Salilyn's Mac-Duff. Duff's first Group win was to be followed by a stud mating. Mrs. Gasow took him to the veterinarian for this purpose, popped him into a kennel without checking a card on the door. It read "Complete Clip." She collected Duff as bald all over as a billiard ball, ears to tail! It took a full year to regrow his coat. While feather regenerated prettily, body coat did not. His winning record was tremendous, he was an exceptionally good Springer, and judges didn't seem to query the quality of his re-grown, soft coat, but by the Standard probably should have done so. Came a major Specialty, and an overseas judge, an Australian, carried Duff just short of the BOB, a difficult decision resolved in the end by the soft, undesirable coat quality.

My own particular aversion is to Spaniel or Setter breeds with heads clipped, bristly forefaces and occiputs that harden expressions and provide a spiky feel where the tactile sensation should be pleasant. As a good judge of my acquaintance once observed, he "disliked getting splinters in his fingers judging dogs!"

The English Springer has a fine breed presence, and possesses further the boon of retaining quality often into quite advanced age. Thus, the Sporting Group at Golden Gate Kennel Club show in San Francisco has twice in a decade been taken by a veteran English Springer Spaniel. Ch. King William of Salilyn brought it off at age 10; Ch. Waiterock Elmer Brown at age 11. The same longevity likely operates in practical field trial competition too. It was not my luck to see little Stubblefield Ace High win his National Field Trial Championship—I was not even in the country. But I did see him in field trial competition at the age of 10-plus, and a great little goer he had still shown himself to be. These are not the only long-lived, success-fully-competing Springers; they merely illustrate what is a very useful quality in any competitive dog. It takes a long time to produce a really top dog in any breed. If the light burns steadily for some years instead of flash-flickering out in a single season, that is a gain not to be underestimated.

It is also worth mentioning how well *women* do with this breed. Mrs. B. Gilman Smith (Melilotus); Mrs. Julie Gasow (Salilyn); Mrs. Lucille Schwede (Schwedekrest); Mrs. Juanita Howard (Waiterock); Mrs. Vivian Diffendaffer (Lee Vee) and English-domiciled Mary Scott (Bramhope) come readily to mind as premier influences likely to be long-remembered, and one can think of many more.

It would have been grand to have lived in the Willamette Valley, Oregon, now my home, in the years when the English Springer Spaniel revelled there in a fantastic wealth of pheasant. The wily Chinese bird had not been easy to acclimatize in America; he took to this area first and best. Old hands tell me of the fantastic wealth of birds in the early years of open seasons. They tell me too that nowadays, the pheasant does not flush so freely, some advancing a theory that those so ready to rise were shot out, and those with instinct to run rather than fly survived, a natural adaptation that sounds reasonable.

English Springer Spaniel, Am. Ch. Salilyn's Aristocrat, foremost winning Sporting dog of 1969. Owner, Mrs. F. H. Gasow, Michigan. —*Bill Williams.*

Another of the breed's remarkable "lasters": Can. and Am. Ch. Waiterock Elmer Brown, pictured winning a Sporting Group from the Veterans' Class, in January 1967, at 11 years of age. Elmer lived to be 15 years. Owner, Juanita Waite Howard, California.

Springer history was well made in the West by English imports, which included those of Mr. George Higgs (Boghurst) who brought in Eng.-Am.-Can. Ch. Boghurst Rover, who was sired by one of the three (only) British Duals. A contemporary, Dr. Sabin, of Portland, Oregon, joined the interest of Mr. Higgs to present good dogs in both venues, with several Duals the result of it—even setting a modest fashion for such in the area.

National Field Trial competition is well-supported, and attendance at the first such event held on the West Coast (at Willows, California) was for me an absorbingly interesting experience. The terrain was tough, glass-sharp rice stubble. Performances were magnificent. A Springer trial is kind to a gallery; one may hike after the dogs as one does in all kind of breed trials in Germany, with no need for a horse. If one is conditioned to admire breed type, not all the dogs will appeal in terms of appearance—some look like long-coated Bassets and some like small snipey Cockers. But there are many that will appeal, and surprisingly, these seem so often to be those turning in the best performances.

In the show ring, the English Springer can more than hold his own. In 1967, Ch. Salilyn Aristocrat established an all-time record for the most best in show wins scored in a year by a dog of any breed (45). Just four years later, Risto's son, Ch. Chinoe's Adamant James, surpassed his sire's mark with 48 best in show wins in 1971, and in followup became one of the very few to have twice won top honors at the Westminster show at Madison Square Garden. One just *has* to like the versatile, beautiful, exaggeration-free English Springer Spaniel as a breed, and wherever one is privileged to see it.

English Springer Spaniel, Am. Ch. Salilyn's Macduff. A dog with a great winning record. Owned by Wm. Randall, Illinois.—*C. Bede Maxwell.*

A group of Welsh Springer Spaniels at a Windsor Soc. show, England, 1968. This handsome breed enjoys increasing popularity in English show rings, and ownership is very enthusiastic. Note evenness of type.—*C. Bede Maxwell.*

The Welsh Springer Spaniel

As an English Setter is variant from an Irish, a Gordon, so too is a Welsh Springer Spaniel variant from an English Springer Spaniel or a Cocker. As, for that matter, a Welshman is variant from an Englishman—as well should be known to me whose maternal grandmother spoke the Cymric.

The Welshie is different in terms of outline, temperament, history, as well as obviously in terms of color and patterning. Granted, in the show ring one sees the occasional Cocker Spaniel type go to the head of a line, but that's dog judging, and one can't sheet home the blame to the breed. The Welshie has his own size, his topline, his degree of feathering, and *very much* his distinctive head type. Distinguished breeder, Mr. H. C. Payne, of Monmouth-shire, emphasized that for me in his quiet direct way: "Cut off a Welshie's head and all you've got left is just another Spaniel." Personally, it is clear to me that there are those other differences too, but it is impossible to withhold agreement that the distinctive, *shallow-flewed* (not snipey!) head is a badge of this breed. That elegant muzzle is shared with the Irish Setter, and this may be no mere accident. Both are Celtic-sponsored breeds, and while Gervase Markham, of the 1600s, who establishes the then-existence of a breed he identifies as the Shallow-flewed hound does not state it as a Celtic possession, he does at least clarify it in terms of what must have been its outstanding badge of identity in Elizabethan Britain. At this distance in time we can do no less.

The Welsh Springer Spaniel is virtually an unknown quantity in American show rings, but registers a modest number each year, many more than the Clumber Spaniel that is so much better known. It teeters about the 104th place in the registration table, sometimes a step higher, sometimes a step lower. The figures for the last few years run: 1965—28; 1966—30; 1967—40; 1968—48; 1969—46; and 1970—16. As the breed is included among those for which I am licensed, it is always my hope to have some entered under me, a hope as yet not realized. My luck was better in England where, in Variety Sporting Classes especially, some lovely representatives of top kennels were in evidence. The beautiful bitch that went Best of Opposite Sex all breeds under me in March, 1968, at Midwestern Gundog Club show, was the 1969 *and* 1970 Best of Breed at Crufts, Sh. Ch. Golden Tint of Tregwillym. It has also been my privilege to see her lovely dam, Sh. Ch. Lady of Llangarna, on in years and yet in beautiful coat and style. Looking at both, it occurred to me to wonder how they would fare, lovely ladies, in an American Group line-up! Rare breeds don't have it easy with us! It remains a pleasure to recall taking Golden Tint to a top spot *before* she accumulated so many honors. Years as a journalist, covering innumerable dog shows, long since crystallized my belief that matches one Percy Roberts once expressed: "Anyone can find champions arrived!"

There has long been speculation as to which might owe to which as between the Welsh Springer and the Brittany Spaniel. Both seem to have some linkage with Celtic shuttlings to and fro across the English Channel as the tribes were harried variously. In modern times there is established an interest in French buyers to acquire Welsh Springers. As late as the 1920s, the boats of the French onion-sellers took red-and-whites from Britain to France and it is reasonable to believe such were absorbed in Spaniel breeding there. In 1970, interestingly, a French-bred Welshie, British-sired, Quetzal des Fretillants, was best Spaniel all breeds at the CACIB show in Paris, France.

Which developed closest to ancient Celtic type is not likely to be now established. The Welsh stayed in the seclusion of the valleys. The Brittany was of a type richly documented by various forms of European art, with his pointed foreface, high short ear, long legs. The Welshie does not have these characteristics. The Brittany retained what may be original pigmentation and in America this is protected by a disqualification clause.

The Welshie has had his original endowment of hazel eyes and flesh-colored nose darkened by modern crossings used to "pretty" him up for show. My kind mentor in all matters Welsh Springer Spaniel, Ray Hood, of the Welsh Springer Spaniel Club, Britain, has carefully explained to me that while, yes, the Standard (English) still permits hazel eyes and flesh-colored noses, in practice the high placing of a dog carrying such would not be well received. Which provoked my reasonable reply—then the permissiveness has no place in the approved Standard. In any breed, a judge has all to do to keep track of Standards as written. He should not be expected further to cope with the *unwritten.*

46

A distinguished champion, Statesman of Tregwillym, shows the type-distinctive head of this breed. "Cut off a Welshie's head, and all you have is just another Spaniel," says Statesman's owner, H. C. Payne, of the Tregwillyms. It is a head *never* to be confused with that of an English Springer. Muzzle is "fairly square," stop defined but slight, ear "vine-shaped."

Ch. Statesman of Tregwillym retrieving.

Welsh Springer Spaniel puppies.

47

The Welshie also belongs to that group of *short-eared* Spaniels that have association with France and Celtic sponsorships—Brittany being anciently Celtic, as those who have blundered their way through Caesar's *Gaul* must remember. The Welshie, like the Clumber and the Brittany, is asked to have an ear that is "vine-leaf" shaped or, as the AKC-approved Brittany Spaniel Standard has it, *"leafy."* Sitting in at an Annual General Meeting of the Club in England, was to hear debate on the desirability of finding different word-age to describe the ear. No one could come up with an exact definition to substitute, and *"vine-leaf shape"* remains. The Welshie ear, by the way, is permitted more feather than the ears of the other two. The Brittany set-on has to be high, that of the other two is required to be low. By those who happily do their dog-judging on a Common Denominator basis such differences will be dismissed as of no account. Yet in fact the altered set of an ear, a shortening or a lengthening, more feather or less, can completely alter head type and expression in any breed.

The patience of the breed interests in Britain has made it possible for me to leaf through a great stack of Welsh Springer Spaniel pedigrees that support the findings in the breed-definitive work on Springer Spaniels by the late Mrs. Morland Hooper. Mrs. Hooper specifically identified the bitch, Goytre Lass, as a carrier of English Springer blood (p. 180). In several matings to Ch. Marglam Bang, she produced litters of red-and-whites that were often endowed with dark pigmentation. The combination is very striking, for the Welshie's red is red, glowingly so. His white gleams, and the dark eyes, nose, eye-rims lend softness not found in the lighter hazel-and-flesh combination. Nor does the Welshie fancier in Britain spend time worrying over the concern that backstops the imposition of the disqualification clause that protects light pigmentation in the American Brittany Spaniel. The Brittany is a pointing breed. The English Springer is a flushing breed. American interests view cross-breeding as hazardous in terms of work pattern.

From Goytre Lass, in direct line of descent, can be traced some very prepotent modern breed influences, to be found in most modern Welsh Springer Spaniel pedigrees. So, in our time, a radical change in pigmentation has been made successfully, at least in terms of eyes and nose.

The red and white coat patterning remains as tenacious within the breed as does the golden liver in Sussex Spaniels. It is still as Caius described it, the most of Spaniels in his time being white, "but if they be marked with any Spottes they are commonly Red, and somewhat great withal." To leap a few centuries, an observation of the year 1800 identifies also a multiplicity of red-and-whites, "with short ear and most usually an uncut, bushed tail." The tenacity of the color and patterning has been siphoned into the American Cocker Spaniel breeding, too, and enhances some of the loveliest of the Parti-colors. One channel by which this color was passed along may have been the

An historic—"Corrin." Originally registered as a Welsh Cocker. Re-registered, when Springer Spaniels were divided, as a Welsh Springer, he was subsequently the sire of an English Springer. He demonstrates some characteristics identifiably "Welsh."

This photo of Belle, a Parti American Cocker, three-time winner of the American Spaniel Club Specialty, fairly screams Welshie type. Yet just a decade later, her straight-line descendants (as exampled by Master Showman) duplicated her only in their spectacular red-and-white coloring—in shape and make they were much changed.

Ch. Idahurst Belle II, whelped 1928

Ch. Bobb's Master Showman, whelped 1940

three-time American Cocker Club supreme exhibit, Ch. Idahurst Belle II, of whom more in the appropriate American Cocker chapter. Her photograph simply *screams* Welshie type.

The Starter, as the Welshie is also known at home, is a hard, useful hunting dog, but usually needs a firm hand. He is wilful and boisterous when young. There is, however, no discernible type-gap as between the show and the working Welshie.

The Standard specifically directs that bodies *"be not long,"* but these Spaniels do provide some illusion of length except when they tend to (undesirable) Cocker Spaniel type. The explanation is likeliest in terms of their being comparatively low-stationed—as compared with English Springer proportioning, that is. Topline is emphasized by the requirement that "loins (be) slightly arched up," and a *slight* uphill run can be discerned in some of the best Welshies.

The head is difficult to visualize from the "Standardese" wording. Maybe one needs to see the really good Welshies to form the impression needed. My thought is that when this tidy, elegant, slightly-tapered, but end-squared head has become memorized it is not likely to be quickly forgotten, and renewal of acquaintance will be exact.

The Welshie does well enough in British show rings, where strong strains compete. Linkhill, Tregwillym, Of Hearts, Brent, Pencellis, Plattburn, Tarbay, not forgetting the Redvia interest of my helpful friend, Ray Hood, are all continually evident in competition. Some great records have been compiled by such as "full" Ch. Statesman of Tregwillym and his son, Sh. Ch. Deri Darrel of Linkhill, who won 7 Bests of Breed at Crufts! Some very good youngsters were on the way up during my stay in England, including the versatile Tidemarsh Rip, then assembling his points, and following the example of his sire, Stokecourt Sam, a notable worker. One had to be impressed by the stock from Plattburn, from Talsarn, because these are strains being fostered outside the reach of interest from the principality of Wales, being located in Yorkshire.

No record of any show or work successes achieved by Welshies in America appear to be available to me, but my thought is that should a flyer erupt to help promote Welsh Springer Spaniels here, this is a breed that could gain a great popularity.

Superficial observation often remarks a "likeness" between Welsh Springer and Brittany Spaniel. It is believed that they may have had common inheritance from ancient Celtic Spaniels, but development was diverse. The Welshie (modeled here by Nobleman of Tregwillym, posed in Wales by owner H. C. Payne, Monmouthshire) appears long because he is somewhat lower-stationed. The Brittany (modeled by Dual Ch. Faulkner's Reddy, show-posed by owner Mr. Ejner Lund of California) appears short because he is "leggy" in accordance with his standard. The Welshie's standard specifically asks for body "not long." The Brittany's asks for body length the same as height measured at the withers—i.e., square.—*C. Bede Maxwell and L. Roberts.*

51

Dual Ch. Tigar's Jocko (Honey's Tigar ex Petite Femme de la Bois).
This Brittany has a most distinguished record of wins that includes
the National Amateur Pheasant Shooting Dog Ch. (1964). Owned
by Mr. John Munson, California.

The name of the game is continuity. Veteran Brittany, Dual Ch.
Pierrot de Fontaine Vallee, with a son.—*Dr. Marlowe Dittebrandt.*

The Brittany Spaniel

I T'S strange about the Brittany Spaniel in America! There he is, way way up in the tabulation of the AKC registrations year by year, fourth in the Sporting Group figures having been his lowest rating for some years now. Yet few breeds have it tougher in the show rings. One wonders why.

There are judges that ruefully confess no particular fancy for Brittanys. Maybe these tend to be recruits from Setter or other Spaniel interests, and have an eye in for different characteristics. British judges, especially can look with astonishment at our Brittany and wonder at its popularity. Thus a famous British dog commentator, conceding Brittany work virtues in an article in *Dog World* (England) wrote that: "judged by our ordinary Spaniel Standards, the Brittany doesn't add up to much" (1958) .

That's the point! A Brittany is not to be judged by "ordinary Spaniel Standards." He has his own! He is no more obligated to resemble a Cocker or a Springer than a cow is obligated to resemble a horse. The late Alan Stuyvesant (Allamuchy) , a notable Brittany pioneer breeder in America, has said it best: "A Brittany should remind one of no other breed. He should look like a Brittany."

Most do look like the breed they are supposed to be. If some critics hold that to be a misfortune, they should not waste too much sorrow over these dogs. If the type appears "foreign" to observers weaned onto heavier British Spaniels, just concede that it is. However, don't neglect to recognize the ancient establishment of the light-bodied, small-headed short-eared Spaniel. Such are identifiable in innumerable canvases all over the world, especially in the greatest of the Dutch genre paintings that one finds much seized upon also by the writers of Toy Spaniel literature. Undoubtedly there is linkage, and one remembers that the Toy Spaniels of the Marborough period were respected as good hunting Spaniels, too. How ancient the type, who knows, but plenty of 17th and even 16th century pictorial evidence abounds—as the Paolo Veronese (1528–1588) in the Palace of the Legion of Honor, San Francisco, California. That Spaniel could go modernly into a Brittany ring but for his long tail. His bodily characteristics and color are exact, even to the pink nose.

All through Belgium, Holland, France, one may see modern variations on the breed theme, smooth-coated ones, hound-headed ones, but always with the characteristics to raise the question. Owners shrug, look with benign possessiveness at their treasure and tell one frankly it is *un batârd,* a word not exactly screaming for translation.

The trouble with the Brittany Spaniel, if such a word as trouble could ever be applied to a breed enjoying such overwhelming public approval, is that the knowledge of its excellencies is not everywhere possessed by non-owners. A Charles Lamb story applies. The great English essayist was walking with a friend when he happened to look across the street and say of a man he saw walking there: "I hate that man!" "Charles," protested the friend, "you don't even *know* that man!" "That's why I hate him," Lamb sighed. "If I knew him I know I'd have to like him."

That goes for men and dogs, for nations and food, everything! One has to have the personal acquaintance to appreciate virtues. It has always seemed to me, in relation to dog breeds, that too many dog judges, male or female, are prepared to "go to the stake" rather than confess that all ramifications of all dog knowledge is not resting within their bosoms. No one is born with acquaintance, let alone knowledge and understanding, of all dog breeds. They have to be learned by personal contact. Some American judges secure Brittanys along with privileges covering the rest of the group. Such may not have been acquainted with even one of the breed away from the show ring. It has long been my thought that those whose judging experience is confined to what comes into the rings may never actually have seen a mature Brittany. Specials classes are not well-supported in the breed. Owners "go for" Dual Championships, in which the Brittany now has a tally close to the hundred. They show-campaign young dogs oftenest between Derby and All-Age Field Trial classifications. Once the Brittany has his show title safely in paw, he returns preferably to the Trial interest, or to familiar hunting chores. Few are the owners that do not know their good Dual Champion will get scant attention in the Group. To see the eminent, and often very lovely Brittany Duals, one has to go to the trials.

For the British judges, an article of mine spelled it out in *Dog World* (1967):

54

This picture may be unmatchable for content anywhere in the world of Sporting breeds. Seven dual-champions, member-owned, competed at the Spring 1967 Field Trial of the Northern California Brittany Club. From left to right, they are: Dual Ch. Lewis's Ringo, Dual Ch. Lund's Trooper, Dual Ch. Tigar's Jocko, Dual Ch. Trooper's Little Frenchman, Dual Ch. Ultra-Mend Maisie, Dual Ch. Tietjen's Red Ranger, and Juchoir's Shady Scamp.—*Dan Buster.*

So many owners of field trial dogs in other breeds are given to acidly commenting that "you can't ever tell when a Brittany is on point." What seemingly they mean is that his height isn't impressive. Actually, his point is unmistakable and often of tremendous intensity. This is Dual Ch. Trooper's Little Frenchman, son of Dual Ch. Lund's Trooper, owned by Mr. and Mrs. E. Burkhart, California.

You will find his skull a bit wide; not coarse, but never narrow. His muzzle runs off. His ears sit way up there, shortish, short-feathered. When you get his attention he cocks those ears right-angled to his face. His eyes are seldom as dark as you, or even his Standard, might actually prefer them, but not to worry. Light pigmentation is linked with his orange-patched coat. He will show you a flesh-colored nose. At least, he *better!* Anything you could reasonably describe as black will disqualify him. He will look leggy. That's right—it's the very word his Standard uses. He is, in fact, what your English Springer Spaniel in England is claimed to be—"the highest on leg and raciest of all Land Spaniels." However, his height is restricted, again by a disqualification clause, to between 20½" and 17½"—maximum and minimum.

If British Spaniel judges trip over his alien type, so do some American Setter judges. Mr. Stuyvesant knew of that: "I have nothing against Setter type—for Setters!" He added the French opinion that a Brittany must never be allowed to lapse into just a small, bastardized Setter. Such do occasionally show themselves; one in my ring very recently had to be discarded by such assessment. Stuyvesant compared the Brittany to "a good riding cob, short-backed, full of fire and go, neither nervous nor high-strung, the epitome of stamina and carrying power for his size." The same authority also defined the work pattern: "Bowing to the great Circuit Trialler, and to the plantation owner's kennel of wide-ranging covey dogs, the Brittany is the dog today for the more modest, but equally keen sportsman whose one dog will hunt for him all day, every day—grouse, woodcock, pheasant, quail."

The American Brittany Club sponsors such an aim, as well as the ideal of the Dual Champion, and proudly approaches now the finishing of Dual Champion Brittany One Hundred. The Brittany is still for the most part owner-handled, less in professional hands than some other competitive breeds. One does notice however that in the pressure of competing against Pointers/Setters that are so relentlessly pressured for pace, the Brittany has become increasingly subject to like pressuring. This could lead to increased relegation to professional handling and training to get the Brittany out wider and wider. If wholly caught up in this same snare, many of the breed's most valued qualities could be lost to the requirement to forcing into the rigid mould of a running dog. This pleasantly versatile and companionable breed deserves to escape this fate. That it might not is not pleasurable to think about, in view of the Brittany's antiquity and rich endowment of virtues long preserved.

The parent club is aware of this endangering of the virtues that made the reputation of the Brittany in the first place, and is not happy with the pressures exerted by a lunatic fringe who have no compunction about changing the dog to suit fashion. One doubts that an average Brittany owner will want to acquire and support a horse to be able to work his dog. And one guesses

The first lesson! This puppy grew up to be Dual Ch. Juchoir's Shady Scamp. Owner, Mr. W. Brown, longtime stalwart in Brittany Spaniel Club activities.—*C. Bede Maxwell.*

Brittany Spaniels don't object to an occasional clowning. Dual Ch. Lund's Trooper, owned by Gilda and Ejner Lund, California.—*C. Bede Maxwell.*

women, who have always so strongly supported Brittanys, may feel less drawn to temperament that too often comes out on the other side of the schooling that serves best to "get it right out."

As a pointing breed, the Brittany is actually out of his element in a classification as a Spaniel, just as is the Irish Water, which is a retrieving breed. The parent club does not press for any change, but long since dropped "Spaniel" as a designation. The club is officially The American Brittany Club. Dr. Z. White's fine definitive breed book is *The Brittany in America*. To owners, affectionately, the dog is a "Brit."

Numerical strength is astonishing, and increase remains steady. In 1965, the Brittany registered 7,644 which took it to 18th place of 115 breeds in AKC tabulation. 1966—8,314; 1967—9,464; 1968—9,620; 1969—10,761 and 1970—13,400. Popularity is maintained, numbers increase, with no aid from promotion or advertisement. This may be among breeds at the top end of the registration scale the least advertised of all.

Introduction to America is purely a 20th century thing. As late as 1927, the writings of even so distinguished a bird-dog journalist as A. F. Hochwald make no reference to a small Pointing breed dog out of France. His mention of the man eventually responsible for the introduction and promotion of the Brittany, the late Louis A. Thebaud, was merely in connection with Wirehaired Pointing Griffons, an earlier enthusiasm of M. Thebaud.

In France, the Brittany could be considered always to have been, in one designation or another, the leggy Spaniel with the light muzzle and the good disposition. The club, Epagneul Bretagne, was first formed in that country in 1907, came to grief in each of the destructive World Wars, and revived after each one was over. It had for motto graphically: "A Maximum of Quality in a Minimum of Size."

The French breed Standard is less restrictive than the American, and the latitudes extended include color, okaying black which of course is wholly out of order in the United States. Undoubtedly, various introductions have been made to the European Brittany, of which English Setter may be the most readily conceded. Which reminds me that a name familiar in British English Setter breeding history came to the United States with early Brittany imports here, Sharvogue. The first champion Brittany was Habask Guid de Sharvogue, and Ch. Patrice of Sharvogue won the first breed Specialty (1946). However, strain names from overseas, in all breeds, have always been light-heartedly grabbed up in the United States, oftenest from some back line in the pedigrees by owners who lack even the faintest notion of where credit rightly belongs. That a famous name is a *property* in dogs is poorly recognized here.

My luck in respect of the Brittanys has been to see some of the greats of the breed, albeit quite often in their advanced age. Thus, my first *ever* Brit-

Dual Ch. Holley Haven Duchess, foundation of the famous American Brittany strain, Holley Haven. Duchess provides interesting comparison with French Dual Ch. Laskar de Saint Tuguen, pictured below. Considerable difference in head type is the major factor, while remembering we are looking at dog and bitch. Owner, Mr. Henry Holleyoak, Michigan.—*Shafer*.

Laskar de Saint Tuguen, a French Brittany with titles for both Field and Show (1966). Owner, Madame Marchand, France.

tany to see was Dual Ch. Penelope of Evanstown, this at a Heart of America show in Kansas City in 1956. It was to widen my knowledge that I walked the long line of Brittany benching, a breed completely unknown to me. There sat this very distinguished looking bitch. "Tell me about her—and her breed," I asked her owner. How lucky it always is to have one's first impression of any breed formed by first-class specimens. Then, at my first-ever Brittany Trial, in California, 1958, there were those two old Duals, Pierrot of Fontaine Valley and Brit of Blaisey Blas.

In California, where the breed interest is also strong, some modern history makers have been delightfully under my attention, such as Dual Ch. Tigar's Jocko, of fantastic performances; as Dual Ch. Lund's Trooper, with his long show and trial career enhanced by an outstanding record as a producer; as Dual Ch. Lewis' Ringo, who moved so beautifully, and his brother, Ch. Rino Diablo, who was so close to the model of modern Brittany type. Years ago, my camera caught old Ch. Ultra Mend Susie, when she was almost 10 years old, and in superb condition, a year before whelping her *90th* puppy! So many others . . .

Imagine that day when someone got around to counting and discovered that at that Trial of the Northern California Brittany Club there were in actual competition *seven Dual champions,* all member-owned, and had sense enough to line them all up for a picture that will not likely be matched in a hurry in any Sporting breed! My misfortune is that this country is so large, for right across the continent, state by state, good Brittanys are being bred, raised, worked, without fanfare, keeping their public by sheer quality of performance and stability of character as house dogs, keeping mother company all week, and out with father with the gun on Sundays. My wish would be to see and admire them all.

The Brittany does not thrive in kennels. He needs a home, such as his forebears have enjoyed for centuries. One cannot change such inherited characteristics just because someone thinks the best thing a dog can do is run out over the county line. A Brittany needs to *belong.* At a show in Brussels (in 1968) it was possible to see all around the Brittany ring, owners sitting with their Brittanys in their laps, even as here. The Belgian Brittanys were all orange-whites, but several had pigmentation darker than one would be able to accept in America. The owners described the color as *tabac.*

It was at the Brussels show, too, that I saw the "other" French Spaniel—*Epagneul Francais.* He looked to me like a scaled-down St. Bernard, which figures, considering that the Saint was once known as the Alpine Spaniel. The French Spaniel unluckily blurred my picture, moving his head, so can't use it here. It is with Nicky Bissell, Secretary of the American Brittany Club, to show her what the breed looks like.

The essential breed characteristics can be quickly learned if only prejudice

Dual Ch. Penelope of Evanston was the first Brittany ever I saw; then benched at Kansas City (Heart of America Kennel Club) 1956. She attained a ripe old age. This picture interestingly depicts the classic spaniel ear that gives modern compilers of the Standards in several breeds trouble to define—the "leafy," the "vine-leafed." It appears to be linked historically with Celtic associations of ancient time. Owner, Louis Oltman, Missouri.

Dual Ch. Penelope of Evanston teaching her kids tricks of the trade. Group includes Ch. Penny's Prince Robin, Ch. Penny's Cactus Kate and Penny's Hi-Jinks, C.D. Owned by Louis Oltman, Missouri.

is shed to make room for accepting them. Though the Brittany is described as leggy, his basic shaping is square, as he is required to match his body length, from the point of the forechest to the rear of the haunches, with his height, ground to withers. A long body is a serious fault. His topline slope is slight, his back taut, his chest deep, his bone elegant but not spindly. His hindquarters provide his motive power, which is considerable, and his feet of necessity have to be good.

Many are born tailless, but not all. Those born with tails are docked, and if more than 4″ be left, the dog in the show ring will be subject to disqualification. The Standard asks for the tail (if any, one takes it) to be set on high as an extension of the spine at about the same level. There seems to be no incentive to peg the tail of a Brittany that carries one, but doubtless there will be handlers to try. The tailless ones are legitimately so, the original mutation (in France) believed to date from the earliest 20th century.

Of the three breeds already mentioned as carrying the "leafy" ear, the Brittany has the smallest head. It could never have supported a long heavily feathered ear. Carriage is important. Again to Mr. Stuyvesant: "For a dog that spends the greater part of his life with his ears alertly cocked, these hold a considerable importance (in judging). Many an otherwise presentable Brittany should be penalized for looking too much like a poor hound dog . . . Stretching a Brit's neck and flapping his ears over his face is a bad mistake in handler judgment. A dog with so short a tail looks out of balance with too long and swanlike a neck. A long neck needs a long tail with a magnificent plume to balance it."

The intrinsic virtues of this breed should secure to it long continuance in public favor. The only fear for it is that new ownerships may not be made properly aware of the disasters that have wrecked other breeds and strains in the past.

"Every breeder of Brittanys ought to know the tragic history of the other breeds," wrote Max Riddle, "and each new fancier should be taught a thorough history of his own breed, its desires and aims, the failures of the others. It is sad that in this and other breeds only one breeder in ten has knowledge of even the elementary history of his breed, and that only one judge in ten knows either the breed history or the aims of it."

For some Sporting breeds it has been for long too late. Too late for the pitiful wreckage of what was once known as the Llewellin Setter; too late for the lower echelons of the type-unrecognizable Pointer residue. One could continue a sad litany, breed by breed. The Brittany however still has much going for him. His appearance *plus his Standard* protect him from serious mongrelization, he doesn't attract pot-hunter patrons, and *the women like him!* That should add up to sufficient to protect him for a long time to come.

62

The English Cocker Spaniel

WHAT but warmth can dwell in the heart for the breed that brought one into dogs? An English Cocker was my first dog with papers. She was prettily blue-roan, and in truth, as her surviving pictures show, she was much to the pattern of cloddy basics in the breed books, the Braeside Bustle sort. Her litter, whelped 1933, was the first ever registered in my name—which puts me back way-way, doesn't it? Fussy had nothing to learn from me, she had been work-trained before she came into my ownership. I was the one that learned—from her! She showed me her quartering pattern, her tenacity of purpose, the use of her nose, her joyousness, her tenderness to carry. One morning she revolved endlessly around my legs, tail a'whirr, and when she finally got across that she had something for me, and I put down my hand, she placed therein an unbroken egg that she must have carried for half-an-hour at least!

She never lost her enthusiasm to hunt. In extreme age, her "game" became reduced to lizards in the garden. By the time she died not a one still carried a tail, all lost to the lightning swipe of that old paw. Colin, my son, was with the Australian Army in Greece when he learned of her death (which did not long precede his own). His letter of regret included all around the margins sketches of a terrified Fussy fleeing through Hell, pursued by tailless lizards with red-hot pitchforks!

She was of the period when the Cocker Spaniel, per se, was the dog of fashion right around the world——the English Cocker, that is, in all the countries of the world other than America which, by then, was busily committed to developing a specific Cocker Spaniel all its own.

No separation into breeds had in the time of the Cocker's highest tide of popularity as yet been achieved, and pending this, there was considerable confusion of type in the American show rings. English types competed with American types and, indeed, the compilation of American Cocker Spaniel champions in the earlier editions of Mrs. Ella Moffitt's American-published breed classic is thickly larded with many that are unmistakeably English— produce of well-known British strains such as Of Ware, Blackmoor, Braeside, Falconers, Treetops, Sixshot, Dobrow, etc. There is even listed as an American Champion an import, Model Maid of Ware, A241872, red-and-white, whelped 1936, whose breeding was the result of a union between two of the greatest English Cocker Spaniels of that or any period, Ch. Whoopee of Ware and Ch. Exquisite Model of Ware (who ended her days in the possession of an Indian rajah). It would be absolutely impossible for a Spaniel to have been more "English" than this American champion. In my edition of the Moffitt (1947) she is listed on p. 237.

Not all champions listed in the Moffitt compilation are of background so distinguished as that, but a great many must, on their breeding, have been very good Spaniels. Mrs. Hartley Dodge's Giralda strain included much imported English blood, she drawing at one time heavily on Blackmoor strain, which of course was also the foundation stone of the famous Colinwoods of later years.

It has been written that Cocker Spaniels came to America first in the Mayflower. True or not, Spaniels were crossing the Atlantic for centuries, representing all the kinds that Britain had in supply, from Toys through Fields, Cockers to Welsh Springers. Not till the present century did there come to be a fostering of a type designed to be wholly American, and decades had to pass before it became stabilized. The ingredients were, as in the case of all newly-formed breeds, the various types that were available. In respect of Spaniels in 20th century America, that represented a very wide sweep.

The English type, however, had been stabilized much earlier—oh, not in terms of ancient history, but from the weldings contrived in the last quarter of the 19th century. There are excellent breed books available for the fancier who wishes to acquaint himself with the whole story of English Cocker development, but no space for more than the briefest glimpse in such a survey as ours. Briefly, the modern Cocker commenced with the black dog, Obo. Till then, a Cocker Spaniel was merely a Land Spaniel that weighed less than a Field. Much hard work and breeder concentration brought the modern English Cocker up from the squat Obo type with thick neck and Sussex Spaniel low head carriage to the elegant pocket-sized Sporting dog that took most of the world by storm. The ideal became as A. W. Collins (Colinwood) has described it: "Square little dogs without exaggerations, built on robust lines, of short cobby appearance, but lots of substance."

64

What the judge should see . . . Classic presentation and correct trim for an English Cocker. He is not, nor ever should be, presented merely as a poor relation of the American variety. The dog shown is Ch. Springbank Ace of Giralda, who was owned by Mrs. M. Hartley Dodge.—*Brown*.

A famous breeder walks his team of English Cocker Spaniels. Mr. A. W. Collins of "Colinwood," Kent, England.—*D. G. Davis.*

"Which one? Oh, I think *this one!*" The author visiting at Sedora K (Cockers and Sussex Spaniels), Lincolnshire, England, 1968.—*E. Orton.*

The operative phrase of most importance is "no exaggerations."

Along with fixed modern type, the Cocker retained his work habit, low-stationed enough to dive under, instead of through, cover. The determination wherewith a good Cocker will face tangles and thorns needs to be seen. He will put up game from most inaccessible places, enjoy doing it, and let his owner know of his pleasure. Joseph Graham (*The Sporting Dog*, New York 1904) tells of the breed's companionability (pp. 180–181):

> The Cocker or Field Spaniel will get into less trouble and make more entertainment than any other dog. You can talk friendly gossip to him and always have a responsive audience . . . you couldn't lose him if you tried . . . While he is not a producer of big bags, his area being small, he will hustle out a wonderful variety of game . . . No dog within my knowledge is so readily brought under command and so human in its companionship . . . In an outing for its own sake, pick the sporting spaniel ahead of everything else canine . . .

In Britain, modernly, a great deal of lip service is paid by the Cocker Spaniel folk to the ideal of the Spaniel that hunts. Increasingly one heard this claim made around the British show benching in 1967/68 as the newly-introduced American Cocker made so many new friends. The "Yankee" couldn't ever hunt, *with all that hair!* No one argues that the American Cocker carries in most specimens far too much coat; a like quantity, if it were possible to plaster so much onto an English, would slow down that one's hunting ability also. Imagine it in thick cover! However, the point is that the British emphasis on hunting ability in their show Spaniels sounds merely superfluous as one assesses the amount of interest actually taken in *working* the Spaniels. The number of Show Champions that round off their title by taking the modest Qualifier in the field, even, is the measure of owner disinterest. In 1967 there were two that Qualified, both very good Spaniels. The black bitch, Ch. Peeler's Cornbow Myth, had the same year taken Best in Show at the Scottish KC show. The blue roan dog, Ch. Lucklena Blue Music, has an excellent show record, and comes additionally from a kennel that has Qualified many good ones, including one of the best-ever performed bitches in the breed, Ch. Lucklena Musical Maid, with 18 Challenge Certificates and multiple Bests in Show. Colinwood also Qualifies most of its stars, as from way back to the foundation stud, Ch. Blackmoor Brand, by way of the post–World War II Ch. Colinwood Cowboy and, of course, Ch. Colinwood Silver Lariot, 57 Challenge Certificates under 53 judges; 10 Specialties, 9 all-breed Bests in Show. The 1970 Best Gundog at Crufts, the Cocker Spaniel Ouaine Chieftain, also gained his Qualifier the previous autumn, still a very young dog. These, of course, are all outstanding Spaniels, blessed additionally with owner interest to Qualify them.

Too many present-day Cocker Spaniels seen on British benches are little nothings that physically might be sorely taxed if asked to bring in a shot quail. They give reasonable indication of being on the way down to the status of Lady's Comforters, with *sweet* little faces and *darling* ears.

The English Cocker Breed Standard in all countries allows a very wide latitude in terms of color. There is none of the rigid requirements such as hedge in the American. The solids are required to be solids, with desirably no more than a smidgin of white on the chest. White feet and such other splashes constitute mismarking. Otherwise, there exists more or less blanket approval. There does seem however to be a certain cyclical thing about color fashion in winning Spaniels, usually linked with the color carried by the current top specimen. Thus, when Colinwood Silver Lariot was the top— and his reign lasted a long time!—the lightest of blues and black-and-whites were fashionable. Goldens have had their innings from time to time. Blacks were outstandingly prominent in the winning list during the recent year of my looking over the show rings in Britain, with such names as Lochranza and Merryborne much in the picture, but by no means exclusively. It did seem to me that there were many lovely blacks. Orange-roans and red and whites were much more rare, with Sh. Ch. Waving Petals of Weirdene and Nontrebor Nonchalent staying happily in the mind. Liver-roans are approved as well as blue roans, but none of the color ever came under my eye till coming to live in California, and seeing those Ken McDonald used to show before he became a judge. A couple of years ago, out of Australia, tiger-brindles were reported, which really serves to startle. The Standard merely okays any color under the designation of "various," and that could reasonably embrace also tiger-brindles. Couldn't it? Or should one cry for help!

The goldens—that is, the solid goldens—in English Cockers seem to have developed from different basics. There was a period of years when type was noticeably different, though that variance has since been ironed out. The great gift that the goldens brought to the breed was an ability to smooth the often shaggy coats of the blacks. A golden-bred black nowadays most often carries a smooth, even a "non-trimmer" coat. Maybe that was put into the breed way back by Sussex Spaniel help. But then, there was that lovely golden bitch that it was my privilege years ago in Australia to show handle to many Bests in Show. In the ring, and dry, she was a most typical English Cocker. In the tub and wet she was a miniature Irish Setter. That was something it seemed a good idea to keep to oneself at the time, though her breeding was in no way questionable, known to me for generations back in terms of the actual living dogs. She had the long thighs, the short hocks especially, and nowadays my thought is that these also are of course the magnificent endowment of the American Cocker. She had Of Ware in her background, and in those days neither the type of the American Cocker, nor the circumstance

A beautiful orange-and-white in classic trim and expert presentation. No overjacketing, no exaggerations, no shearing. Her "separate breed" status is unmistakable. She is Sh. Ch. Nostrebor Nonchalent, a distinguished winner in England. Owner, Mrs. E. S. Robertson, Worc. England.—*1968 photo, by Fall.*

Eng. Ch. Lucklena Blue Music, handsome example of the blue roan English Cocker. A full champion (1967) and BIS winner (1968). Owner, A. Mansfield.—*Cooke.*

that Mr. H. S. Lloyd had imported and used some in his breeding program was known to me.

There is of course tremendous type variation as between the head of an English and of an American Cocker Spaniel. The English Cocker has a good length of functional muzzle and good accommodation of jaw. His stop is minimal by comparison with that of the American, and his eyes are of a different shape and setting. His eyes can at times displease with loose haw, which is a most undesirable throwback. No loose-hawed Cocker could ever look good to me, having had my share of trouble with such in my own time in Australia where an otherwise very-usefully prepotent English-bred stud, generously distributed the fault. Never to show any dog-judge the fault that plagued his own breeding is a recognized truth of dog-showing policy. Apart from giving a dog a miserable expression, the loose lid is a receptacle for all manner of junk.

The bodily characteristics are as A. W. Collins described them (*above*) and one adds importantly a reference to neck. The Standard says "long," and makes "short, thick" faults. Quite true, but "long" can also be "too long," though the fault may not have been evident when the AKC-approved Standard was compiled in 1955. There were many Cocker Spaniel necks to see in England, 1967/68, that were so long as to destroy type in outline. Warner Hill has noted such with the comment (*Dog World*) that while undoubtedly there have been in the past Cockers with stuffy necks, now they were being bred with necks long enough for grazing from trees! Some with this fault very noticeably, shown under me in England, hailed from a kennel that was also interested in breeding Americans. Maybe some brood bitches had been doing some pre-natal gazing into neighboring kennel runs.

What a true-type Cocker can't say with his eyes, he conveys with his tail. At work, it beats steadily as the dog quarters, quickens as scent is recognized, whirrs when approach is being made. The "wanton Tayle" the Elizabethans recognized is the badge of Spaniel character. A judge who merely ignores a handler pushing-up a Spaniel's tail is not doing his job. If the fault is the handler's, the judge should merely brush the hand away and allow the tail to resume a natural position. If the fault is the dog's, i.e., if it actually has a pegged tail, the obligation is to penalize it. The AKC-approved Standard asks for tail to be "*set on to conform with the topline of the back. Merry in action,*" and the opposite characteristics are defined as faults.

A Spaniel that *moves* with a pegged tail is wholly out of type. One that, alternatively, clamps the tail down as though against violation, is an abomination. A Cocker is not allowed to be a craven.

In judging, it always provokes me to see English Cockers hung about the after-ends with pathetic attempts to ape the patterning and volume of the American Cocker coat. In the days of creation and to come the English

70

English Cocker Spaniel, Eng. Ch. Peelers Cornblow Myth. A beautiful black. Pictured the day she qualified in field, 1967. Her wins include Best in Show, Scottish K. C. 1967. Owner, Mrs. M. France.

A royal occasion. Prince William of Gloucester, then aged four, makes a presentation to the winner of a Puppy Sweepstakes at Canberra, Australia. Fromelles Tomahawk later finished his title and became a well-known, prepotent English Cocker stud. Owners, Mr. and Mrs. J. Mercer.

Cocker will not be able to match the lush quantity of American coat. And so, when the English is brought into the Group and stands next to the Americans with wisps of tatty garbage dangling from his thighs, all the impression he gives is along the lines of being a poor relation. He is *not* a poor relation of the American Cocker's, but a distinct breed, proudly possessed of its own individual characteristics, jacketing, and patterning. It favors cleaned hocks and neat, muscled thighs.

Separation of the two breeds was imposed officially in 1946, when AKC granted separate breed status to the English, following a lot of hard work and pedigree clarification on the part of such sponsors as Mrs. Hartley Dodge. They had a spur to drive them to seek separation in the developing judicial climate of the time.

Mrs. Ella Moffitt's definitive work on the breed, *The Cocker Spaniel,* has gone through many editions. The more recent have been subjected to politic editorial revision, likely following some considerable protests against comments such as that on p. 180 of my copy, which includes copyright up to 1946: "To a fancier of the American type, a poor specimen of that type is less a hardship to look at than a good specimen of the other (English)." Yet, on an earlier p. 29, the writer had already conceded how mixed the American type still was, and that it was often difficult for a judge to find four to place that looked reasonably alike.

When one runs down the Moffitt list of Cocker Spaniels with AKC championships, and is further knowledgeably aware of how high must have been the quality of those representatives of the great English strains that are included up to the date of breed separation, it is clear how much prejudice must have been involved. By her 1953 edition, however, the lady was in full retreat, reporting her chapter on the English Cocker and its influence on the American deleted: "This is a very controversial subject on which there is the widest difference of opinion" [p. 191].

This is by no means the only breed in which examination of earlier editions of an author's work can yield up some pay gold. So often in later editions, provocative matter gets screened out, and useful information becomes lost to present-day students.

Since the 1946 official separation, the English Cocker has been entitled to appear in his own guise, and under necessity to ape no other breed. His sponsorships may have failed him in not insisting on the emphasis of his type individuality, his right to presentation in accordance therewith. It should not be necessary to go to Canada to see a ring full of English Cockers properly presented—as indeed it is. Which reminds me of having an English Cocker import under me in California (1969) that by sheer coincidence had won under me the year before in England. In England he had been classicly presented. In California he was hung all over with hair to resemble rather a

Ch. Ancram's Simon established two marks in 1969. He became the first English Cocker to win Best in Show at the American Spaniel Club show (a win he repeated in 1971), and his win of 12 Bests in Show and 34 Groups in that year set a record for the breed. Bred and owned by Joyce Scott Paine, and handled by Ted Young, Jr., Simon is pictured here in win of the Sporting Group at Hartford under Mr. Clark Thompson.—*Gilbert.*

English Cocker Spaniels, WB and WD at Westminster, 1960: On Time Dorrie and On Time Benjamin Blue, homebreds, owned by Mr. and Mrs. Seymour Prager, New Jersey. Both dogs later finished to title.

little Afghan. It was a major surprise to have him identified to me later as the dog at the head of my English Cocker line in Kent. It should not have been necessary to delve so deep to find his virtues.

Continually one seems to meet Americans who tell one how much they prefer an English Cocker before the American—but never seem to own one! And Americans who tell one the English Cocker is by far the better dog to hunt with—and who don't hunt and don't trial any. Club sponsorship of competitive venues is minimal. The ownerships in England are not the only ones that talk a great game, but hold back from playing it. The Cocker Spaniel out of England carries within his inheritance, most remarkably, good hunting qualities. One faithfully believes that neglect will not destroy them.

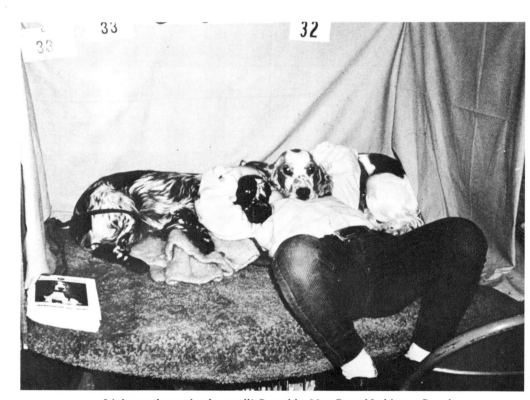

It's been a heavy day for us all! Owned by Mrs. Grete Mathiason, Canada.

The American Cocker Spaniel

THE word "American" is not put before the title of the nationally-recognized Cocker Spaniel in this country, but is reasonable to employ in this work that is taking a geographically-wide look at the various Sporting dogs. The Spaniel has become as American as the Golden Gate Bridge, and as readily so identified across the world. It is a breed of ultimate glamor emphasis, appeal, superb in movement, and rewarding to present in the show rings. Europeans have always acquired the occasional specimen, but the insular British, happy with their own Spaniels, stubbornly refused to admire or to acquire. With the like approach to the "foreignness" of the Brittany, the English dog folk repudiated the "difference" of the American Cocker. He didn't look like *their* Spaniels, was not to be regarded as admirable by "ordinary Spaniel Standards." Until recently, that is . . . We'll discuss the change, and what precipitated it, in a moment or so.

The American Cocker may reasonably be considered one of, if not *the* newest breed of dog known in the world today. Ownerships may not all realize how very new, nor for that matter care. The dog *is!* That he cannot be described as always having been is seemingly of little interest to them. Not only to newer ownerships, either. There was that long-term breeder who recently told me she was considering writing a book. She wasn't going to go for any of the historical stuff though, she added. Only what was happening *now!* My unspoken thought was that the least stable factor in dog interest is what is happening *now* because, by tomorrow, there will be a different *now.* Nothing is so lost to fancier interest as the competing dogs of the immediate past. Not till they become part of a pedigree compilation will the average

Ch. Midkiff Creme de la Creme, wh. 1915.

Ch. Midkiff Miracle Man, wh. 1922.

Ch. Stockdale Town Talk, wh. 1939.

All were involved in furthering the development of the American Cocker Spaniel; all were good winners, good dogs in their period. Variation of type in such characteristics as topline, tail-carriage, head qualities is very wide. May one do less than marvel at the skill of the breeders who formed the type we see in our time from basics such as these? The 1939 dog, of course, is already a distinct preview of modern type, lacking only the added-on exaggerations with which we have become familiar.

fancier even concede that the big winners were worth feeding—and by then, oftenest of course, he is proud of owning some of their blood. If he wishes to boast of it, he has to turn to the "historical stuff."

It is nowhere in this book my intention to deal in strings of names, dogs or people. There just isn't the space. The interested must go for such to the several comprehensive breed definitives. My specific interest is in matters the breed definitive books don't always spell out, perhaps because usually these are written by people currently active in their breed and so under various pressures to avoid the controversial.

My approach to the subject of the American Cocker is wholly in terms of How Come? For that question the answers appear to be elusive. Like any new fancier who might happen to get his hands on dog magazines of, say, the 1930s, or who leafs through well-supplied photographic galleries in the breed books, my amazement is concerned with the question of how This developed out of That and Those. If one asks the question direct, the answer is likeliest to be the same one a field trialler will advance to explain radical type change —he calls it "selective breeding." This, one is asked to believe, is a process whereby something is plucked from somewhere and added unto something that didn't have that whatever-it-was in the first place.

No sporting (hunting) breed of Spaniel appears ever to have carried the head, the jacket, or even the anatomical construction providing the distinctive outline of the American. These radical differences must have come from somewhere. From where?

Spaniel breeds have traditionally been in a state of flux, and not until the present century did the Kennel Club in England get all the various types sorted out into recognizable compartments. In America, the sorting-out was made much more difficult in that there came to be a strong urge to produce an entirely new type of Spaniel altogether. The early decades of the 20th century could not have been easy periods for American dog show judges who had to fumble their way through the maze of type changes presented for their attention. In my edition of Mrs. Ella Moffitt's *The Cocker Spaniel* (dated 1947) she wrote (p. 29) :

> . . . it is still often true that when a judge gets through sorting a good entry of Cockers he will find that it has not been possible to assemble four to which he has given *Winners* that look alike. This naturally would be the ideal finale, but too often cannot be attained without disregarding essential details and soundness. For this apparently inconsistent result he often draws the adverse criticism of ringsiders and exhibiting critics.

For a montage of American Spaniel development it was necessary to go back no further than 1927 to come up with an American Cocker champion that was still a long little low carrying its head straightforward in what, from my agricultural livestock reporting days, recommends itself to me as "sick pig" style. In the 1940s, it was still possible to come up with a major winner that was in all respects predominantly English Cocker type. By then, however, the developing American type was in competition already clear to see. Heads had become re-shaped. Necks became an item of major importance. Shortness of back became emphasized by handling pose. A lengthened thigh favored the development of the magnificently-spectacular gait. Coats were lengthened —and lengthened—and lengthened. . . .

Many people now middle-aged grew up in households that included the favorite breed of the time, the Cocker Spaniel. The name still retains for such a warm connotation. The dog was for the children a playmate, for father to use with the gun. Mother appreciated the comfort of a proffered paw when pondering the more disturbing of her domestic problems. A family member in good standing, the Spaniel was not particularly glamorous. Usually he could have done with a trim. At times his ear feather matted and his ear-canals become unsavory. His upkeep was likeliest minimal. He was bred and bought by the thousands. As his glamor was promoted, his public support fell away. The Beagle toppled him from first place in all-breed registration tables, and by 1968, he had been deposed even in the Sporting dog tally by that pudding-plain breed, the Labrador Retriever. He had become a fancier's breed, no longer the homely, comfortable Cocker-remembered. It is in dogs an oft-repeated tale. As the fanciers take over, the public bow away in droves. One plus in that calculation is that the puppy-farmers also fall away and take their destroying influence to some other luckless breed, leaving serious fanciers to mop up the mess that had been made by indiscriminate production of pups bred only to sell.

All these vagaries of fortune have befallen the American Cocker Spaniel in our very own time. Now the fanciers continue to fight the uphill battle to restore the dwindling prestige of their breed. They are doing in the main a very good job, screening for faults of conformation and importantly of temperament. It was a sad time when the average judge, in or out of the judging ring, learned to be careful in his (or her) approach to the Cockers. Many still remember incidents. It was a very eminent all-rounder who warned me that the dog that would eventually bite me in the ring would be an American Cocker. He was right, too, and the considerable blood drawn from me by a pretty 8-month-old has also washed into *my* consciousness the need to be wary. The mistake made by me, that day, was in not ordering the puppy from the ring. It is a mistake that will not be made again—for it has become obvious to me that only by penalizing bad temperament is a judge able to assist the ethical breeders in their very earnest endeavors to screen out this undesirability. The AKC officially supports the action of judges who rid their

ASCOB Cocker Spaniel, Am.—Can. Ch. Biggs Snow Prince, top winning Cocker Spaniel of 1963–4, and top Sporting Dog in America for 1964. A prepotent sire as well. Owned by Mrs. H. Terrell van Ingen.

Cavalier Toy Spaniel, Eng. Ch. Vairire Osiris (1969), owned by Major W. W. Wild. This beautiful dog, with his characteristic round eye, blocky head, magnificent ears, provides an interesting study for those concerned in speculation as to whence the American Cocker, years ago, may have acquired such like endowments.—*Cooke*.

Mrs. Hartley Dodge (Giralda), though the first strength in the promotional interest in the English Cocker Spaniels, here awards Best in Show at the 1960 American Spaniel Club show to Ch. Clarkdale Capital Stock, black American Cocker, owned by Leslie E. and Elizabeth Clark.

Ch. Hugo Headliner, tricolor male, winning under judge Mrs. Anne Rogers Clark. Owned by Albert Siekierski, and handled by Ted Young, Jr.—*Klein*.

rings of dogs that, to quote the official letter, "give any indication that they *might* bite." (The italics are mine.)

From whence came this snappishness and nervous instability? Always and always, the commercial/puppy farmers are saddled with the blame and, reasonably, they may have earned it. But there could well be more to the story than that. One gathers the impression (documentation of any exactitude appears still lacking) that the unique characteristics in the American Cocker, such as his head, outline and spectacular coating, were fixed by weldings of Toy Spaniels with the sturdy Fields and the smaller Cockers. If this be true, then may one look to the Toy Spaniel side of the experimentation for a degree of temperamental change?

Maybe, in time, some other researcher will find the answer to the Cocker type change riddle. Meanwhile, there is little to go on other than the confusion that the pictured types represent. The sons of Robinhurst Foreglow (Judge Scudder's), the stud that is credited with influencing type development, putting in a longer-legged, shorter-backed outline, are regarded generally as the taproot of modern American Cocker Spanieldom. Go look at their pictures and see what you can make of them—Red Brucie, Ch. Sand Spring Surmise, Ch. Midkiff Miracle Man. No hint of radical change in those, though one is told that Brucie was able to endow longer legs. Heads? Nothing strikingly variant there. So, is one to guess that the type change factors rested not with the successful show males, but with the unpublicized broods those served?

There is a most intriguing suggestion implicit in the breeding of two American Cocker Spaniel champions, litter brother and sister, Billy Obo Jr. 305419 and Junette Obo, 305420, whelped 1919, bred and owned by F. J. McGauvran, by Moore's Cavalier out of Patricia Obo. Having recently strolled the shelving at the British Natural History Museum storage annex near London, and seeing how many of the longer-nosed types of Toy Spaniels preserved there, some as much as a century dead, strongly suggest the heads of modern American Cockers, my reasonable query, scanning those breeding particulars of 1919, is to ask in respect of the sire of the two champions—Moore's Cavalier WHAT?

If it were done it were well done, to mangle a familiar quotation.

Meanwhile, everything *went*. See the photographs of Mrs. Moffitt's own Rowcliffes, workers all, including a Dual Champion in her Rowcliffe Hill Billy (whelped 1933). That was still a time when working interests were richly valued, and one does tend to wonder what Mrs. Moffitt *really* thought of the pictorial production that her breed eventually became; she who confessedly believed "a poor specimen of the (American) type less of a hardship to look at than a good specimen of the other (English)." That is on p. 180 of my 1947 edition, but it was edited out of subsequent printings.

The famous breeder Herman Mellenthin (My Own) was also concerned to work his Spaniels, as one might reasonably expect from a man partial to harness racers, and who had actually driven Dan Patch. Several very well-performed Spaniels came from his strain in the years between the two World Wars, including Dual Ch. My Own High Time (whelped 1928) and Dual Ch. Miller's Esquire, CDX (whelped 1938) whose sire was Ch. My Own Peter the Great. Once again one is inclined to think that the modern paucity of Cocker Spaniel performance on the working side is as much the fault of the American Cocker owner as the paucity of work performance is the fault of the English Cocker owner. Every well-performed dog, any breed, is the result of exertions made by his *owner*. An outstanding example in American Cockers is, of course, National Field Champion, Prince Tom. Unfashionably bred, trained to such excellence as to make him first an Obedience, then a Field champion, this one owes to the tenacity of purpose that animated his proud owner, whose constant companion Tom was. One simply *cannot* reasonably look at a beautifully-presented, lush-coated Cocker Spaniel and say didactically that it cannot work. The only valid judgment to be made is in terms of what opportunity was given the dog to prove his abilities, yea or nay. And shearing off the jacketing of a middle-aged show champion and hurling him into Field Trial competition isn't a fair measure either. The opportunity to parade his instincts should be provided earlier than that.

Most discussion, especially the "agin" kind, zeroes in on the American Cocker's coat. After all, it is so *visible!* Though early breeders labored to produce and fix it, early critics tended to report as in connection with the appearance in 1942 of Ch. My Roy Masterpiece, a son of the excellent Ch. Stockdale Town Talk. Masterpiece had "so much coat ringsiders could not see his conformation at all. His brisket and belly coat dripped to the floor, and his legs floated in an enveloping blanket of hair" (*Denlinger, The Complete Cocker Spaniel, p. 76*). Our modern show-goer and/or breeder will shrug and say so what? That's exactly the quantity of coat a show American Cocker carries in our time, nearly 30 years later. The Standard disapproves of it, of course, setting forth that feather *"shall not be so excessive as to hide the Cocker Spaniel's true lines and movement or affect his appearance and function as a sporting dog. Excessive coat or feathering shall be penalized."*

Now, that's really for *laughs,* and provisions of a breed Standard officially-approved should never be for laughs. Yet, of course, this is not the only breed Standard that has provisions that are wholly ignored by fanciers and by most judges. The American Cocker Spaniel with a coat in tune with the Standard requirements would be in the like case with a Welsh Springer Spaniel with light pigmentation that his Standard approves; i.e., his win would not be well received.

However, it is not necessarily true, as some galleryites proclaim, that *be-*

cause a Cocker is excessively coated, his body underneath is faulty. There is very often some remarkable dog-engineering under all that hair! It can be a pleasure to feel the strong rib spring, the wonderful thighs, the short hocks that provide the tremendous, spectacular drive.

The thing is, however, that if the Standard was really intended to be read and respected, then there would be teeth put into the requirement that excessive coat should be penalized. If color and patternings can be burdened with exact requirements in terms of disqualification for non-conformity, so can the degree of coat. Unlike the English Cocker, the American is rigidly restricted in terms of color, with proportioning in Parti-colors carefully spelled out. Also operative is a height restriction, operative however only at the top of the scale. A male may not be over 15½″, a female over 14½″. At that, it is interesting to note how far up in the world the modern American Cocker has actually come. An original Obo son, imported in utero into Canada decades ago was reported as 9½″ high, and weighing 23½ pounds.

Before moving right away from color, it is worth taking a look at the picture (p.49) of three-time winner of the American Spaniel Club Specialty (1930/31/32), Ch. Idahurst Belle II. She has most successful descendants in straight-line down, handsome Spaniels in red-and-white Parti-coloring that run through the breed books. Within a decade down from Ch. Idahurst Belle II one can come up with Ch. Bobb's Show Master, by way of several generations between. The only thing these several direct descendants have from her is the spectacularly red-and-white patterning. Their shape and make is as variant from hers as is possible to contrive. They look exactly like the best of their contemporaries, Spaniels such as Ch. Stockdale Town Talk and the rest.

Anything further removed from modern American Cocker Spaniel outline and type than Idahurst Belle is just not to be imagined! She came from a strain "noted for a particular head type, very clean skull, pleasing expression, low fine ear, stop lacking in the depth breeders were working for" (*Denlinger, The Complete Cocker Spaniel*). Her outline, in terms of body-leg proportioning and characteristic topline is unmistakeably Welshie. If we could trace down the processes whereby her produce *within a decade* changed so radically and completely, we might have a better understanding of how the modern show Cocker evolved in the way he did. All one has however are the photographs of the more famous of the Spaniels that ornamented the breed's high tide of popularity, the 1940s, the 1950s. One has looked at such as Ch. My Own Brucie (twice Best in Show at Westminster KC) and at Ch. Torohill Trader, and in between at Ch. Nonquitt Notable, who was so near as makes no matter 100% English in type, and any dozen or two dozen more, every shape and head type there is, and it is impossible to withhold the greatest of admiration from dedicated breeders who over so short a period have

Am.—Japanese Ch. Whitfield's Why Certainly, top winning Cocker Spaniel, all varieties, for three straight years. Owner, Briarcliffe Kennels.—*Ludwig*.

Ch. Be Gay's Tan Man, Best in Show at American Spaniel Club, 1970—first tri-color ever to take this honor. Judge, Dr. Gilbert Taylor. Bred, owned, and handled by Bill and Hay Ernst, New Milford, Conn.—*Gilbert*.

managed to weld all this divergent material into a single, and most pictorially admirable type that now breeds true generation after generation.

That is one aspect of the remarkable story of the modern American Cocker. The other is the remarkable story of English acceptance of this breed. In July, 1967, it was my historical privilege to judge the first-ever classes specifically put on in England for American Cockers. The venue Stevenage, near London, sponsors the Rare Breeds Club. The black bitch, Sundust Merryborne Leading Lady, was my Best of Breed, and went on under another judge to take Best in Show. By January 1970, the Kennel Club had assessed the breed strength in the land to be sufficient to justify providing Challenge Certificates, and so champions could be made. The first American Cocker Spaniel champions in England were made in 1970. Entries continue to rise. Thus Manchester Championship show, 1970, less than three years after the first showing of the breed, attracted 55 Spaniels making 88 entries, way ahead of many breeds long approved in England.

Promotion was contrived first by a charming girl out of Holland, Yvonne Wayland (now Knapper, and Club president). When she had proposed to bring her Dutch-bred Americans into England she had been told they would *never* be accepted! With Dutch stubbornness she brought them over, and Leading Lady, whelped in quarantine, spearheaded the interest. Now, with English acceptance, spread to Australia and New Zealand can be confidently forecast.

This is truly history. This little lady. Sundust Merryborne Leading Lady, imported to England from Holland, was the first American Cocker Spaniel to win a Best in Show in England. Shown with her owner, Mrs. R. Knapper, whose privilege it was to introduce the American Cocker to England.—*C. Bede Maxwell.*

"Marking the Covey" by Harry Hall, from the Art Exhibition of the British Institution, as reproduced in the *Illustrated London News*, March 10, 1854. Rare, indeed, is the fortune to find a Setter picture of this period. The artist clearly differentiates between type, and one notices that the Irish is on lead, while the English stands free, supporting the long-term understanding of temperamental differences. Note that the game includes fur as well as feather.

The Setters

THE first thing to write of Setters is that the varieties differ. English, Irish, Gordon——each is in its own right a distinctive breed, differing in heritage, habit, anatomy. Identification merely by color is not enough. Anatomical "experts" who provide a single skeletal drawing to cover all three do no one a service, and are for ranking with cheap ceramic makers tipping all three from one mould and painting to suit. Judges should not operate on any same slick basis.

Earliest identified, best documented, is the English. The Irish may be even more ancient but remains very poorly documented. The Gordon is an amalgam, and has been further bolstered from breeds outside the Sporting group. The English is basically a Spaniel. The Irish is basically a scent hound. The Gordon partakes of both groupings.

A close-up of the Setting Spaniel in the "Falconry" Tapestry of the Devonshire Hunting collection in the Victoria & Albert Museum, London. Expert opinion dates this tapestry in the 1400s, woven at Tournai. It clearly establishes that the Setting Spaniel was not only ancient, but was also the forerunner of the breed we've come to know as the English Setter, body characteristics being unmistakable.—*C. Bede Maxwell.*

The English Setter

ANCIENT writings and medieval tapestries establish the long existence of the dog the French knew as a *Coucher,* and that Johannes Caius, the Elizabethan, identified as *Index,* the Setter. We know it as specifically the *English* Setter, but that it actually is an English dog rests on no better evidence than that offered in proof that the *Spanish* Pointer originated in Spain. The name was accorded the "improved Spaniel" (as Edward Laverack has described it), by long custom and consequent on the considerable improvements added onto the original type by the long-term interest of English breeders of great skill.

The distinctive work pattern that gave the breed its name has been described as far back as the time of de Foix, the 14th century, but for its look-like, what manner of dog it actually was in medieval times, it has been necessary to wait centuries for the opportunity to see publicly. Now, in the Victoria & Albert Museum, London, there are on permanent view the Devonshire Hunting Tapestries, woven in the 15th century at Tournai, in Flanders. These four great spreads of pictorial splendor, restored at the expense of the British taxpayer and by the skill of Dutch technicians, have been in the Devonshire family for so long that no one knows any more how they were come by—maybe as loot of war. The most beautiful of them, "Falconry," is rich in flowers, castles, prancing palfreys, princes in gold ornamentation, ladies in court hunting dress. By a millstream, a falconer is launching his birds against flying duck. A little Setter is his helper, and one easily recognizes it for what it was, 500 hundred years ago, in France.

However, the English were using the Setter in Elizabethan times, as Caius attests. We also have other evidence. A letter survives in British archives as of January 23, 1563, written by Ambrose Lord Warwick to his brother the Earl of Leicester, Robert Dudley, Queen Elizabeth's Master of Horse. Lord Warwick, at the time, commanded the English forces beseiged in Le Havre, England's last foothold in France: "I thank you for sending me so fine a horse. In return, I send you the best Setter in France, with a paper bearing a list of its qualities, written in French and in English" (*Ref.: Forbes. Public Transactions in the Reign of Elizabeth I*).

The English had Spaniels of course, but of a different kind, heavier, closer to the ground, lacking the elegance of the airy-fairy little dog of the Tapestry spread, with its exactly recognizable Setter shape and coat patterning, differing only in head from the fundamentals of the dog we recognize today.

Dudleys, as a family, were patrons and participants in every form of hunting sport. Ambrose was the patron to whom George Turberville dedicated his great work, so little quoted by those 19th century dog writers on whom everyone draws, perhaps for the rarity of the surviving copies, of which three only are cataloged. Those same 19th century writers make many a mention of one Robert Dudley as being first to teach a dog the "setting" work pattern. No one who quotes this ever seems to provide any exact reference of source, and there is also disagreement in which century this was effected. As a matter of fact, all over medieval Europe, century by century, hunting dogs were being schooled and worked, documented too. Thus John of Avis, of the 14th century, compiled in Portugal his *Livro de Montaria* as a distraction from the troubles of ruling his realm, "a treatise on the hunting of bears, wolves, wild boar, deer and hares, which along with falconry were the main sports of noblemen of the time. He expounded in his matter of fact way the proper care of horses and the training of hunting dogs" (*John Dos Passos, The Portugal Story, 1969, p. 79*). It was entirely in the character of the times that a princely ruler should take practical interest in the care of the creatures that furthered his sport. It is also interesting, by the way, to notice that the game as quoted by the Portuguese ruler is exactly the same as that depicted in the Devonshire Tapestries. Turberville translated earlier works by Italian and French falconers and huntsmen. The country that still stubbornly lags in providing documentation remains Spain.

Actually, there does exist a reference to the effect that a particular Robert Dudley taught a dog to something or other in relation to the hunting of Partridges. As happens most often, it was my reading outside doggy interest that provided the clue, a reference in the work of Elizabeth Jenkins, who specialized in the Elizabethan period. She identified the quote as from *Athenae Oxoniensis,* a scholarly work covering the biographies of all graduates of Oxford University from establishment till the compiler, Anthony á Wood, put down his pen in the later 17th century. The spur then was for me to find and photocopy the reference in the copy seen in the British Museum. A Robert Dudley, born 1574, son of the Earl of Leicester and Lady Sheffield, is subject of a long biography that ends: "He was an exact Seaman, Navigator, excellent Architect, Mathematician, Chymist, and above all celebrated for Riding the Great Horse and for his Being First of all that Taught a Dog to Sit to Catch Partridges" (*Vol. II, Column 127*).

Whatever Dudley taught a dog to do in relation to Partridges, it was not the Setting Pattern, for that work had been described already centuries before he was born.

The Caius' description of the Setting Dogge's manner of work has been often used, and has been re-copied continually since his time. Let us then draw rather on Gervase Markham (*Hunger's Prevention, or the Whole Art of Fowling, London, 1621*) whose name is well known enough even in our time. The Retriever people copy a paragraph from his work continually, his description of the Water Dogge, and the Gordon Setter people reuse the reference "Idstone" makes to Markham's praise of "black-and-fallows." His entire work, however, is crammed with delight, by all measures my favorite dog writer:

> If you chance to see your Dogge make a sudden stop or stand still, you should make unto him (for he has set the Partridge). As soon as you come to him you shall bid him "Go Nearer! Go Nearer!" but if you find he is unwilling to do, or to creepe nearer, but lies still or starts shaking his Tayle as who would say "Here they are, under myne Nose!" and withal now and then looks back as if he would tell you how neare they are . . . then you shall walke about . . . looking before the Dogge's nose till you see plainly how and in what manner the Covey lyeth. You shall then charge the Dogge to lie still, then drawing forth your Nette as you walke, having pricked down one end to the grounde, cover all the Partridges therewith (then) you shall make a Noyse, the Partridges will rise, and be entangled in the Nette . . .

Markham was clearly a conservationist. He advises letting go the Old Cocke and the Old Henne so they might rear other broods. Besides, he added, they were poor eating in any case.

The exact documentation of the work habit of the Setting Spaniel by writer after writer throughout the centuries establishes that it is indeed an ancient pattern. That it is bred into the very fibre of the Dogge is not to be disputed. Besides, what is it, after all, but the hunting habit of primeval dog. All man needed to instill was the discipline to prevent the dog from leaping in to seize the game. There always have been, and likely will continue to be, Setters that defy even the most sadistic of training practices and insist on creeping up to, and falling in front of their game. Not even the force of cross-breeding can, in every case, blot out the strength of instinct.

Dog men of earlier centuries than ours worked *with* instinct, not against it. There is probably no illusion more disappointing to harbor than that because modernly some form of fashion favors certain stylized procedures and posings, the ancient ingrained instincts can be turned around in a generation or so.

The style for bird dog hunting developed by those who were satisfied to work with instinct rather than against it was that the dog that actually had the bird went *down*. The dog that backed stood *lofty*. It is also believed that when the fashionable emphasis on high stance became first engendered, selective breedings were made with the dogs that stood loftiest of the backers. It worked better with Pointers than with Setters; better with Irish Setters than with English—and for the reason that the Pointer and the Irish Setter are basically hounds and the work of the Setting Spaniel was never part of their heritage. Standing lofty came to them naturally.

There is a great wealth of artistic evidence to demonstrate the partnership between the dog that went down and the dog that stood lofty to back. Famous examples are those Louis XIV paintings in the Louvre. It is the very root and branch of the tragedy that overtakes so many strains of sporting dogs—the Llewellin Setters, now an extinct strain, being a handy example—that training is often in the hands of those who have no understanding of dog instinct and inheritance, and whose rule-of-thumb measure, often a heavy pressure indeed, is applied to all breeds without distinction.

Edward Laverack wrote that "many of the best Setters fall as if struck by lightning, though many have been induced to stand by imitation, being broken with the old Spanish Pointer who never fell to game." Those Setters that could not be induced to "stand by imitation" stimulated the ingenuity of the trainers to keep them on their feet. Some day, some one should get around to arranging an exhibit for Madame Tussaud's Chamber of Horrors of the various inventive contrivances whereby, over the years, dog trainers have sought to keep on their feet Setters with strongly ingrained instinct to go down.

The strongest force to keep them up was undoubtedly the natural, painless one of inter-variety breeding. Purcell Llewellin used a considerable mixture to form his original "field dog strain," and legitimately too, for in his day inter-breeding of Setter varieties was not regarded in other than a reasonable light. We know he had weldings of Irish; we know he kept Gordons; and we know he introduced a strong coarse not-specifically-analyzed Setter strain from "out of the north," his Duke-Rhoebe introductions. We do not know whether these weldings produced the high tails that American field trial judges for many decades classified as a "Llewellin fault," but we can reasonably guess his other infusions helped to get the Setters up on their feet. The high-carried tail in those Llewellins that happened to carry it,

Laverack type English Setter. The early imported Laverack Setters were also useful hunters, but of course lacked the speed of the later-introduced Llewellin strain. However, they possessed in full measure the beauty that Laverack valued so highly.

Llewellin type English Setter (Scottijohn, owned by Richard S. Johns). Though founded on Laverack bitches, Llewellin type was radically different from Laverack. The high tail was introduced in this country by Llewellins, described by judges for long as a strain fault. It became acceptable early this century, fashionable by the 1930s, and mandatory ever since. Though the "straightbred" Llewellins were competitively finished by 1915 (La Resita's National year), many dedicates carry on with good hunting dogs.

didn't by the way, come via the Laverack English Setter brood bitches that Llewellin used so consistently, those scatty spooky ones. We know from "Stonehenge" (eminent dog writer and editor of *The Field*) that in his time the Laverack Setters carried tails "trailed like a fox."

"The Setter's inherited tendency to crouch, still observed in many of the best and highest bred of the present day is accounted for undoubtedly by the former habits of the breed. Where the instinct is very strongly ingrained it is a fairly hopeless task to overcome it" (*Vero Shaw, The Illustrated Book of the Dog, 1890*). This classic writer's summation is matched in many other works of the 19th century. The cumulative advice was that the trainer get another dog, call the battle quits. The Germans, too, were aware of the strength of the instinct to go down in the Setter, but then they approved of it; by their hunting fashion it was fine. "In search and movement the Setter differs from the Pointer who takes a higher station and quarters his field, while the Setter goes forward with wind-use and drops before the scented game, whereupon his usual instinct is to lie down in front of what he has located" (Gorny: *Ein Hundebuch*).

There is seldom any percentage in attempting to beat out of a dog instincts very strong within him. That the Llewellins in their heydey in America also carried the instinct is established by that best of 20th century Bird Dog writers, A. F. Hochwald. Discussing two National Field Trial Champions, sire and daughter, he wrote:

> Mohawk II (National Champion, 1904) . . . sometimes showed the catlike traits in approaching his game that Tony Boy, his sire, seems to have imparted to some of his sons. He was not habitually feline in movement when approaching game, but when he did it was held that his keen nose detected what most dogs might miss, at long distance, so that he was prone to steal up till sure of the body scent, when he would go to his game with thrilling snap.

Here, clearly, was a dog whose instincts warred with his training. His sire possessed the instinct and passed it along, not only to Mohawk II, but to a half-brother, Lanark Lad, who showed the same trait. Mohawk II, in turn, passed it to his daughter, Monora, National Field Trial Champion of 1910: "On game she was catlike, crouching frequently on her points, or actually dropping" (*Hochwald, Makers of Bird Dog History, pp. 33–58–59*).

Tony Boy, who was also the sire of Geneva, the National Field Trial champion, and one of the greatest of all-time competing Llewellin bitches, was himself bred in the most exactly-dyed of Llewellin strain purple, being by Antonio, he by Roderigo, he by Count Noble.

Plainly, judges of that time were good dog men, which not all who ride the saddle in our present day Saturday and Sunday field trials necessarily are.

94

Those of the earlier day could perhaps better estimate dog performance on an all-over basis, instead of tripping over the minutae of technicalities of lesser importance.

The tenacity wherewith instinct lives on in Setters was demonstrated for me years ago by a great show bitch of my own, an Australian–New Zealand champion, show bred for as far back along the many generations we could take her pedigree. She had never had opportunity to work in Australia—my State of New South Wales was virtually devoid of upland game but rich in lethal snakes. Taken to New Zealand, which is rich in upland game and wholly devoid of snakes, she pointed quail in the hedgerows and pheasant when we walked afield. We spent a lot of time on walks going back to flush something or other for her. Every second male acquaintance wanted to borrow her to, as they said, "make a dog of her—with all that instinct she has to hunt." However, we had serious show commitments, so that was that. Every day we surfed down on the long grey beach of Pegasus Bay (Christchurch). When her swim was over, she played a game with dedication and daily attention. One morning, the sense the good Lord gave to geese prompted me to take the camera. So it was possible to preserve the record of the strange circumstance that this untrained Setter re-enacted *with exactitude* the routine of the Setting Spaniel just as Markham and his contemporaries described it, as do the modern Germans: "going forward with wind-use . . . drop before scented game, whereupon his usual instinct is to lie down in front of what he has located."

She played her game with the sea gulls feeding on the pippy-shell beds. She would use the wind (who taught her that?) and creep down to them. And when she had come up as close to her unsuspecting quarry as could be without flushing them, she would go down: "here they are, under myne Nose!" Wet from her swim in the surf, seasonally out of coat, she shows in those pictures taken with a battered old Box Brownie, all the mechanism of dog progression in the anatomical sense. These are valuable pictures to use in lectures both for the anatomical reason and for the proof of instinct preserved. "Instinct, like a desert river, may disappear during parching years of drought, but will reappear without bidding when times are right" (Robert Ardrey's magnificent work, *African Genesis*).

It would seem, from discussions heard from time to time that there are dog-trainers (not necessarily only in Setters) who regard such demonstrations of strong instinct as providing them with a challenge. Modernly, it can happen in the case of German-trained dogs in breeds such as the Shorthair, mature dogs whose natural instinct to go down has been bolstered by German training to drop to shot. There are some sad stories in connection with such, and the most usual outcome appears to be a ruined dog. In Setters—English Setters specifically—another inherited characteristic is carried down into

Dr. A. A. Mitten's Happy Valley Kennels could well have been the greatest-ever Setter kennels in the U.S. This photo (with Dr. Mitten in profile at left) pictures half the Happy Valley entry at Philadelphia show, 1934.

present times, thoroughly documented along the way, century by century. That is the inability of the English Setter to cope with severe punishments. Only strong infusion of hound influence balances this hindrance to the "taking of training." Whatever influence got working Setter tails up in the air may also have provided some "fight back" or "the patient endurance of mistreatment" that so many 19th century authorities especially document in relation to Pointers. Truebred Setting Spaniel inheritance has never been able to cope with harshnesses, nor seemingly can to this day. Jeff Griffin (*Hunting Dogs*, 1960) holds it against that pitiful little bag of bones, the modern field trial Setter, that it "must be trained with kid gloves." There never was a time when this did not apply, even to the sturdier specimens of an earlier period.

> The Setter breed is possessed of a constitutional timidity which induces it to fear severity of correction, avoid means of disgrace, perpetually alive to the fear of giving offence and incurring bodily punishment by claiming ever little tender affections, at home and in the field——Taplan, *The Sportsman's Cabinet*, 1803.

> Setters cannot be broken with a severity that too often (and unnecessarily) accompanies the breaking of a Pointer. The Setter has not the patient courage of a Pointer. If too much chastened it is made into a blinker—Youatt, *The Dog*, 1836.

96

The other half of the Happy Valley benching at Philadelphia, 1934. The exhibit included all of Dr. Mitten's "greats" of the time, active showing stock and broods, etc. The lineup included his great bitch, Ch. Inglehurst Reward, his Maesydds, and the imported Ch. Pilot of Crombie—who on the day took Best in Show. (The photographs were donated toward this book by Dr. Mitten, shortly before his death.)

Europeans recognized the trait. The most heart-breaking dog picture of my knowledge is that by the great German sporting artist, Sperling, called "Setter under Punishment" (*Feine Nasen,* 1889).

One inclines to wonder about the Elizabethans, how they schooled *Index,* their Setting Spaniel. Okay, come in, Gervase Markham, come in again and tell:

> When you have, either by your own industry made such a Dogge, or else by your Purse, Friendship, or other Accident, obtained such a Dogge, you shall . . . cast him off with Words of Encouragement, according to the Custom of his Education. Then shall you cease from more words except any Faults or Mistakes enforce you. You shall have great and special heed that he never raunge too farre from you, but beate his Ground justly and even, without casting about and flying now heare now there, skipping many places, which the Heate and Mettal of many good Dogges will make them do if they be not reprehended.
>
> When any Fault shall happen, you shall presently call him in, and with the Terror of your Countenance so threaten him that hee shall not dare all that day after to do the like, but shall raunge with modesty and temperance, ever and anon looking you in the face as who shall say, 'Doe I now please you or not . . .' You must then give him Cheerishment and Encouragement.

Markham wanted his dog "happy, with a wanton Tayle, a constant companion to learn from your Frowne and your Smyle, your Gentle with your Rough, the Terror of your Voyce." He used food to reward and withheld it as punishment:

> If hee has been very wilful . . . take him up into your Stringe and lead him Home, tying him up for the Night without more than a bit of Bread and Water to maintain Life in his Bosome. Then, next day, take him to the Field and so as before, yet withal with somewhat more Terror and Hard Countenance of Face, so that hee may not only call to mind his former fault but also see that hee hath not gotten your Favour, and will be more careful than hee was before. Then you must by no means forget to bestow upon him all the Cheerishments that may be, tone of Voyce, Hands, Food, also wherewith the Dogge may be delighted and encouraged.

A modern professional American field trial trainer will laugh himself to stitches, reading that. He, with clients conditioned to demand Instant Everything from Coffee to Gundogs. Besides, his preoccupations are different. He is not trying to produce a dog that a man will find a companionable, bird-finding booster for hunting sport, such as men of Markham's day delighted to own or, for that matter, many men also in many parts of this our modern world. "Words of Encouragement" won't get a Setter out where bullwhips, pellets of shot, and/or electronic aids will shove it, and that of course is the modern American trainer's problem. But it is also true that in so many places, in so many lands—including this—there are those who like to hunt with a companionable dog that can find them game. "Meat dogs," I guess, is what the dedicated field trial buff will call them. Owners of such dogs would enjoy Markham. He wrote in the language they enjoy to speak.

All 19th century authorities of distinction do discriminate between the collapse of a Setter under punishment and the same Setter's courage in occasions that call for guard. This was also an instinct thoroughly proved by that same Setter of my own. One evening, out walking far from any human habitation, on that same long grey New Zealand beach, her breeder and myself were accosted and badly frightened by a burly exhibitionistic pervert. Rohi, who was on lead, swung a sweeping arc continually to and fro in front of us, facing the pervert, snarling with her fangs bared, making roars and lunges that would have done credit to a Doberman. We were Her People, and she defended us. The pervert, thoroughly intimidated by her performance, covering protectively with his hands what he had been proudly displaying, made off and away.

"Didn't I tell you when you first had her from me, that she'd never let anyone touch you!" gasped her breeder. My, we had been two scared gals!

It was also true that the same Setter would cower visibly if I yelled at her for any faults.

98

There is a wonderful record of a Setter at war, one that saw the "rockets red glare" over Fort McHenry and the bitter retreat from before New Orleans. In her time, officers took their hunting dogs to the European wars, and between battles had their sport. We do not know her name. Subaltern George R. Gleig, her owner, refers to her only as "my brave Setter" or "my faithful Setter." He was 19 and she 9½ months when first they landed in northern Spain, at San Sebastian, towards the close of the Seven Years' War there, where the Duke of Wellington set a sporting example by having his foxhound pack along. Gleig hunted over her, and by night she may have been his Linus blanket, for they were both so young. She made rounds with him, and they survived the battles. Then, that war over, they went by transport to the Chesapeake, were at the burning of Washington, the attack on Baltimore, the awful debacle before New Orleans. There was no hunting sport for them in America. Gleig wrote that this was no gentlemanly-conducted war:

> The Americans send riflemen to fire among the parties around the watch-fires, while one or two, stealing as close to each Sentinel as possible, act the part of assassins rather than soldiers. In one such situation, I was saved only by the barking of my faithful Setter. Amid all the bustle of landing, and through the tumult of nocturnal battles, never once did she stray from me, or if she lost me for a time, she failed not to trace me out again. As soon as order was restored I found her always at my side.

Only once did she fail him. It was during the terrible retreat to the ships after New Orleans. Gleig struggled back with the remnants of the 85th:

> Every step we took we were to our knees. Men drowned in mud. We had no tents, no coverings, no food. I took my firelock and went in pursuit of wild duck that abounded over a bog, killed three. They dropped in water but my Setter, more tired than her master, would not bring them out. I pulled off my clothes, broke ice, plunged in, and shivering like an aspen returned with them to camp, losing along the way one woollen stocking sucked down by mud, so till we rejoined the ships had only one leg warm at a time.
> —George R. Gleig. *A Narrative of the Campaigns of the British Arms at Washington & New Orleans . . . in the Years 1814–15.* London, 1821.

She survived to go home with him where, eventually, he took Holy Orders, became Chaplain-General of the British Army.

A Gordon Setter also figures in a strange war-dog story, to tell presently.

The Great Names of English Setter development are of course Laverack and Llewellin. They were good friends, Laverack dedicating his breed book to the other. Llewellin's field trial breeding was based on spooky Laverack bitches that in mating with coarse but sturdily practical Setters of a strain from the north known as Duke-Rhoebe (from the names of the dog and bitch he acquired) added in the nervous energy and fire.

Llewellin built up as the Laverack strain collapsed. The last days of the famous strain are documented by Vero Shaw (*The Illustrated Book of the Dog*). The constitutions of the end product of the decades of inbreeding could not withstand distemper (in those days uncontrolled) or even normal ills. Nov. 13, 1874, Laverack writing to his friend Rothwell: "I am quite broken in spirits to think that after all my trouble and a lifetime of expense I feel I have, or shortly shall, lose the breed. I have only one brood bitch left, Cora, and I fear her too old to breed. The only dog I have left is Prince . . ."

A fantastically-extended pedigree was published in 1897 in an Australian work, *The Dog in Australasia,* by Walter Beilby. There is likely no equivalent extant anywhere else in the world, as it has been extended all the way back to the Laverack basics, Ponto and Old Moll, and clearly depicts, for those with the background knowledge, the degree of inter-variety breeding practiced. The dogs one stumbles over continually in English Setter (and Irish Setter!) history are there even to Llewellin-bred Flame, the Irish Setter that went to the Mallwyd (English Setter) kennels and put in that rich red that many orange-beltons carry to this day. Llewellin's weldings can be easily picked up. A "pure Gordon bitch" was his, and "Judy (MacDona's)" has to be an Irish, MacDona a famous breeder of such. There is much name duplication, as in all 19th century pedigrees, such as a Cora, a Cora I, a Cora II, a Cora (Blair's) etc. However, one can be hauled up as is a horse on a Spanish bit by the exact identification of Prince and Cora, mentioned in the pathetic Laverack letter (*above*) as the parents of Carrie, the Irish Setter Llewellin showed consistently at that time, and she the dam of the famous Mallwyd basic, Flame (*above*).

There was nothing underhand about all these weldings and re-weldings of the varieties at that time—they were merely the introductions by which the modern breeds of Setters we presently recognize were shaped and polished. But the compilation, in its exactitude, does make hay of the claims of those who labor to convince us that the breeding background of the Setters of today is possible to trace in unsullied purity of separation way back to the ancients. Dog breeds have *never* been kept pure, and a sizable percentage of the modernly-recognized in all Groups are not kept pure to this day. The only difference is that in our day the requirements of registration do not permit the whole truth being told. It still remains true that the only person who really knows what dog covered which bitch is he who witnessed the mating.

There are several Laverack letters of like pathetic content. We find space for at least one more. "March, 1875: "I have reared only one dog out of 30,

The classic English Setter head, full face. Am. Ch. Clariho Bit O'Candy, owned by Laurel Howe and Jane C. Slosson, New Jersey.—*Gilbert*.

The classic English Setter head in profile. Australian—New Zealand Ch. Enzed Laurent, bred by Enzed Kennels and owned by the author.—*Ben Gabriel*.

101

and have many requests from America. If I approve of your young ones, I may perhaps get you a customer."

Thirty years later, Joseph Graham (*The Sporting Dog*, New York, 1904) wrote: "there were in truth here more highly-perfected Laveracks than anything old Laverack himself ever bred" (p. 84). Americans that had imported Laveracks brought in, as did Llewellin also, fresh blood, and restored the constitutions of the in-bred strain.

Llewellin's activities can be traced through old English show catalogs, for he was a dedicated show exhibitor as well as a field trialler. The ideal of the Dual Champion would have appealed to him, and one would not be troubled to guess what he would think of some of the pathetic rubbish that is in our present time memorializing his name. When Laverack showed Dash at the Crystal Palace show, 1870, Llewellin showed his Gordon Setter. In 1871 Llewellin showed his Laverack-bred blue belton, Countess, a famous one; Nellie, who would become the dam of the famous American-owned Llewellin, Count Noble; and Carrie, his Irish. All these are in the background of that mythical, never-was creature, the "straight-bred Llewellin."

When he acquired his Duke and Rhoebe, Llewellin cleared out his Gordon and Irish interests, deciding to concentrate henceforth on developing a field trial strain, but their legacy was still in his breeding stock welded from all their multiple excellences. From Duke and Rhoebe he got his Llewellin's Dan, and from there was off and away. The first contribution he made to the American scene was in 1874, sending Bergunthal's Rake, first of what came to be known as The Famous Six. Rake, by Llewellin's Dan ex a daughter of Laverack's Fred, was a coarse, almost black Setter of whom it is recorded that "if he possessed a nose he lacked the judgment to use it" (Graham, *The Sporting Dog*, p. 65). Of his maternal grandsire (Laverack's) Fred, the distinguished author, "Idstone" (*The Dog*, 1872) wrote that he was "very superior of form and texture of coat, but far too heavy in shoulder, and too wide in chest for speed, a fault he persistently handed down to his descendants, including Fred II and the blue-mottled Dash." All of which, by the way, was recorded in the extensive pedigree published by Walter Beilby.

The character of the spooky, scatty Laverack bitches used in the Llewellin breedings has been thoroughly documented, including by the published works of the most eminent American bird-dog writer, A. F. Hochwald. In England, "Stonehenge" left us the description of Countess, whose sister, Nellie, threw Count Noble: "When fresh, she would break away, defy the whistle till she had taken her fling over a thousand acres and more. On good scenting days she was a pleasure to watch, and both she and Nellie could find game well enough with a good scent. They were useless on a bad one." Such unruliness as Countess displayed in the English trials was new to the game, but when introduced in America provided an astonishment and set a fashion. The fashion became described as "class." The most famous of all bird-dog trainers in the heydey of Llewellin fame, J. M. Avent, provided an apt description of the quality. This was after he had won the National Championship of 1900 with Lady's Count Gladstone. This Setter, he said, "would get away from him if he didn't know how to turn it," and added the definition of "class" as "a dog that runs away but not quite" (Hochwald, *Makers of Bird Dog History,* p. 19). What the eminent trainer was describing was a dog that was on the ultimate razor-edge of control. One has seen many of the like in other breeds in this our own day.

After Bergunthal's Rake came the brothers, Leicester and Lincoln, whelped 1872. Orange-whites, by Llewellin's Dan ex Laverack's Lil II, they were entirely different in type. Leicester was handsome, refined, fast, and as spooky as his erratic, gun-shy dam. Lincoln was a steady one, and took from the Rhoebe side of his breeding her physical qualities, that is he was short-legged and common-looking. He was however a first-class bird dog, heavily-marked, richly-coated, with what is described as a "ropy" tail. His eventual influence on Llewellin breeding was exerted most strongly through his son, Gleam, one that the fanatics wanted to discard anyway, holding that Gleam was not "straightbred," i.e., that he carried blood other than that of just the Famous Six. Restriction to the blood of the Famous Six was the measure of "straightbred Llewellin" status. Only as one digs into the multiplicity of material Llewellin used to produce those Famous Six does one realize fully how absurd the claim to "straightbred" status actually was. Llewellin himself avoided continued breeding along such restricted avenues, his continuing aim to produce not only good field trial, but good *looking* dogs.

Next came Gladstone, imported in utero, whelped in Canada, sold as a pup into Tennessee. Also by Llewellin's Dan, he was ex Laverack's Petrel, another spook. It is extraordinary that as one tends long since to bracket the Laverack name with show dogs of a solid citizenship often classified as "dull," how consistently the evidence provides that the Laverack bitches behind the Llewellins were as Hochwald and others described them—"rattlebrained," etc., etc. Gladstone was reported to have been 22½" high, 50 lbs., "finely built but quite thick in shoulder, short in head, snipey in muzzle, with high ear-set and a tail carried like a foxhound, but with excellent legs and feet" (Graham, *The Sporting Dog,* 1904, p. 60). So, then, *that* must have been at least one source of the high tail carriage in field trial dogs described by the judges for so long as "a Llewellin fault"—until the proliferation of the character additionally in field trial Pointers into the 1930s forced them to about-face and consider the one-time fault a virtue. Nowadays it counts as "style," and a dog that lacks it might as well be in his hammock, as the navy used to say.

After Gladstone, came Druid, 1877. A 4-year-old, ex (for a change) a

The indestructible nature of instinct! A Setter, showbred for generations, plays her game on the beach, mirroring exactly the routine of the Fowler's Setting Dog of centuries past. Wet from swimming, out of coat, she also demonstrates the use of anatomical parts, the necessary "front and flexibility" that permits her to drop between her shoulders as she gradually lowers herself to the ground in progression.

The closer she approached her quarry, the lower she dropped. Her hocks lie flat on the ground as she creeps forward, her belly feather brushes the sand. Such a routine would not please an American field trainer or judge, but this untrained show bitch obeyed only the bidding of Setter instinct.

Using the wind (note her back-blown ears) she always contrived to come very close to her quarry without disturbing it. Then she would go down and hold. How did she know to do this?

These snapshots, taken with my old Box Brownie years ago, shows the construction, shoulder placement, clean throat (see shadow in water) and classic head of Australian–New Zealand Ch. Enzed Laurant. Gervase Markham, whose work so much delights me, would have known what she was by her pose conveying: "Here they are, under myne nose . . ."—*C. Bede Maxwell.*

docile dam named Dora, this blue belton was a better bird dog than any that came before him. Steadier too, thus providing a useful "dampening" influence. His daughter, Sue, provided classic nick with Gladstone.

In 1880, came the Noblest Roman of Them All. Count Noble was by Count Wind 'Em, that Llewellin would eventually rate as the best dog he ever bred. The dam was Nellie, already discussed. Count Noble is described as having been "long and low, most unimpressive standing, but all style and intensity in work." Eventual weldings of his stock with the Gladstones represents a concentration matched likely only by the family of Fletcher Christian on Pitcairn Island.

English sporting dog interests went into gales of laughter when it was learned that the Americans considered "Llewellins" to be a *breed*. The best of contemporary American dog journalists also stubbornly refused to consider these field trial dogs as other than merely a strain. There are three (only) breeds of Setters, it was pointed out regularly—English, Irish, Gordon. There was long a fashion to dub the produce of imported stock by the name of the exporter—as the black Pointers were known as "Papes" after the English breeder, and the "Llewellins" fell into a like. There are still those in this our own time who talk glibly of "Llewellin Setters" and identify the present-day field competing English Setters as such. Actually, the strain has been dead for decades. The last successful "straightbred" Llewellin was La Besita, the National Champion of 1915!

Hochwald (for one) could not resign himself to the belief that the Llewellins were gone for all time, though his knowledge and reason told him this was so: "While it must be admitted that no representative of this strain has become remarkable for outstanding achievements since La Besita's day, it could happen at any time that a new and unexpected star may arise, phoenix-like from out the ashes of a glorious past and again bring prestige and fame to a cause that has been practically ruined by ill-considered over-zealousness" (*Bird Dogs and Their Achievements*, p. 80).

No such Llewellin star did ever appear. However, that is not to say that no *English Setter* ever had a taste of glory after 1915 and La Besita. It's that there was never again a "straightbred Llewellin" star. Indeed, from within a very few years after her, there were no field trial English Setters that had other than the merest courtesy claim to the famous name. In modern times the English Setter, Mississippi Zev, snatched a victory from the Pointers in the National Championship of 1946. The next one came nearly a quarter-century later, Johnny Crockett in 1970. As proverbially one swallow does not make a summer, these two victories, by so many years divided, meritorious as undoubtedly they were, do not constitute a resurrection of a "breed" that never *was*, in any case.

The force that wrecked the Llewellins was the same that wreaks its harm on competitive field trial strains in our own time. It spells itself out as a

Irish Ch. Banner of Crombie

Irish Ch. Banner of Crombie (the dignified one at extreme left) poses with his Australian family, including his son Dual Ch. Manoah Moonlight (tall one, back row). Owners, Manoah Kennels, Melbourne, Australia.—*C. Bede Maxwell.*

106

concentration on some single aim at the expense of the whole dog. A dog always has been, as are all other creatures that live, the sum of *all* his parts. In dog breeding, as in all else, no one beats the percentages.

Llewellins also suffered, of course, from extensive inbreeding. Additionally, many great ones died without produce, and others left but nominal get of little importance. Thus Tony's Gale and Joe Cumming scarcely survived the rigors of their National wins. Sioux, greatest of all Llewellin bitches was mowed down by a train and left no descendants. Geneva left nothing of value. Phillipides was killed in a kennel fight. Pioneer was a failure at stud. Prince Whitestone sired gundogs, and of Eugene M., Hochwald makes the remark that "at this late date it is best not to disturb the skeletons mouldering in old field trial closets all these years" (*Bird Dogs and Their Achievements*, 1927, p. 61).

Skeletons still moulder in our own time in field trial closets, including closets of other than English Setters. As did Hochwald in his time, those in the know keep their mouths shut.

The fanatical graspings after "straightbred" status, the scorning of helpful introductions as "dirt in the veins," had also much to do with the destruction of the strain. A glimpse at the table of the National Champions gives the picture of the degree of inbreeding:

1896	COUNT GLADSTONE IV	Count Noble ex Ruby's Girl, by Gladstone.
1897	No competition	
1898	TONY'S GALE	Antonio, by Roderigo, he by Count Noble ex a granddaughter of Gladstone & Count Noble.
1899	JOE CUMMING	Antonio ex Picciola.
1900	LADY'S COUNT GLADSTONE ...	Count Gladstone IV ex Dan's Lady, she by Dan Gladstone by Gladstone.
1901)		
1902)	SIOUX (B)	Count Gladstone IV ex Hester Prynne.
1903	GENEVA (B)	Tony Boy, he by Antonio, ex Lena Belle.
1904	MOHAWK II	Tony Boy ex Countess Meteor; she by Count Gladstone IV ex Fleety Avent; she by Roderigo (above) by Count Noble.
1905	ALAMBAGH	Dash Antonio, he by Antonio, ex Eldred Lark.
1906	PIONEER	
1907	PRINCE WHITESTONE	These five were all by Count Whitestone, he by
1908	COUNT WHITESTONE II	Lady's Count Gladstone ex Jessie Rodfield, she
1912	COMMISSIONER	by Rodfield ex Clarke's Maud Gladstone.
1915	LA BESITA	
1910	MONORA	Mohawk II ex Tankas, a daughter of Prime Minister, he by Count Gladstone IV ex Hester Prynne (above) ex Cado, by Roderigo.
1911	EUGENE M	Roscoe Gladstone, whose background is given as almost solidly Count Gladstone IV and Dan's Lady, both sides.
1913	PHILLIPIDES	Prince Rodney, he by Lady's Count Gladstone ex Jessie Rodfield (above).

Irish Field Trial and Cert. of Merit winner, Mab of Fairy Thorn, with her owner, the late R. L. Russell of Ballymens, Ireland. "Only the best hunting dogs in all Ireland will please me," Mr. Russell wrote me, "but the Irish eye of me has to see beauty as well." Mab was entirely show-bred. Her sire, Sh. Ch. Ripleygae Mallory, was a prominent show winner in England in the early 1950s, and sired several of the breed's full champions. I also knew a daughter in New Zealand, Ch. Fantail of Sandylands, by Mallory, a fine show dog and a magnificent hunting aid.—*C. Bede Maxwell.*

Many men still active in the sport have personal recollection of the Llewellins, or recall what their fathers had to tell. "I'm glad you came to our place to search for Llewellin material," writes my friend, Richard S. Johns, of Pennsylvania, whose help with several sections of this book has been so generous, "For me it was a raking over of ashes almost dead, the fires of memory rekindled. I have killed hundreds of grouse over a Llewellin you would have loved, with fire popping from his huge dark eyes, drawing himself on point so high you could swear he stood upon his toenails. But memory apart, it is over." Dick mourns as did Hochwald—La Besita was the last!

Dick once had aim to make an English Setter Dual. When that proved impossible he turned to Shorthairs, and made *several* Duals. He has never seen an English Setter Dual Champion. Two are known to me, both Australian, a country of course where the American type of field trial is not favored. Bird work is the measure, as in the 19th century in America, before the coming of the Llewellins and the fostering of the ideal of "class" to the exclusion of most all-else. Australian Setters still work towards field points much as the Irish Setter used to do in America until Llewellin speed shoved him aside. Dual Ch. Manoah Moonlight, and his son Dual Ch. Manoah New Moon were bred by Mrs. C. Nance-Kivell, in Victoria, and their background was 100% "show." Both were excellent hunting dogs. Moonlight's sire, imported Ch. Banner of Crombie, was a most famous post–WWII sire in Britain before export. His dam, unshown, was litter sister to a B.O.B. bitch at Crufts that had her "full" championship, having gained her field Qualifier.

One will never make an American field champion from a show-bred, but it is just *not true* that show breeding cancels out practical working qualities by some automatic process. English Setter inherited instinct is very strong. What lacks in 99.05% of show dogs is the opportunity to show whether they have instinct or no. My best time ever with any breed of hunting dog was across Tullygrawley Bog in County Antrim, Ireland, in 1955, with the late Mr. R. Russell, Irish schoolteacher, working his Pegamoid of Fairy Thorn, and her daughter Mab of Fairy Thorn, an Irish Field Trial and Certificate of Merit winner.

"Shooting sport is my life interest," Mr. Russell said, "and I've hunted Tullygrawley all my days. Nothing but the best hunting dogs in Ireland could please me, and these I have. But the Irish eye of me has to see beauty as well." For that, he sent Peg to a well-known English show stud, Ch. Ripleygae Mallory. At the time of my visit, there were pups of Mab's in the yard. Some went to Sweden, where a dog has to qualify as a worker before even being allowed to show on the bench, and became champions. And son, Rollo of Fairy Thorn, went to Wales, and in 1968, Rollo's grandson, certainly unknown to me, went to my Best in Show at the Midwestern Gundog Soc. show at Cirencester, England. A beautiful blue belton, upstanding fellow, with good wins, this Haulfryn Biddybegan Blue Boy, is a practical shooting dog used by his owner, Mr. W. Stephens, just as was his grandsire.

Ch. Ripleygae Mallory sired several dogs that got their Qualifiers, and the president of the Franklin Kennel Club, New Zealand, worked for years a most beautiful, almost snow-white Mallory daughter, Ch. Fantail of Sanderlands, another personally known to me.

One hears plenty about "work qualities lost to show-breeding," but one needs to clarify what the speaker means by "work qualities." If he's talking about "run," that isn't necessarily the same as "work qualities." One hears little, either, of field trial breeds that don't possess the desired qualities, but in this venue many indeed are bred, as the weekly columns of the *American Field* establish. Match those numbers with what actually survives to compete and there you have (as also in Pointers) the whole sad story of so much of this kind of breeding in which the wastage is so extensive.

The Show English Setter

There is no intent to trespass on the English Setter breed book preserve, but it may be reasonable to quote a provocative matter which probably belongs in there rather than here. It is from Graham (1904), his *Sporting Dog* (pp. 94–5):

> . . . in 9 cases out of 10, the modern Laveracks in this country (America) seem to me to breed such blemishes as bad pasterns, hocks, ill-shaped feet, wrongly-set shoulders. Almost invariably (though) they reproduce a coat of fine quality and good Setter expression . . . My observations of these breeding defects are confirmed by reports from a few other breeders.

Present-day breeders are still proud of coats and expression, and there are still too many English Setters with poor running gear.

English Setter *heads* actually never have given breeders much trouble. One finds the occasional "lippy" one, and the occasional slanted eye that gives a look of hauteur unbecoming to this breed. One meets the occasional one with light pigmentation—very unbecoming—and also, but more rarely, black pigmentation on an orange-belton. Davis Tuck held this indicative of Irish Setter cross. So, who denies inter-variety breeding as from centuries past. However, the combination is striking, and the Standard says noses *may* be dark in the colors other than blue, leaving it to the discretion of the judge, whose penalization of such a character would be close as makes no matter to nit-picking.

Setter *ears* are really important. A useful quote is from "Frank Forester" (Henry William Herbert) a first among American sporting writers: "The only permanent structural difference between the Spaniel and the Setter is the size of the ear, which in the Setter is smaller and looks as if it has been

110

English Setter of the 1920s: Swedish-Danish-American Ch. Tula Jager-hem, owned and imported by Erik Bergishagen, Michigan.

Lest we forget how good they were also in the 1930s: Ch. Inglehurst Reward, a beautiful Best in Show—winning bitch, owned by the Happy Valley Kennels of Dr. A. A. Mitten.

111

Star of the 1950s: Ch. Rock Falls Colonel, with 101 Best in Show awards. Pictured competing in the breed at Westminster K. C., 1956. Owner, Wm. Holt, Virginia.—*C. Bede Maxwell.*

A 1960s beauty: Am. Ch. Valley Run Dinah-Mite, owned by Mary Beth Nichol, New York.

1970s winner: Am. Ch. Guys 'N Dolls Shalimar Duke, pictured winning Best of Breed at Ventura K. C. under the author.—*Ludwig*.

113

rounded by art." The AKC-approved Standard reads: *"slightly rounded at the ends,"* and the English: *"tips to be velvety, the upper part clothed in fine silky hair."* This requirement was probably better understood years ago than modernly, if one takes photographs for guide, as in the Davis Tuck Gallery of Champions.

"Forester" has also well-defined Setter body: "it should be high and thin in the withers, snaky in neck, roomy in chest, long in arms and quarters." English Setter forehands should have considerable flexibility. The Setting Dogge had to lift and drop his body continually between his shoulders, and the requisite flexibility is a long term inheritance in this breed, or should be. A judge may accept a *slight* degree of looseness in this area in an English that he should not tolerate in Irish. That is not, of course, to approve a shoulder that swings out and away, as one does see at times. The Irish, of different work habit, never needed to depress and elevate himself between his gaze-hound angulated shoulder assemblage. These factors influence outline, among other things, and an English Setter's correct outline is wrong for an Irish.

The Standard requirement that "shoulders should be so formed as to permit perfect freedom of action to the forelegs," is usually taken to relate only to gait. Up-and-down flexibility is an English Setter tool of trade, and and can be observed in work, the properly built one able to draw his foreleg back quite a long way along his ribs if a work requirement demands it, and drop his body between.

English ribs, also, are more rounded, Spaniel ribbing as compared with hound ribbing in the Irish. Tail set also varies between these two, consequent on pelvic assembly differences. However, it is also true that extensive inter-variety breedings have (unfortunately) reduced many basic Setter differences to Lowest Common Denominator terms.

The American Kennel Club Standard permits the snaky neck to be *"not too throaty."* The English Kennel Club Standard is agin throats pendulous, and asks for elegance. The heck of it is that the American Setters appear to have necks long and elegant, the English short and stuffy because many American Setters are neck-shaven to the skin, the English less often, though there is a hint of American style to be seen there now occasionally.

Swampy *backs* are the ultimate Setter abomination; a roach is ugly, but preferable.——one representing weakness, the other strength. Another prevailing fault in show Setters is muscle-lack. "Loosely-twanging banjo strings for muscles" have figured in my critiques before this day.

Standard requirement in *gait* is for *"free, easy, graceful movement, lively tail, high head carriage."* I incline to shy from those folk who try to make a mystique of gait. In confined ring space, especially indoors, the ultimate assessment of a dog's worth cannot be made solely on the basis of what he

114

does with his back legs especially. Hung up, as so many are, on a gallows' lead, dogs cannot find their proper center of gravity (*McDowell Lyon, The Dog in Action*) and legs can sprawl every-which-way in consequence. A judge can satisfy himself as to construction while a dog is standing and if a dog is built right he can move right—under reasonable conditions. Which, alas, too many show rings do not, repeat, do not provide.

Setter gait was taught me on the long grey New Zealand beach where a distinguished Setter breeder, once described to me by Percy Roberts as the best amateur handler he ever saw, made me study the dogs as we took our daily walk, two dogs of mine, one of hers. My Patrick, blue belton, dripping coat and glamor but stick-straight at both ends, had the *showiest* prance, which he could accelerate only to galumphing canter. My friend's old Best in Show winner bitch, plump in retirement, could cover ground very fast, but had lapsed into favor of a lazy pacing gait. Coming head-on, Jolly rolled like a harness horse heading into the straight—two-off-two-near; two-off-two-near. Rohi, the daughter of Jolly, also a Best in Show winner and in her age prime, used a reachy diagonal trot which she easily lengthened to a skimming gallop. The three, it was drilled into me, moved differently because they were *built* differently. Jolly was structurally correct, except that she was far too fat. Old Patrick always had the passers-by hooked. No one looked at our Best in Show bitches when *he* was around. He was past showing age, but one day we took him just for the heck of it. A visiting Irish judge said: "If it's winnin' with your good bitch ye be wantin' to do, then take me advice and be lavin' the owld felly home. Not ivery judge has me own fine discriminations, and such could be puttin' him over her, so they could!"

Many the time, standing ringside in various countries, have I seen some equivalent of my old Patrick, dripping coat, glamor, and structural faults, go over sound and beautiful bitches.

In addition to watching the Setters gait, we photographed their paw prints in hard wet sand. Such instruction can be of value beyond the price of rubies. It is not beyond the ability of breeders to contrive if so minded.

Show and field, there is emphasis on positioning a Setter tail. A show Setter lashes his tail side to side. A field trial dog on point skies it. There was in America for a time also the fashion to sky the tail of a Setter in the show ring, and some of us remember a forthright young Australian judge who told a famous handler: "There's nothing the *matter* with that dog's tail, it's just the way you're holding it!" The AKC-approved Standard for almost every Sporting breed, is for "carriage in line with, or below the level of the back."

Color: English Setters are blessed with the freedom of a very wide color range. Ticking and patching are anciently verified. Blue, especially, is associated with this breed, and seems to have come from out of Asia, through

Europe. Gaston de Foix mentions small hounds, white flecked and mottled, centuries before Caius records the "marble-blewe . . . newe kind of Dogge from France." The blue-ticked pattern has been anciently, and still is, favored in that country. Benedict Henri Revoil explains the beautiful blue hounds, the Gascons, in his *Histoire Physiologique et Anecdotique des Chiens,* Paris, 1867, as ". . . *quelques chiens d'origine asiatique, aussi remarquables par la beaute de formes que par leurs excellentes qualites."*

There is still a wealth of blue in France. There are still Basset Hounds, *Bleus de Gascogne,* to see in the show rings, and the classic big fellows, the packhounds, the *Grands Bleus de Gascogne.* Too, there are still those Blue Luzerners (hounds) in Switzerland. Most exciting of all, to me, was to see come alive a page from the famous 1905 compilation of Baron de Bylandt, a living *Braque Bleu d'Auvergne.* Nora du Creuzon, L.O.F., 7 Br.Au. 6290/ 137, owned by M. Wallard, Chelles, France, whelped 1964, is one of a rare breed indeed. Bylandt described her race as *"importe par les Chevaliers de Malta."* He praised the "beautiful outline, gentle eye-expression, white with black markings making a blue color." Never saw a dog it would have been a greater delight to own than Nora. She was literally *azure* colored, but if one had her in the United States most breeders would get around to describing her as an off-type Shorthair! We became acquainted, and she posed for my camera at the show in Brussels, Belgium, in 1968.

England has always kept up blues, as from Laverack's Ponto and Old Moll, favoring the lighter shades. There was a time in America when the blue seemed about to vanish. Rumor held that "judges didn't like it." One presents the thought that judges are not free to penalize colors the Standard approves. Breeders should come to terms with the well-documented truth that English Setters *need* their several colors. Many qualities in the breed appear to be color-linked, and in screening colors, qualities are also screened. "I suffered much from sticking too much to one colour in past days," wrote "Idstone" (*The Dog,* 1872) "I lost size. That I did not care about so much, but I also lost courage." Davis Tuck (1950) is not the only modern that learned the hard way that "there must be some multiple factor between coat color, eye color, and vigor, because when orange-beltons are bred together for too long a time, the eye color grows lighter, and vigor, vivaciousness, pep and steam, seem to lag."

A reason given for the decline in English Setter popularity in modern America is that the dog is dull. The rings are *full* of orange and lemon beltons—and the "judges don't like blues" and they "wouldn't look at tricolors," or so runs exhibitor opinion.

Davis Tuck held the belief that tricolor indicated field trial breeding, which interpreted means that he connected the color with the rag-tag residue called Llewellins in his (and our) day. He made some experimental crossings

116

Some English Setters get stuck with the baby sitting. (Dual Ch. Manoah Moonlight has company on the show bench.)

of show-field stock and didn't like what he got. However, the Llewellin patterning of black-white-tan is not the tricolor of the show Setter breeding. The show tricolor is most often prettily light-blue, with tan spotting on muzzle, foreface, and especially front legs providing delicate emphasis. Many of the best English Setters known to me have been tris, including the two Australian Duals. The list of English Setters with their Qualifier gained to become "full" champions in Britain is over-weighted with tris. The latest list available to me counts 5 blues, 1 orange, 1 lemon and 11 tris. There could be acceptable belief that the tris unite those several desirable qualities that are linked with the various color inheritances.

AKC-Champion, Valley Run Dinah-Mite, a tri, whelped 1962, is closed-meshed into the pattern of those English full Champions, this by way of her grandsire, imported English and American Ch. Ernford Highflier. Her great-grandsire, Ernford Easter Parade, has two full champion get, including Sun-top Carnival Queen, a tri of remarkable prepotency, and Ernford Evening Flight, who shares Highflier's dam. Highflier himself, before leaving England, sired an Irish Field Champion, Faithful of Fermanor (1962). Space lacks for full analysis along these lines, but could be rewarding for fanciers in America to examine.

Patches, held catastrophic in a show dog, should not deny stud opportunity to a dog with otherwise much to offer. And for a final thought, the Standard's Scale of Points allots 3 of 100 to Color AND Markings.

Coat is mandatory for a show Setter. Laverack wrote that for him a Setter could not have too much coat. Even Llewellin worked for coat, and indeed, the picturization of the great American Llewellins most often present well-coated dogs. Those modern know-nothings who hold appearance of no value should occasionally take a look at the pictures of the great Llewellins in such works as those of Hochwald. Their looks didn't hamper them, and no modern bag of bare bones has ever after all duplicated the performances of the Llewellins of the strain's heyday. "Forester" wrote that without a good coat a dog was not a Setter at all. However, judges should not fall into the opposite trap and accept a Coat without the Dog underneath, as at times can happen. Davis Tuck wrote me years ago that: "American English Setters *in general* do not carry heavy coats. Food, climate, have no bearing, as individuals with heavy coats carry them summer and winter, on different diets, in different latitudes. Pups from heavily-coated parents do not necessarily have the same. My feeling is that the English Setter is not fundamentally a heavy-coated breed, and in wishing for such we may be wishing for something not a breed trait at all."

The distinction necessary to make would be between *sufficient* coat and over-lavishness.

Overseas, the belief prevails that all American Setters are monsters for *size.*

The English Standard actually makes provision for larger ones than ours, males 25½–27", females 24–25½", compares with our males "about 25" and females 24". The Davis Tuck Gallery of Champions provides interesting figures; none recorded reach 27". Most top the measure at 25" to 26". However, tall-posed stance and oodles of coat help convey impression of a larger dog.

The breed has undoubtedly lost public favor. Even the Chesapeake Bay Retriever tops it in registration figures now. Economic considerations and the deaths of prominent, wealthy supporters, have cancelled out many kennels, and the breed is today much in the hands of one-dog owners, who are often sadly unaware of vital facts connected with the descendants of the ancient Setting Dogge. The dogs need something to *do,* and indeed, the whole tide of dog fashion and public support in the Sporting breeds is setting in that direction. Owners like to have *something to do* with their dogs other than merely to give them to handlers to show. It seems to me the sponsoring breed interest could do more to provide opportunity to work English Setters outside the actual competitive field trial sphere. Irish and Gordon Setter interests do a great deal.

The English Setter, beautiful and dignified, is not a lap dog. In denial of the deeply ingrained instincts it possesses, vital processes are hindered, and in our time, truly, the breed could die of it.

The extremes in Irish Setter head types:

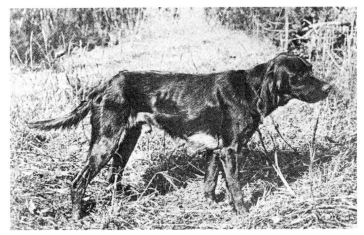

Ch. Morello, K.C.S.B.—1114 L

Ch. Finglas, 21569, imported to USA 1891.

120

The Irish Setter

STATISTICAL history of the Irish Setter in America has been thoroughly covered by the late William C. Thompson (*The New Irish Setter,* 1968) and attempt to rehash this could be only presumptuous. However, even in the provision of detail matched only by the Begats in the Bible, Mr. Thompson contrives to probe no distance into the mystery of Irish Setter breed and/or type origin. His successors need expect to do little better, for this breed is virtually undocumented in the sense that the English Setter is by such lucky provisions as the Devonshire Tapestries and the writings of dog men of centuries past.

Even Anna Redlich (*The Dogs of Ireland,* Dundalk, 1949), the only writer who has bravely attempted the frustrating task of delving into the mess of fabled nothingness that is Irish dog history, can provide no reference to a Sporting dog earlier than the writings of a 17th century Primate of Ireland which includes nothing that the works of Caius cannot duplicate.

Inevitably, researchers grasp after the red-and-white Celtic Spaniels of which the Welsh Springer Spaniel is the modern example. Red-and-white Irish Setters predominated before the tide of fashion declared for solid reds and still had separate show classifications into comparatively recent times. If there was, however, exact linkage with the Spaniel we have as yet no acceptable evidence of it. In his construction, and his working character, the Irish Setter is a hound, but he has the red-and-white Spaniel's "shallow-flewed" muzzle, and he has a handsome coat that is more Spaniel than it is hound. Over more than a century of interested speculation, no one has apparently fathomed whence the red Setter came, full-fledged, into the world of dogs, but his "difference" has continually been emphasized.

121

Dual Ch. Molly Coddled Misty, C.D., one of the several Irish Setters proudly holding in the three avenues of dog activity—show, field, and obedience. Owner, Robert Frisch, Wisconsin.

Dual Ch. County Cork's Red Knight, U.D. The three-tiered achiev ment of this dog is to be credited additionally to the dedication his owners, complete novices in all spheres when they acquired hi Owners, Buck and Laverne Stines, California.

Dual Ch. Tyrone's Mahogany Mike, C.D.X., another with the distinction of title in three spheres. Owner, W. McIver, Michigan.

The Thompson translation of Lt.-Col. Corn. Schilbred's 1927-published *Irish Setter History* notes that: "it is odd that of all the Setters, the Irish is the farthest removed in type from the Spaniel. We know (however) little concerning the early Irish sporting dogs except what may have been derived from old pictures and paintings through which the light flickers" (p. 3).

Thompson himself tries. He fires a scatter of shot in hope to hit the target: "Most investigators believe that the foundation stock of the Irish Setter was the Setting Spaniel (but) there is a difference of opinion as to what crosses were used. Bloodhound, Pointer, Irish Water Spaniel, Gordon Setter, English Setter, and/or their progenitors have been variously described as possible ancestors" (p. 9). Leaving out the obvious comment that Thompson must have been unaware that the Setting Spaniel and the English Setter were one breed, none of the above-named, other than the Pointer, have even an approximation of Irish Setter anatomical construction—and the Pointer is also a hound.

Let us move over to France, as one must do with virtually every breed of Sporting dog—the France of the 1500s, when the English diplomat, George Turberville, examined the hounds of the French hunting pageantry (*The Noble Art of Venerie or Hunting*, London, 1575). Turberville classifies the hounds by color, and carefully describes their characteristics, the Whyte, Blacke, Dunne, Fallow. Of the Fallow he wrote:

> The Fallow Hounds do not endure Heat as well as the Whytes, but fear neither Cold nor Water. They are hardy, endure Pain and Travayle, and are some of a lively Redde, such as have Whyte Spottes on their Foreheads, or a Ring about their Neckes, and some have their Tayles shagged like Ears of Corn, and are on the whole commonly good and swift. Princes of these days have mingled the Races of Fallow Hounds, one to another, but such Hounds are to yield pleasure to Kings and Princes, nor meet for meane Gentlemen, because they are commonly but for one Chace.

The exact reference to "Tayles shagged like Ears of Corn" proves the presence of long-coateds, as well as smooth. That these were of distinct varieties is established by the reference that "Princes of these days have mingled the Races of Fallow Hounds," so we may guess that the Fallow Hounds came smooth-coated and long-coated, as, for example, do Dachshunds in our day, and—as these in our day—were inter-bred. That Turberville so exactly establishes that these dogs were "to pleasure Kings and Princes . . . not for meane Gentlemen," should mollify moderns unhappy to have their Setter shackled to hound origin.

That Turberville found these in France should trouble no one. There has always been close association between French and Irish, as from ancient Celtic relationships and the sharing of the common enemy, England. There

Australian Ch. Tatlow Irish Melody was also possessed of the inimitable Irish Setter expression, lacking which, as Frank Warner Hill insists, a dog is not an Irish Setter at all. Melody's show career was phenomenal, and her only litter produced eight champions. Owners, Miss M. Deane and Mr. A. Thorn.—*photo, Olive Longmore.*

Irish Setter expression has defied the pens of dogdom's best writers. Possibly contributing most to good or bad expression is the eye, and its placement. This photo is of Eng., Irish, Can. & Am. Ch. Delaware Kate. Old hands in Britain still rate her as the best ever. Owned by Dr. A. A. Mitten.—*Tauskey.*

"When Irish teeth are smilin'," tha[expression, too. Ch. Tirvelda Cat O'Rinn, owned by Mrs. Wm. Brool Virginia.

124

were centuries of shuttling the Channel, and over to the Irish isle, all of which is established by whole libraries full of historical matter dealing with the Celtic peoples, their wanderings, their customs, their horses, their dogs. Brittany was the land of the *Celtae* in Caesar's time, and for centuries thereafter. That the Celts had a red hound as well as a red-and-white Spaniel is also historically established. The hound was commonly described as having disappeared, while the Spaniel survived. Where the hound likeliest disappeared *to* may have been the shelter of a long coat and the "Tayle shagged like Ears of Corn," a process of absorption which has been witnessed in respect of other breeds right up to and including our own time.

Irishophiles may prefer to believe their Setter sprung full-formed from among the shamrocks, but history yields no proof of it. History is however crammed with references to the Irish hounds (German: *Keltenbrache*) the running hounds of the Celts, long of leg, flattened of rib, deep of chest, long of neck set into wide-angled (obtuse) shoulder assemblage, with long, slightly upward curved tails, of character fierce, often to the intractable, brave to endure "Pain and Travayle" in pursuit and-or combat.

Certain such identifications, emphasizing courage and endurance crop up for centuries. Thus Taplin (*The Sportsman's Cabinet,* 1803) describes this factor of endurance: "this Setter . . . identified as peculiar to Ireland, where it is favored because Irish fields are large and stony." The type difference was early understood, too, as established in *Cynographia Britannica,* London 1800, from which comes a much-used picture of the three Setters. The English is down in the classic *Coucher* position, his ear-carriage Spaniel-low. The Irish stands lofty, his forehead "Whyte-Spotted," his ears high-carried, his eyes light and fiercely hawk-staring, his tail differently-feathered as compared with that of the English, literally "shagged like Ears of Corn." (see *The New Irish Setter,* p. 8)

Decades after the publication of that picture, Laverack went to Ireland in search of something to use in his breedings (he who swore he bred only in-and-in from Ponto and Old Moll! and described:

> the best Setter in Ireland . . . long in head, particularly low, very oblique shoulders, wheel or roach back, very deep and broad in chest, remarkably wide behind the shoulders, very short in back and legs, immense profusion of coat, with a tinge of black on the tips of his ears. I would have bred from this dog, but for the reason that no one was ever able to break him, and his stock was frequently black.

One marvels that such a dog could have interested Laverack—one suspects he was looking for coat, and that he did eventually produce orange-beltons and tricolors in stock he swore owed only to his blues, was always a matter of comment among rivals. However, the very oblique shoulders and the roach are not for overlooking. Long legs or short, the Irish retained his hound characteristics: "The Irish Setter (has) a back rather arched at the loin, is flat-sided, back ribs short, a tucked-up appearance, longer in leg than the English. A good Irish Setter should look a trifle leggy, all wire and whipcord." (Vero Shaw, *The Illustrated Book of the Dog*, 1898)

Publishing six years later than Shaw, the American, Joseph Graham (*The Sporting Dog*, New York, 1904) wrote:

> . . . higher on leg, narrower all through (than the English). A lightness of muzzle and lip which would be recognized as a defect in the English, is entirely permissible in the Irish (which brings us back to Markham's Shallow-Flewed Hound, of course, CBM). Many of the best have the flank tucked-up and the loin curved, suggesting the contour of the Greyhound. These Greyhound lines, however, do not make for extreme speed. A good Irish Setter is fast, but the speed is not that of the field trials, it is galloping rather than running (p. 104).

This quote from Graham is important, and it astonishes me that writers on the breed (including Thompson) giving evidence otherwise in their work that they are acquainted with Graham's, have denied modern readers the opportunity to be aware of the *very* revealing comments that Graham's book contains. For one thing, he provides rebuttal of that weary old tale wherewith every second field trialler challenges one in the course of conversation: "Look how the *show* people RUINED the Irish Setter!"

Graham, as contemporary observer, a practical dog man, explains that the Irish Setter lost the favor of field triallers on the score of lack of pace. The Irisher was the most popular 19th century hunting dog, and did well in field trials when these were judged on field and bird work. He pleased the ordinary hunter, was pictorially pretty at stance, lofty, and merrily lashing his tail, a sight in those days much enjoyed, and in our time heavily penalized. What happened was the coming of the Llewellins, whose speed he could not match. As the new-coined word "class" became the measure of performance, the Irish was soon out of contention. Graham defines "class" as:

> . . . the ability to do at high speed and rapid accuracy what the mediocre can do only with deliberation, and under favorable circumstances . . . Just why "class" in the field is attractive to most men, and especially to Americans, is explained in the remark of an old foxhunter: "I don't keer much for these extry fast hounds, but I always feel a little better when old Brag is out in front." Hardly one man in four will say, theoretically, that he admires particularly fast dogs; but three out of four will look for the fastest dog they can find when they are either buying outside or selecting from their own breeding. This merely means that the American does not propose to see some other dog taking the lead from his. [pp. 211–212]

126

The weary belief that "Obedience ruins a dog for show" is not supported by facts. Here are two breed greats to deny the belief out of hand: Dual Ch. Red Arrow Show Girl, U.D.T., was the first dog in any breed to gain every title in AKC gift. Also the dam of eight champions, most of whom displayed her versatility. Ch. Innisfail Color Scheme, C.D., proved himself a remarkably prepotent stud. The pair are pictured scoring Best of Breed (dog) and Best of Opposite Sex (bitch) at Harbor Cities, 1958, under judge J. G. W. Head of Australia. Handled by owners L. and E. Heist and C. R. Webb.—*Schley*

A unique presentation. The Irish Setter Club of Southern California was to have honored the 13th birthday of Dual Ch. Red Arrow Show Girl, U.D.T. When she died just before, the presentation was made to her memory. Shown are owners Larry and Eleanor Heist, and club president Sean Byrne.

Those early trial dedicates, however, still placed emphasis on "the ability to *do.*" Speed was that bonus, that extra, and every competing owner wanted it. The beauty of the Irish, the thrill of watching his lashing tail, became secondary. He just didn't have Llewellin speed. As to the lively tails, some decades later there would be attention to getting those up in the air like flagpoles, maybe through Llewellin crosses made in hope to boost the speed. Until well into the 20th century, high tail carriage was marked by the judges as "a Llewellin fault."

Additionally, an Irish Setter:

> ". . . took longer to train; often in his first year he would not point at all, he had to be taught. It is certainly true that (the Irish Setter) has not the natural pointing instinct or judgment in locating birds to the degree shown in (other) breeds. . . . They are however hardy hunters, excellent retrievers, ready for either water or weather; they do not reach their best till 3 or 4 years (which) operates against them . . . and though the good ones are bold even to recklessness, the timid ones are the most creepy and exasperating potterers I have seen in any breed . . . In public field trials the Irish Setters have not been able to compete with Pointers and English Setters. It seems impossible to give them the dashing getaway speed which judges expect in a good stake, and they usually waste too much time on their game when they find it . . . After field trials were placed on a settled basis, the Irish practically ceased to compete, and their entries became rare. Breeders never gave up entirely the idea of beating English Setters and Pointers in the field, but their success has not been very flattering." [*Graham,* pp. 98–99–100]

Dedicated owners who *liked* Irish Setters perservered, and some Irish have always been in competition right to our own day, when the modern show folk are turning increasingly to the interest of discovering if *their* dogs can work. There will be those who fiercely will challenge the Graham summary, but Hochwald, the most respected of all Bird Dog writers in America is in support: "When the early Laveracks and the so-called Llewellins came over, well-heralded in the press . . . and demand was created for them . . . the Irish Setter breeders of the day seemed to lose heart, and with the exception of a desultory specimen as the years went by, the handsome red dog was practically out of existence as far as field trials were concerned. However, many an owner continued to breed his Irish Setters along utilitarian lines, and as a shooting companion he is still popular" (*Bird Dogs and Their Achievements,* 1922, pp. 115–116) .

Hochwald added that the breed was "taken over by the show and pet people . . . and consequently working qualities became lost to the breed." Actually, nothing was *lost to the breed,* merely to quote an old Maurice Chevalier song, Nobody Was Using It Now. There was no incentive to persevere with a breed discarded by the experts as lacking what modern field

"On the double!" Irish Setter, Ch. Bayberry Kincaide.

Rear-end movement in large dogs, as seen in small indoor rings, is seldom satisfactory. But outdoors, on a loose lead (as Irish Setter, Am. Ch. Webline Golden Jubilee, C.D., illustrates here) a dog can find his center of gravity and produce action beyond reproach. Lift and thrust here are excellently depicted, as is the necessary showing of the pads.—*photo, Richard Golden.*

trial competition demanded. Here and there, owners desperate to try and keep their favorite breed in the running tried various "selective breedings" which put the high Llewellin tail in, and the Greyhound underline and outline, and the rest of the signature tunes that are to be found in this breed still today, in and out of the show rings. When none of these optimistic attempts produced what was sought, there would seem to have remained but two alternatives in terms of what to do with the Irish Setter. These seem to have been: Shoot him or Sell him to the Show People.

So, let's have done with that nonsense one has heard for so long about the "ruin" of the Irish Setter. Field trial people discarded him as from now almost a century ago, and for their part he could have become extinct as has become the Llewellin strain that superseded him. The show people set high store by his beauty, and *liked* his active waving tail. They sheltered, fed, bred and showed him. Most importantly of all, they preserved him as a recognizable breed, admired all over the world. He lives! The Llewellin is dead! So, might one not reasonably bat the ball into the opposite end of the court and say: "Look what the *field trial* people did to the *Llewellin* Setter?" And don't quote me the 1970 National Champion English Setter as a rebuttal. There has been no "straightbred Llewellin" Champion since La Besita of 1915. Modern Field Trial English Setters carry "Llewellin" only by courtesy and in the minds of the less-than-well-informed.

The early historicals, as their pictures show, were not all endowed with Greyhound outline; some were even quite squat, but their hound characteristics of construction yet were plain. In the Thompson book one can follow the "streamlining" that went along with the establishment of a popular modern American show strain which not only showed taller hound outline, but is reported to have been short of bird-sense, nose, intelligence, all by the way as recognizably Greyhound endowment as the topline and underline. One would not dare to whisper the famous name even among the reeds down by the riverside, but one can establish by available documentation that early basics to the strain were field-owned. Which figures—*show people* have never had the incentive to try make their dogs run faster!

The greatest praise must be given the modern American Irish Setter clubs that pay so much attention to finding work for their red fellows to *do*. Apart from the emphasis on giving Irish Obedience training, there is ever-increasing interest in getting show-breds out into work via Fun Matches, picnic occasions, and eventually AKC-licensed trials. Gordon Setter folk are increasingly building the same interest, though English Setter interests continue to lag. The Dual Champion Irish Setter represents modernly not merely an ideal—he (or she) is a reality of which the breed can be proud. Most Irish Setter Duals also carry Obedience titles. There are, as of time of writing, as yet no English Setter or Pointer Dual Champions, but the Irishers keep on

The day that Ch. Enchantment of Varagon came out of retirement, three litters behind her, to take BOS to her son at a regional Specialty in California, she had her photo taken with the author and judge. However, in competition, on the day, she was handled by her owner, a privilege he was never inclined to concede—they were a team, Ray and "Trinket." Owner, Ray Gonsor. Judge, Helen Walsh.—*Cammar.*

Field Trial Ch. County Clare's Jiggs, whose West Coast competition record has yielded him Open All-Age wins. Owned by Sean and Kathleen Byrne, and handled by John Merrell.

Am. Ch. Shiralee Beguiling Bridget is six generations down from old Ch. Korere Belle. Owner, Kyra Kompinsky, California.—*Ludwig.*

131

coming along, increasing their tally. The latest, Dual Ch. Merry Kerry Quite Contrary, C.D., interestingly has been show-bred for the four generations that her published pedigree provides. Her paternal grandparents are Ch. Michael Bryan Duke of Sussex and Ch. Enchantment of Varagon, which is about as "show-bred" as one could contrive. Her dam line is overwhelmingly Thenderin, which is also a show signature tune. Many of the Irish Setter Duals have been owner-handled, often by those who came into the interest with their show-breds via the Fun Matches. That novice owners can take a dog all the way was proved by the owners of Dual Ch. County Cork's Red Knight, U.D., who made up this, their first Irisher in the 1960s, and did it without having him ever sleeping one night out of his own home! The first dog *in any breed* to take every title in the gift of the A.K.C. was an Irisher, Dual Ch. Red Arrow Showgirl, U.D.T., also throughout her career in unprofessional hands. No one, *but NO ONE!,* is at liberty to make little of achievements such as these, measuring these arrogantly in terms of single-aim field performances. In cultivating *all* aspects of dog excellence, performance, companionability, good looks, plus prepotency, the "show people" are doing very well indeed by the Irish Setter and "ruin" is not the word to use in describing future prospects.

As show ring interest does however occupy the greater percentage of Irish Setter owner concern, one quotes "Stonehenge's" opinion that "there was no reason to suppose any improvement had taken place in the Irish Setter in its native country until very recently, when institution of local shows stimulated breeders to fresh endeavour." This was Palmerston's time, a discarded field dog, slated for drowning, rescued by show folk. Here was the Stone that the Builders Rejected becoming the Keystone of the breed Arch. His surviving picture shows him poorly posed, but with classic head, long and lean, neat muzzle, moderate stop, setter-short ears. Moderately-curved hound ribbing, deep chest, long hound thighs, short hocks, were all to pattern. He came at a time when Irish suffered great judicial disapproval, many literally thrown out of the show rings faulted for type. There is still a very wide type diversity to be found in modern Irish Setter competition. Heads still range all the way from such as Ch. Morello, KCSB 1114L, Mrs. Ingle Bepler's foundation bitch with a profile virtually straight as if ruled, to that of Ch. Finglas, 21569, imported to the U.S. in 1891, and described by Thompson as "occurring in the pedigree of almost every American-bred Irish Setter." The Finglas picture is in the *New Irish Setter* and Ch. Morello's is in the Thompson translation of the Schilbred work. Comparison will demonstrate the nature of the problems that can face judges of Irishers in the show rings nowadays as in the past.

Whenever there is discussion of Irish Setter heads, someone will come up with the mention of expression. No one seems as yet to have succeeded in

Sh. Ch. Raycroft Call Boy, who brought sound, strong masculinity to his show-ring successes in England. A multiple Best in Show winner, and usefully repre-sentative of best contemporary Irish Setter type in Britain, where there tends to be sometimes less positiveness in the males than ideally might be desired. Owner, Mrs. E. Furness, Chesterfield, England.—*Anne Roslin-Williams*.

Sh. Ch. Brackenfield May, distinguished English winning bitch with 9 C. C.'s. Owner, Miss Sybil Lennox, Derbyshire.—*Anne Roslin-Williams*.

133

defining classic Irish Setter expression in print. The words elude everybody. One just has to "learn" it from Setters that carry it—which, by the way, does not include every Setter registered as an Irish. It has come under my own notice far more often in bitches than in dogs, but then that merely matches with my firm belief that Irish Setter bitches in general possess a greater share of breed-identifying excellences. It is not easy to breed a good Irisher male. This side of the line he is "coarse," that side he is "bitchy." Highest praise is merited by the breeders who succeed in presenting true-type masculine males, but I often wish the gals had more American recognition. The elegance of a beautiful bitch should oftener grace the Groups. One can count on almost a single hand the Best in Show Irish Setter bitches in the United States breed history, yet go listen to the Old Hands talking of Best Evers, and almost always they are talking of bitches. One for remembrance of all dedicates was English-Irish-Canadian-American Ch. Delaware Kate, described not only as undefeated by any American Irisher, but as handsome, big, slashing, and beautiful-moving. Likely no other Irisher ever held all those titles. Yet Thompson dropped her picture from his latest edition! She is my candidate, along with a very successful Australian Irish Setter bitch, Ch. Tatlow Irish Melody, to model "Irish Setter expression" for this book.

The commonest definition of the breed expression is "wistful," but this is not temperamentally a wistful breed. Anything but! Irish Setter temperament (barring inter-variety crosses) is well-documented, wilful at best, and at its worst as "Frank Forester" (*Upland Game*) described it:

> . . . often savage ferocity of temper, always extreme courage, high spirits, indomitable pluck . . . They are naturally wild and given to riot at the edge of indocility, require much breaking, a jealous eye, a resolute wiil, a tight hand over them. With these, they are of undeniable excellence . . . The breed is unsuited to the young sportsman, or to any but those that are constantly in the field, whatever the game in season. For such, their hardihood and pluck render them invaluable.

Always, then, one comes back to the accepted characteristics of hardihood and pluck, just as Turberville, in different words, described almost 500 years ago. The other characteristics have also always been well understood by the experienced. A novice has often to learn the hard way from that "lovely red-setter pup" he acquires. Not every one can live happily with an Irisher, but those who can will consider no other breed worth owning. This is not a breed to cage in solitary idle confinement, either; in my day more than one stir-crazy Irisher has made my heart ache to see. The ultimate mismanagement may be overmuch confinement in a crate, All that energy *must* have adequate scope. Mrs. Florence Nagle (Sulhampstead) wrote: "It seems to be often forgotten that the Irish Setter needs wise discipline and an outlet for

A brace of remarkable litter brothers:

Above:
Am. Ch. Shannon's Erin, BIS and Specialty winner, owned by Lucy Jane Myers.

At left:
Am. & Can. Ch. Major O'Shannon, the top winning Irish Setter in American show rings from 1968 through 1970. Owned by Albert M. Greenfield, Jr. and handled by Tom Glassford.

Dual Ch. Merry Kerry Quite Contrary, C. D., completed her dual in 1970, latest of the sequence of versatile Setters sponsored by the Irish Setter Club of Southern California, with its multiple encouragements to owners to work their show dogs. From wholly show-bred stock, Merry Kerry is passing on her own versatility, with a promising daughter already in the limelight. Owners, M. and K. Gerdis, California.

135

energies. Abounding stamina and fertile brain, its best assets as a working dog, prove handicaps in the dreary life of a kennel. No wonder gangster instincts can develop. But it is from these gangster Irish that I should look for potential good workers with necessary guts to stand the hardship of real work."

Sulhampstead has abandoned the strain of Irish Setter working stock that became world famous, as Mrs. Nagle's attention turned more to her interest in training thoroughbred horses, but one more comment from her is worth quoting: "If an owner's way of life does not permit him to give his Irish Setter the privilege of a daily period of free galloping, he should be in some other breed." And here one might add the words of the late MacDonald Daly (England) : "The right of every dog is at least a daily period of free and collarless galloping."

Owners persevering with an over-ebullient Irisher pup, if they help it spend energy, will usually find Youth a Malady that Time Soon Cures. Those unlucky enough to acquire a mean one should cut their losses. It is not ethical to pass such along to other ownerships. For the mean-natured, denial of stud privileges, and indeed, elimination is the answer. For the merely ebullient, the answer is Obedience class. The 1966 Thompson compilation of Irish Setter champions around the world (but he left out Australasia) counted almost 1000 American Obedience-titled Irishers, and many have finished since then, all the way to U.D.T.

The British ownerships display less than token interest in giving show-bred Irish something to do. It was possible to identify only 2 C.D., though some others may have finished since. In working tests, one notes that several of Mrs. E. Walker's famous Hartsbournes gained their fully-Qualified titles. British owners in this breed, as in Cocker Spaniels, talk a great game about valuation of working qualities. They criticize American-breds on this score; "too heavily coated," "oversized to work," they say. This always struck me as completely absurd in that those heavier-coated American-breds have such a fabulous record of achievement in various spheres, and that the British breeder interest to promote energy-absorbing activity for show-breds is even less than minimal. Merely *talking* about work potential and what may help or hinder this just isn't enough.

All in all, and excepting the usefulness in the brood sense of some supremely elegant bitches, which Britain has in quite considerable richness, the British-bred Irisher is not really for American interest, and indeed few are brought here other than the occasional bitch as above described. In a practical exposure to the breed in various British show rings it seemed to me that there were more spooks than one would expect to find in American rings— but that might well be because the cost of showing dogs in America tends to screen out the undesirables. That doesn't, however, prove that such are not produced in the United States by the poorly-oriented, or commercially-inclined breeder, just as, no doubt, their likes are produced by such in Britain. Poor little substanceless things, how sad they make one feel!

It is needful to differentiate between a spooky Irisher and a mean one. Both can cause grief. The spook is the fear-biter, and as much a hazard as the aggressive for that reason. Lonely caging, lack of association with people helps to foster spookiness, but aggressives are usually born so. The definitive breed books tend to tiptoe around the subject, fearing to give offense.

Every modern-day breeder, for his education, should have access to the W. J. Rasbridge article in *Our Dogs*, England, of Jan. 23, 1959. Therein he traces the inheritances conveying sharpness of temperament, the fighters, the spooks. Many dogs from such inheritances have been introduced to America, and breeders should be able to identify which these were. There is no mandate, or space, to re-copy the Rasbridge article, but such specifics as Achcha—whose daughter, Aryan, was imported to America—should be known to breeders. Mr. Rasbridge pin-points the Achcha inheritance as producing stock "metaphorically speaking, a skin short. When they lash out they do so in fearfulness rather than aggressiveness. That to my mind accounts for the wild look they so often have in their eyes, the look of terror rather than of the brute . . . (and) explains too why so often temper manifests itself as somebody passes it by on the bench, or other dogs crowd it in the ring."

Familiar? Take the Thompson compilation of world Irish Setter champions in one hand and the Rasbridge analysis in the other, and as in "watching T.V." the chances are you'll learn something!

Distinguished Irish Setter breeder, E. Irving Eldredge has written me an interesting commentary on the Rasbridge survey. His personal requirement is that a dog shall be "of good disposition, gay, friendly, birdy, get along with humans and dogs. . . . Oddly enough, my original I.S., obtained when I was 10, has influenced my entire thinking. I got him as a 4-month-pup, when we visited J. R. Carberry of the Boyne kennel. He was a son of Int. Ch. Sarsfield of the Boyne who now, 35 years later, I find in the Rasbridge article noted for bad disposition and producing it. My puppy grew to be a terror with my parents' dogs and we gave him away because of it to people who had no dogs. For several years he lived with his new owners; they let him sleep on the bed. When, one night, the husband climbed into bed with his wife and Tara bit him, they forgave him. When it happened a second time, and there were close calls with the neighbors, they put him down. Never have I had a mean dog since, nor have we allowed our many house dogs on the furniture."

Most Irish Setters publicly seen today are stable, youthful ebullience a mere transience. However, to maintain such qualities of stability should be every breeder's concern. Who *wants* Irishers that bite judges—as of my own witnessing? Who would risk such a scarring as was shown me by an exhibitor with Irish benched at the Brussels (Belgium) show, 1968? His shoulder and arm were shocking to see. The perpetrator, from a famous English kennel, had been shot.

Work—work—exercise to burn up energy—provision of things for idle paws to do, fertile brains to conceive—these are the answer in the case of the naturally stable dog. The screening of bad inheritance is however the obligation of the breeders. And let it never be overlooked that much of the stability of the best of American-bred Irishers is fostered by breeding from Obedience-titled parents, often down several generations, successive proof of good trainable temperament.

If, as discussed above, head type in Irishers is varied, so is body type. The Irisher still comes in a multiplicity of shapes, outlines, sizes. In size, much latitude may exist, the good ones come in all sizes, small to large. Yet in no respect does a judge render himself more vulnerable to ringside criticism than when he "mixes sizes" in his line-up in Irish. The late Leo C. Wilson taught me the rights about that: "Your first-place dog in a class is the best dog you have in there. Your second is the second-best dog you have, irrespective of his size, up or down, in relation to the first, provided both are within the size limits approved for the breed. A dog must be judged on his *own merits,* not by mere reference to the size of those that happen to stand either side of him on the place pegs."

Try selling that opinion to the gallery! All you'll hear is that the judge "doesn't know what he's looking for!" Yet, of course, he is looking for so much more than merely size, which is just one quality. He's looking for breed type, heads, bodies, feet, soundnesses. In short, he is judging *Setters!*

In any case, Irisher size can become a mania with some, including those who carried measuring tapes until the AKC decided that there should be no "measurings or weighings in the ring in breeds where no disqualifications apply." It was Isaac Sharpe (Stylish), a famous British Sporting dog breeder of an earlier time, who scorned "those who come with measuring tapes in their pockets!" Your measurer, often enough, gets lost completely in terms of judging *dogs* (Setters!) .

Ringside acidity also becomes applied to most heavy coated Irish. "I'd like to see what's *under* that coat!" is a usual turn of phrase. Surprisingly enough, many the Irisher under a huge coat that is beautifully-put together in the structural sense. Mr. Roy Jerome (Innisfail) gave me, years ago, the color slide reproduced herein. It has proved worth its weight in precious metal to me as a lecture aid, recording as it does one of his Setters, a well-made, well-balanced typey one, that had been shaved all over for medical reasons. This is the most wonderful slide to pop onto a screen right after some lushly-coated champion—*what's under that coat!*

138

"What's UNDER the coat" of a true-type Irish Setter. Shaved for tick-infestation, this unusual picture of a first-class specimen illustrates the constructional elements that separate Irish from English Setters. Owner-photographer, Roy Jerome, "Innisfail" Kennels, California.

It seems to me, having looked at the breed around the world, and over many decades, that the best of the modern American show-bred Irish Setters may be the most beautiful of the breed now to be found in the world. In addition, so many are admirable in terms of versatile trainability, and in the main, good temperament. There seems to be nothing one cannot ask of an Irish Setter nowadays. A team of Irishers has even gone with its sled to Alaska and beat the Huskies there in snow-sled races right on the Huskies own doorstep! At home, he plays with the kids. On the weekend he goes off to the field trial or fun match, or alternatively to the show ring. If one worries a little about too many of him being currently bred, maybe the emphasis being modernly placed on all types of population explosion may serve to tramp on the brakes and slow down the excess.

But, even with over-popularity, how necessary it is to concede that over the decades of this entire present century, the show people have done wonderfully well with the breed the field trial people discarded because it couldn't out-run those subsequently lost Llewellins.

How was that again—that bit about Who Ruined the Irish Setter?

The Gordon Setter

THE 4th Duke of Gordon, by now already a century and a half gone to his rest, gave to the handsome black-and-tan Setter the name by which it is everywhere known. However, that is not to say that the Duke actually originated a race of Setters of such coloration. Black-and-tans have been known as from centuries before his time, the "black-and-fallows" of Elizabethan documentation providing the reference most often used. Merely, it would seem, the Duke favored the color because he held it easier seen on his Scottish hillsides. He seems to have left no actual documentation in connection with the breed, and most of what attaches to his name is in terms of legend and, modernly, surmise. There are, for example, those in modern times who venture even confidently to second-guess what His Grace would or would not have done, as in relation to the rumor that he introduced a "Colley" cross to his Setters. A man of his experience, declares a 20th century opinion, would not have dreamed to do any such thing: "he would have been far too knowledgeable to wish to introduce Collie characteristics into his strain" (*The Story of the Gordon Setter*, Adams, p. 6) .

There seems to be no valid reason why he may not have made such an experimental crossing. If it didn't work out, he would merely have scrapped it, as did all breeders before his time (and since) who were concerned to try to improve the dogs they had. "We bred a lot and drowned a lot" was not employed only by pastoralists that formed the Australian Cattle Dog or by the Germans forming their Shorthaired Pointer. In any case, there exists an interesting record that would seem to cast considerable light on the possible tolerances of the 4th Duke of Gordon insofar as cross-breeding of dogs was

141

concerned, published by a contemporary (*Captain Thos. Brown, Biographical Sketches and Authentic Anecdotes of Dogs, Edinburgh, 1829, p. 30*) :

> Mr. Brooks, proprietor of the celebrated menagerie, put together a Wolf and a Pomeranian Dog (*a biggish breed in those times, CBM*). Ten pups were the produce. Mr. Pennant saw one of these at Castle Gordon, Fochabers, the seat of His Grace, the Duke of Gordon, in Aberdeenshire. Strongly resembling the Wolf, and in its nature similar, being slipped on a weak deer it instantly caught it by the throat and killed it. Whether the mongrel continued the species I could not learn, but another did, and stocked the neighbourhood of Fochabers, in the County of Moray, where it was kept, with a multitude of curs of most wolfish aspect.

My hope is that the skimming speed reader will not gather I am claiming that the Duke put Wolf into his Gordon Setters. Merely, the story is apt to illustrate the tolerances His Grace had for experimental cross-breeding even of quite a drastic sort. Undoubtedly, he would have conducted his Setter breeding with considerable care, but that need not necessarily have cancelled out ventures of one kind or another. We discover, for example, that the Duke fostered his Setters in association with the most dedicated livestock improver of the period, "Mister" Coke of Norfolk, Earl of Leicester, discussed in our English Springer Spaniel Chapter. The authority for this is "Idstone," p. 95 of his famous publication, *The Dog*, 1872. "Idstone" is the most used of all 19th century source material by Gordon Setter historians, but it is just possible that they passed over the name of Mr. Coke, unaware of who or what that remarkable man was in his time.

It was "Idstone," too, who first resurrected that much-used quote from Gervase Markham, of centuries earlier, the praise of the Elizabethan "black-and-fallows." It has served breed historians nobly ever since. However, attempts to link the Elizabethan black-and-fallows with Castle Gordon black-and-tans, let alone our modern strains, might defeat even the best intentions. There was considerable variation at Castle Gordon, even in the time of His Grace, and his black-whites may have been produce of the English Setter brace he received from Captain Robert Barclay of Urie, this a famous name of course. An earlier Robert Barclay of Urie was the famed Quaker Apologist, the friend of William Penn. The Barclay's Bank, familiar all over England today, was also founded by the same family. Beyond doubt, however, the black-tans were strongest during the lifetime of His Grace. Edward Laverack, visiting the Castle two years after the Duke's death, saw mostly such, but a few years later, again visiting, he found only black-white-tans.

"Idstone" also preserved for historians the record of the Tattersall's sale of Castle Gordon Setters after the death of the 5th Duke, whose enjoyment of the title had been brief. His widow regarded the sporting dogs as "incum-

Dual Ch. Windy Hills Lucky Chance, whose many honors include the siring of a Dual Champion. Owner, Nathan Putchat, Pennsylvania.

The Gordon Setter is at his best as a Man's Hunting Pal. Ch. Midshipman Ready, owned and trained by Travis Look, N.Y.

brances" and cleared out the lot at auction. Tattersall's report was likely found by "Idstone" where, also, I found it—London newspapers reporting the July 3, 1836 sale. Colors were various: black-tans, black-white-tans, black-orange-tans, black-orange-whites, black-whites. "Idstone" also preserves for us his belief that Irish Setters were used at Castle Gordon: "for in every litter, provided it descends from the Duke's kennel, there is a brace or more of red whelps." He added that: "these have the peculiarity of being almost white until they moult, when they take on the brilliant red and follow the form, have the pantherlike noiseless gallop of the Irish Setter" (p. 100).

The red has never been completely eliminated. It is entirely possible to register as Gordon Setters dogs that are wholly red, provided they stem from registered parents, this in both England and America. Such however, are not eligible for showing. The English Standard, lacking disqualification clauses, identifies undesirable colors merely as faults. The American Standard imposes disqualification. As an AKC spokesman clarifies the situation: "Such a dog would be eligible for registration in our Stud Book as long as the litter of which it is a part is duly registered with the AKC. This registration would be made in spite of the fact that the Gordon Setter that is predominantly red in color would be automatically disqualified under the Standard for the breed were it to be entered at an AKC licensed or member dog show." The spokesman added that "Our rules . . . would not prevent us (either) from registering an albino Boxer or a parti-colored Poodle, provided they were part of an AKC-registered litter . . . An applied-for dog's color is always known to us (providing the applicant is honest) because the color of the dog must be stated on the application form."

What action owners take modernly in respect of red whelps in litters is of course a private matter here as elsewhere. O. Winge, Danish writer on color inheritance, reporting reds in Gordon litters in his country, advises that: "they are not spoken about too loudly, and breeders as a rule do away with them in silence." That would likely be the way of it here too, though Winge felt the better way would be to report carriers so they could be eliminated from breeding programs.

In days long gone, when Australians could have dogs registered by "certification," i.e., get papers provided they looked like the breeds they were claimed to be, an English Setter breeder of my acquaintance, keeping his mouth shut, took to its championship a "Gordon Setter" handsomely resultant of an accidental English-Irish mating in his yard. In New Zealand, a few years later, another litter of black-tans was shown me following another unplanned mating between a blue belton English and an Irish Setter bitch. That litter was, however, honestly described, and sold unregistered as hunting dogs. Several of them became known to me as adults, owned around the district, valid for the black-tan, but "Irishy" in bodily characteristics. Now,

Head study of a Gordon Setter of the late 19th century, reproduced from the life-size portrait by Maud Earl.—*Courtesy, Howell Book House.*

A Gordon Setter is his own dog, wholly distinct from the other Setter breeds.
—*C. Bede Maxwell.*

when here and there an "Irishy" type of Gordon appears in my show ring, inevitably the thought is provoked—Is he or isn't he? Only his breeders, maybe even some generations back, know for sure!

A Californian owner of Gordons, not so long ago, stonewalled to me that the production of black-tans from an English-Irish mating was "impossible." Reminds me of the old gentleman who looked at the Giraffe and said there was no such animal! The use of Irish is verified also in the breedings of the famous "Heathers" (established 1875). British judges took time to accept "Gordons of a type flat-sided, long-legged, narrow-fronted, lacking loin." "Heather" was, like "Stylish" (Isaac Sharpe's) a "shooting-dogs-for-hire" kennel, with usually a couple of hundred dogs available. "Stylish" probably harbored even more, enduring far into the present century, type in Gordons mixed, some very good, some so-so. The "Heather" establishment went out of Gordons eventually, the reason given as "following a disagreement with the Kennel Club over the matter of authenticity of some of the dogs' pedigrees." The famous name was later carried on by a son interested in Scottish Terriers.

Obscure backgrounds did not apply only to the "Heathers," either. The most famous of English Setter breeders, the Rev. Turton Price (Of Crombie) finished a Gordon Setter Champion—Crombie King—that is regarded now as a main stem-male of Gordon Setter breeding though his pedigree is given as Unknown (*British Gordon Setter Handbook,* 1958). Ch. Bonnyside Don (1926) was of unregistered parents.

If, then, the occasional red whelp appears, no reason to panic. Merely combine the producers somewhat differently next time. The Bloodhound influence, reportedly used by Lord Rosslyn in his Gordon Setter breeding years after the 4th Duke, could also be a source of recessive red. The black-and-tan, a very ancient patterning in dog jacketing, was carried into Europe following the Crusades, and fostered in the St. Hubert's Monastery in France. But St. Huberts also turned out hounds in whites and it turned out reds. The German scent hound breeds, stemming from this source, lean heavily towards reds, as in the still extant, handsome Schweisshunde, richly red with black masks (see photograph in section discussing Germanic breeds). However, many German-formed breeds carry the classic black-and-tan, with the tenaciously-maintained exactly-defined distribution of the tan. Dachshunds, Dobermans, Rottweilers come readily to mind, and England, of course, has its black-and-tan Terriers, America its black-and-tan Cockers.

If the disputed "Colley cross" showed up anywhere, it may have been in such guise as "Idstone" reported—a "Colley or Teapot Tail" and the habit of one of his own Gordons of "going round her game as a Scotch sheepdog would gallop around a flock" (p. 97). If it matters . . .

"Idstone" was a dedicated owner of Setters, Gordons especially, holding

146

The foremost show winning Gordon Setter of all time, Ch. Legend of Gael, C.D., owned by Mrs. Cheever Porter of New York City, and handled by Jane Forsyth.

these to have certain properties the English did not, and vice versa: "He has not so finely formed a head. It inclines occasionally to the heavy Bloodhound type. His ears are frequently too large and weighted with coat as well as leather" (pp. 98–100). He could have been describing his own famous Kent, KCSB 1600, described by judges as "thick in shoulder, with elephantine ears, high-domed head, goose rump, weak hind legs without second thigh muscles, pendulous lips and a Bloodhound voice."

"Idstone" knew all this, but did a great deal of winning with Kent, including the Grand Prix de Paris. "He won mostly on the richness of his color, the majesty of his size, plus a knack he had of showing himself to his utmost." In this summary of his dog's virtues, "Idstone" could be summarizing the winning attributes of many a show Setter of our own time. But "Idstone" was not kennel blind: "Kent propagated his own faults and others besides," he conceded (p. 101), so leaving for posterity explanation of the various problems that faced the owners of this dog's many descendants. My own eye lights on that reference to the weak hind legs that lacked second thigh muscling, for among modern Gordon Setters, in Britain especially, some most extraordinarily weak-looking rear-end assemblage can be seen. Words to define such as these were provided not so long ago by distinguished American breeder, Mrs. Jean Look. She calls them "back-to-front back legs," so simplifying my own endeavors to explain amazing rear-ends in terms of backward bent bow. Maybe the compilers of the 1962 AKC-approved standard had disapproval of such rear-end assemblage in mind, asking that when a dog is *"standing with the hock perpendicular to the ground, the thigh bone shall hang down parallel to an imaginary line drawn upward from the hock."* Such structure would cancel out a "backward bent bow."

Modernly, a specific head type has come to be recognized as "Gordon," though the historicals show considerable variation. The Standard description includes such requirements as *"deep rather than broad, with a nicely rounded skull, broadest between the ears . . . with flews not too pendulous, lip lines square . . . expression intent, penetrating, of a nature peculiar to a Gordon."* Here again one is facing a requirement that is defiant of attempts to describe it in words, just as in the case of the "wistful" expression of an Irish Setter. One knows the expression when one sees it or not, according to the extent of one's experience with the breed. My own description would run along the lines of an expression conveying a suggestion of solid citizenship.

Occasionally, one comes upon references to topknot, further described as "a superfluity of hairs on top of the head." This is not peculiar to Gordons—may even be a legacy of Irish Setter incross long ago. Irish Setters, English Cockers, Goldens especially, English Setters, can all grow luxuriant crops of light flaxen stuff up top. In my own days as an exhibitor, my fingers developed a reflex action, stripping the soft stuff away. Shearing is quicker but tends to

148

leave the hair butt-ends to somewhat thicken a skull. Thinning shears plus Duplex razor are modernly used to tidy skulls, but plucking plus sand-papering is better if an owner will take the time. The growth has been described as the vestigial remnant of an ancient endowment, and of course several breeds do legitimately carry topknots, including some very ancient—the Afghan for one.

As with the re-reading of all dog breed Standards, the perusal of the present-day Gordon Setter description can raise some provocative thoughts. The 1962 revision pushes up heights by 2 inches overall, as compared with its predecessor. Males went from 22–25″ to 24–27″. Females went from 21–24″ to 23–26″. Weight provides for a wide variation: 55–80 pounds for males, 45–70 for females. By comparison, the British ask for males to 26″, weight about 65 pounds; females 24½″, weight about 56 pounds. The increase in the height of the American Gordon Setter may well have been added with the aim of counteracting the always-operative tendency of field trial interests to shrink breeds to the not always desirable minimum.

The surprising thing in the 1962-approved Standard however seems (to me) to be the considerable emphasis on the word "short." Thus, backs shall be *"rather short"*; body shall be *"short from shoulder to hips"*; loin shall be *"short and broad, not arched"* and tail shall be *"short."* Against this, the British are clearly asking for quite a different kind of Setter, their standard desiring a body of *"moderate length,"* and loins *"wide and slightly arched."* Here again is a fair example of the difficulties that complicate dog judging of identical breeds that, in different lands, have different requirements. Reasonably, too, one wonders whether or not the end product of taller dog heights allied to telescoped body proportioning might not eventually result in a Gordon that gives such a tripod impression as, by the way, do some of those British-breds one sees standing on those queerly-shaped long back legs. My files do include a most graphic picture of such a British dog, taken on the occasion of a big win, but alas, it is impossible to publish photographs of recognizable living dogs and pinpoint their faults.

Another puzzlement in the American Standard is that color, allotted disqualification when out of tune with the classic pattern, is yet rated at only 5 points in a suggested scale that totals 100. As a major breed-identification characteristic, 5 just doesn't seem to be an adequate mark.

Europe has long liked Gordon Setters, introduced in the 19th century by Prinz zu Solms Brauenfels, closely identified with all sporting dog interests of his time. Scandinavia received fine Gordons from zu Solms breeding, and distribution in Germany was wide, especially in the south. Some magnificent Gordon paintings appear in German dog literature, especially in Sperling's *Feine Nasen,* 1889, he being the outstanding sporting artist of the century. Rudolf Freis in *Unsere Jagdhunde,* 1960, also writes nostalgically of *der alten Münchner Gordonsetter* (one word) so versatile, land and water. He complains of British judges faulting these dogs for thicker, shorter, slightly wavy coats, describing these as best suited to the work of the Setters in that country: *"Jammerschade um diese Hunde, denn es ist zehnmal leichter schöne Hunde zu züchten als Gute!"* ("Darned shame about those dogs, as it is ten times easier to breed pretty dogs than good ones!") But then, of course, there was alternatively that Pointer breeder of my acquaintance who insisted to me that while a working dog can be *made,* a show dog must be *bred!*

That German sportsmen wanted their Gordons to work in water is not surprising. German sportsmen require *all* their sporting breeds to work in water, Pointers included. Enquiry of Mrs. Look discovered for me that she is aware of the Gordon Setters' fancy for water, but so far as competition is concerned could only tell me of Timberdoodle Dan of Avalon, U.D.T., a very fine competitive retrieving Setter who, alas, was denied privileges when retrieving trials became closed to Setters.

In the 1950s, my English Setters and Pointers exercised on the opposite bank of an Australian river that flowed past a fine kennel of Gordon Setters, the O'Argyles of Mr. George Edwards. Overseas judges had nothing but praise for the Setters of this strain, big and handsome, classically colored, and strong. My own recognition of Gordon Setter type was formed on their model. There came to be several Dual Champion O'Argyles, and Best in Show winners, and even a Best Exhibit at the Gundog Society Specialty, a toughly-contested annual occasion catering for all Sporting breeds.

Now this was in the State of New South Wales, where upland game just *isn't,* and so a sporting dog had to get its field (working trial) points in retriever competition. Day after day, working my own side of the river with my dogs, I watched George Edwards training his in that convenient flow past his kennel door. I remember them all of my time, but the strain was long established before that, actually from 1923. It was founded on a Mary O'Argyle, and for decades from then on there was always a Mary O'Argyle in the kennel. The Mary of my time was a notable Dual Champion, familiarly known as "Bloody Mary" in competition, field or show. She was always the dog that had to be beaten.

How lovely they were, those of my remembrance——Mary, Royal, John Haig, Mysie and the rest. Mysie O'Argyle was the Dual Champion that made me some cherished slides of a water-retrieving Gordon, handled by young Johnny, the Edwards grandson, aged 13, in a Stake they won that day. When George Edwards died just a few years ago, however, all his dogs and all his proud papers were by his testamentary direction destroyed. All but Mysie, and how she escaped destruction is not known to me.

The few passing years have seemingly removed from the memory of dog-

150

interested Australians all awareness of this strain of great Gordon Setters, close on 40 years fostered. On my return to New South Wales in 1969, to judge, no one could tell me of the O'Argyle influence, whether the blood still flowed anywhere. This then, my remembrance, may be the last that will be penned:

> *Once there was a most beautiful lady,*
> *Light of step and heart was she.*
> *I think she was the most beautiful lady*
> *That ever was in the West Country . . .*
>
> *. . . but when I crumble, who will remember*
> *This lady of the West Country?*

> —WALTER DE LA MARE.

If the memory of those Gordon Setters is destined to die with me, let me also recall that scene from *The Bluebird* (Maeterlinck) in which Myttyl and Tyltyl visit the Land of the Dead. Grandma and Grandpa sit at the cottage door, the canary is quiet in its cage. When the children speak, the old folk wake from sleep, the canary begins to sing. Grandma explains—when the living think and speak of the dead, these come temporarily again to life. So, pretty Mysie, Royal, and Bloody Mary, while I've been typing this, you've been bound-deep through the riverside reeds, looking back for the directing hand of George . . .

That Gordons like the water so well may have to do with Bloodhound infusion that probably provided also the sensible temperament. "Idstone" also told of Bloodhound liking for water. Of Bloodhound temperament, too: "Temperaments in dogs are varied, as in Christians, but after diligent enquiry I am led to believe that as a rule the Bloodhound is amiable, sagacious, faithful, obedient and docile" (p. 50) . Mrs. Look worries lest Gordon Setter trials not being "shoot to kill" might lose the breed its retrieving instinct. Not to worry—the genes are longer-lived than contemporary field trial fashions, can last even centuries through.

No record of a British Dual Champion comes under my notice, only the narrowness whereby Fld. Ch. Rowney of Grafnant missed the honor, his record being one Challenge Certificate and 6 reserves. American Dual Ch. Gordons have not been numerous but include some very distinguished, such as Dual Ch. Windy Hill's Lucky Chance, who was also a National Specialty and a Shooting Stake winner and in his turn sired Dual Ch. Glascott's Scottish Majesty. Dual Ch. Gunbar's Dare Devil, C.D. joins the select company of titleholders in the three venues of AKC competition, and that Dual honors are still being sought is established by the 1970 finishing of Dual Ch. MacGeowl's Macdougal. Best in Show wins have been rarest of the rare, but

151

modern increase of interest in Gordons has seen the prestigious Windsor Gundog Show fall to a Gordon in England, and Ch. Legend of Gael, C.D. is establishing a precedent for his breed with the many supreme awards (17 at this writing) secured to him in America.

A story of a British-bred, Bell, is of honor of a different kind. As was once usual in British war service, Bell the Gordon went with her owner Captain Reginald Sartorius to all manner of engagements that soldiers of the Queen had to keep in her time a century ago. These included crossing the Himalayas by a 19,000 foot pass into Tibet and Central Asia. However, 1874 found them in Africa, involved in the Ashanti War. Advancing with a British column on the Ashanti capital, Coomassie, the word filtered back that Coomassie had been burned by another British force. Sartorius was sent ahead to reconnoiter, and at his pony's heels followed Bell. They threaded through the still smouldering capital, seeing no one, hearing no one, but eyes there must have been. When Captain Sartorius caught up with the other British column, native envoys from Coomassie were behind him with tribute and offers to surrender. They had been frightened by the apparition of the big black dog at the heels of the pony, having seen none like it before, feared it to be the rider's Familiar Spirit and held it in superstitious dread. In Camberley Museum, England, may still be seen the gold dog collar presented to Bell by admiring ladies when the gallant Captain brought her home with him, as well as the silver goblet presented to the Captain by the Prince of Wales, following the award of the distinguished Victoria Cross.

There is a considerable plus in that a Gordon Setter is likely to be blessed with a long life. It takes time to train a dog and adapt it to one's ways. That it should survive many years thereafter to give pleasure is a definite bonus. One notes, in this connection, that Ch. Sangerfield Tillie and Ch. Sangerfield Tracy count among their honors the Best Opposite Sex awards as successive Specialties. Tillie took one such at age 9, another at age 11. Tracy took hers at age 11. From this strain, too, stemmed the distinguished Ch. Sangerfield Jed, one that promoted the best of public relations for his breed, winning many honors, though denied the long life of the gals quoted.

By and large, these are dogs, as a breed, of good disposition though of course, as in all breeds, the occasional bad actor can appear. Association with your Gordon is best furthered on a personal basis. It is not suited to kennel confinement: it needs to be a People Dog. "You have to get to know your Gordon," wrote William Cary Duncan in an AKC Gazette column, some years ago. "You should make his acquaintance at an early age. It is not a breed to kennel, and professional methods of training do not always suit, factors which may tend to affect popularity with owners unwilling or unable to do their own training and handling." Mr. Duncan emphasizes the difference between Sporting breeds that can, and those that cannot "take training." Briefly, it would appear that while an English Setter may go to pieces under tough handling, and an Irisher can go stir-crazy in confinement, the Gordon is likely to attend to his own defense very competently. Mr. Duncan points out that what a Gordon needs is firm but reasonable training methods, preferably on an individual, even a personal, basis.

My publisher, Mr. Elsworth Howell, reading through a draft of this work, has pencilled in the margin—"Maxie—you like Gordons, don't you?"

The answer is in the affirmative!

Pointer Work, 18th Century Style. This famous painting clearly establishes that in original use, the Pointer also went down to birds. The lofty stance is held by the dogs backing, and it is believed that the lofty stance on birds was eventually developed through breeding with the most stylish of the backers. Note all the short tails.—photo lent by *L. L. DeGroen*, Australia.

154

The Pointer

THE Pointer is the towering giant of modern Sporting breeds history. He has been used in his own person, and to help in the formation or the improvement of many breeds we presently recognize, not only British breeds, but European as well. He came with two great gifts—his patience to stand to game and his magnificent nose. With these gifts went certain minus qualities, such as lack of the courage against predators which European interests always have and still do demand in their Sporting breeds, as well as in general a distaste for cold conditions and for water work. Additionally, while early-type Pointers in England were regularly pictured in retrieving work, retrieving was never actually one of the breed's enthusiasms. It has been the aim of many breeders in many countries to secure into their strains the Pointer's virtues while screening out the minus qualities that were not desired in a utility dog (such as Europeans value) or a running dog (such as American field trial fashion demanded).

He has been siphoned into Setter strains and into retrieving breeds, and in what one might call the Pointer-type range, he influenced strongly pioneer development of the German Shorthair and the Hungarian Vizsla. In fact, one might reasonably consider that with the exception of the Weimaraner, who was always what the Germans would call *Vorstehhund-frei* (Pointer-free), his assistance has been generously invoked, and few the strains that were not the better for it.

He was for long identified as the "Spanish" Pointer, but one still lacks documentation that can actually verify a long-held belief that he originated there. Even wealthy, dedicated William Arkwright (*The Pointer and His*

155

Oft-disputed—what actually was an Arkwright head? Here is that of the famous F.T. bitch, Arkwright's own Sea Breeze. Preserved in the Natural History Museum, England. Presented by Wm. Arkwright, 1905.

The only "Spanish Pointer" so far found by me in Spanish art: "The Verger of the Cathedral (Seville)," Murillo (1617–1682) .—*Metropolitan Museum of Art.*

Predecessors, 1902) who spent time and money searching Spanish archives for his magnificent book that remains the breed classic, found no support for the claim. One does not even have the support that the art of the great painters and weavers give to the history of other Sporting breeds. Few indeed are the dogs of any kind on Spanish canvases. The only one of my own acquaintance is the Murillo (1617–1682) in the Metropolitan Museum of Art, New York, but of course there just *have* to be others, somewhere—don't there, she asked plaintively! The Murillo—"The Spanish Verger at the Cathedral in Seville"—includes a large, parti-colored hound with a head far from classic Pointer type, one that rather than suggesting "dished" qualities has even a hint of Bull-terrier downface!

"Spanish Pointer" came into England as a name for a dog that seems to have been introduced in the 18th century. The Elizabethans give no hint of having known of such a one in their earlier time. Maybe introduction was made as from the time of the British armies fighting in Flanders. The pages of all dog history, right into our own time, are crammed with evidence that

156

Australian Dual Ch. Stonethorpe Swift (imp. England) carried the hint of ram-nose, such as one finds on the best German Shorthair studs. However, his breeding background is mainly *Herewithem* (Robert Maloney's famous Pittsburgh strain, USA) through post-war introductions to England.—*Olive Longmore.*

A typical Pointer head of the 1960s in England, following introduction of Continental blood. Cassius of Eastlands, owned by Mrs. Shakespeare, Winborne.—*James.*

after wars soldiers brought home dogs as, after cruises, sailors traditionally brought home parrots. This was the period of Spanish occupation of the Low Countries, and beyond doubt Spanish officers took their hunting dogs to war as did the British. Gentlemen wanted their recreation between battles in those times. Then, if a novel kind of dog was "acquired" (that lovely navy term!) by British officers from Spanish opposite numbers, the dog would reasonably have been dubbed "Spanish" when his new owners took him home. Just in the same way as the Flemish country dances, taken home by the Spanish troops, gained in Spain the name of *Flamenco,* which they retain also to this day.

Undoubtedly medieval Spaniards hunted as did their Portuguese neighbours, but while the Portuguese produced a book to which reference can still be made, a Spanish equivalent still remains to be found. That there would have been good dogs available to Spanish hunting interests is also reasonably to be presumed for she was in her heydey—as the world's great power—as certain to attract the world's treasures, animal, vegetable, mineral, as the United States attracts such in this our own time. Likely enough, the Spanish acquired their breeds as this country of ours acquired its breeds originally—by importation. The teasing question is, of course, from *where?*

Despite his present classification in the Sporting Group, the Pointer, like the Irish Setter, is a hound. However, he is within hound classification entirely unique. Not in terms of shape and proportioning, for many breeds match these, but in his classical endowments of work pattern, head shape and the intriguing endowment that is his tail. The head and the tail are both extremely vulnerable to cross-breeding, but as a duetted signature tune they are of major importance.

157

Of blacke hounds aunciently come from Sainct Huberts abbay in Ardene. Chap.5.

The houndes which we call Sainct Huberts houndes, are commonly all blacke, yet neuerthelesse, their race is so mingled at these dayes, that we finde them of all colours. These are the hounds which the Abbots of Sainct Hubert haue alwayes kept some of their race or kynde, in honour and remembrance of the Sainct which was a hunter with Sainct Eustace. Whereupon we

The Blacke Hound of St. Huberts.

hounres , but J will wzite heereafter of the nature and complerions, as well of white hounres , as of fallowe , dunn, and blacke , whidy foztes are moste commodious foz Prince and Gentlemen.

Of the nature and complexions of whyte dogges, called Baux, and furnamed Greffiers. Chap.₂.

The Whyte Hounds of the King.

In the 16th century, when Turberville published, there were no Pointers (recognized as such) in England. But in the French hunting circles, the royal kennels and sponsorship, the famous Whyte Hounds of the King began to include a distinctive-headed dog with the clear preview of what modernly we came to call a dish. Many pictorial representations and statuary depict Whyte Hounds working in which both the "dish" and the straight profile appear, supporting Turberville's continual mention of "mingling of the races" of the various hounds by "princes of these times."— From George Turberville, *The Noble Art of Venerie, or Hunting,* London 1576. Courtesy, British Museum.

159

It was the late Frank A. Longmore, Australian Kennel Club executive who loved and understood Pointers and taught them to me along with most all else that has best served me in the years of dog-interest since then, who provided a capsule description of Pointer type that, within my view, cannot be bettered. Describing an English import to Australia, in the 1950s when Pointer type in England was at a somewhat low ebb, he wrote: "This bitch has excellent shoulders, neck, legs, feet. *So have thousands of other dogs!* Two things a Pointer *must* have—a head and a tail. No Setter heads. No Greyhound tails!"

The classic Pointer head is not pretty, nor ever was. One meets even knowledgeable dog folk who will tell one they don't care for it at all. The point is, characteristics counting as exact breed identification cannot be made the subject of personal preferences. Alone among the Sporting breeds the Pointer has this unique profile, a head that is all roundnesses of a Norman arch style plus a prominent stop. Frank Longmore also wrote that: "A Pointer has a head like a Pointer. If he should wake one morning to find he has one like a Setter, be sure the Setter head is wrong."

On what other breed of dog, within the Sporting or any other Group, then, may one seek an equivalent or even a near-approximation? Whence derived the heavy roundnesses and the archings? The only linkage that has been reasonably proposed brackets the Pointer originally into the group of breeds classified as the Mastiff. Many authorities have bracketed all the "drop-eared" breeds into this grouping, and were of course aware that whatever had been the original form, the geographical dispersal of dogs across the world, the endless cross-breedings, had everywhere developed variety of size, general appearance, jacketing, and employments. Perhaps the best modern examination may be found in the pages of a 1970 publication of Natural History Press, *The Natural History of the Dog,* by Richard & Alice Fiennes. These authorities discuss modernly recognized sporting and "spaniel" breeds firmly in terms of Mastiff derivation: "The breeds considered all came originally from the same geographical region, the mountain spine stretching from east to west across Asia and Europe, comprising the Himalayas and the mountains of Tibet, the mountain regions of Anatolia, the Alps, the Massif Central of France, and the Pyrenees. In these regions were developed breeds of dogs, which despite diversity of form, size, color, resemble each other in the acuteness of their powers of scent, the possession of a pronounced stop, a tendency to produce fine silky coats and large floppy ears, and to have short or very short muzzles . . ." (p. 111) .

The authors include within this group of Mastiff origin not only Bulldogs and related breeds, Great Pyrenees, Great Dane, St. Bernard, Newfoundland and other very large dogs, but also the "true scent hunting hounds of variable size and form from bloodhounds to dachshunds; dogs of Pointer type, retriev-

The fame of Italian Pointers has circled the world. It is impossible to discuss the breed, and leave the Italians out. Italian and Int. Ch. (Dual) Ora del Doro has a big winning record across Europe.—*Luis Zavaterro.*

Italian Field Ch. Brio. In Europe they named this one "The Supreme Stylist."—photo, *Luis Zavaterro.*

International Dual Champion holding the Dual title in Italy, France, and Belgium: Barnabe de Valesia.—*Luis Zavaterro.*

"Elhew" has long been a famous name in field trial Pointers. Champions all—Elhew Marksman, Elhew Zeus, and Elhew Jungle. Owner, Robert Wehle, Scottsville, N.Y.

162

ers, spaniels, setters, comprising water spaniel and poodle group, the mina-
ture spaniels and small dogs of the pug and pekingese type" (p. 111).
Interbreeding provided infinite varieties, the authors note, emphasizing also
that "breeds with similar traits (appear) to have been developed independently in more than one area . . ." (p. 112).

Perhaps the most important observation made in this connection by these
dedicated researchers is that "nevertheless where canine breeds are crossed,
usually one breed leaves a greater imprint than another . . ." (p. 112). This
is strongly applicable to the Pointer. He publishes his signature tune wherever he has been introduced. But we are still left wondering what basically
formed *him* in the first place—how he comes to be within the Mastiff-in-
heritance group a Pointer rather than, say, a Bloodhound, a Spaniel or a
Peke!

The Fienne bibliography does not include any mention of the work of
the Elizabethan, George Turberville (*The Noble Art of Venerie or Hunting*,
London, 1575), so one takes it these authors did not have access to the classification Turberville provides in respect of the hunting hounds of the French
courts of his time as a British diplomat in France. Turberville not only
describes the separate hounds, he also provides pictures—probably the first,
and certainly the best, of dog illustrations provided to that time. We have
already drawn on this work in respect of Irish Setter history, examining the
Fallow hounds, as apart from the Whyte, the Dunne, the Blacke. The pictures are explicit also in defining differences—the Blacke (St. Hubert's)
Hound with his distinct downface, and the Whyte all roundnesses and a
pushed-together foreface. There can be no doubt but that the two drew their
characteristics from different sources, or that the profile of the Whyte Hound
is clearly a preview of what would come to be recognized as "Pointer" in
subsequent centuries.

The Whyte Hounds of the King, as these French hunting sorts were historically known, were the brave fighting hounds. One can find their like on
many tapestries, in many paintings, battling bear and boar, pulling down
deer. Statuary also honors them as even from centuries before Turberville,
bas-reliefs most ancient, even to periods B.C. Their bodies were strong and
free of exaggerations of type. Mostly their heads were smoothly "hound."
They can be identified even as anciently as those "white boarhound bitches
in whelp" paid by the Greeks as tribute to ancient Crete. Then, here and
there, in statuary especially, creeps into view, wherever more than one
hound is involved, a variation of head type—some with straight profiles, some
with visibly dished. By the time of Turberville (16th century), as his illustra-
tion suggests, the Whyte Hounds carried the rounded, dished type of profile.
One guesses that Mastiff courage had been needed to further bolster fighting
hounds.

163

Mary Montrose. "Peerless Mary" they called her. She won three National Championships, the first in her Derby Year. She went from that performance to Madison Square Garden, and took the breed honors in the show ring. She could have been so easily a Dual Champion if any one had cared. The Pointer breed still lacks its first Dual, and type changes have cancelled out any chance that it will ever possess the honor of such in any foreseeable time.—picture courtesy of *The American Field Publishing Co.*

Stonethorpe Hup De Chasse was imported from France to England in 1950 by Peter Woodford (Stonethorpe prefix) of Aylesbury, after an extensive search in Europe for a stud with the breed type and elegance desired. Stonethorpe leans more to working Pointers than to show, but the elegance of the stock following the importation is still much in evidence in English show competition, too.

Now, let us go to Turberville's text. Noting that the Whytes splendidly endured heat, he adds, "but they do fear Water a little, especially in Winter when it is Cold . . . A proportion of the Whelps are spotted with Redde or Blacke or Dunne or Fryse (which may be *Fraise*, French for strawberry, i.e., some form of liver-roan. CBM). The spotted Whelps," Turberville added, "are possessed of Small Valor." In other words, their courage was minimal.

In an extraordinary faithfulness we have here a record centuries old listing characteristics that the Pointer carried faithfully right into modern times. He endured heat very well, he disliked cold water, and in terms of facing predators he was for "including out." Some of these characteristics have been masked in individual dogs by cross-breeding into present times, but in fact are still recognizable in modern Pointers wherever such still look like Pointers rather than cross-bred hounds.

The ability to endure extreme Heate intrigued Turberville: "I have this day," he wrote, "at Rochell, Fraunce, a Seaport, enquired of Pylottes and Mariners . . . and an Old Man told me that all the Hounds of the Barbar's kennels were Whyte, and all the Dogges of that Countrie also (and) I think the Whyte Dogges do come out of (w) hotte Countries for they give not out over the Chace, however (w) hotte it bee . . ."

Mention of Barbary immediately suggests an easy linkage with Spain. Maybe this was the real country of origin. However, one must also examine those "Spotted Whelpes from Whyte Hound litters." The colors Turberville lists are still carried by Pointers to this day, and one cannot overlook that he distinguishes so clearly between Spotteds and Pure Whytes in terms of character. How *came* the Whytes to throw Spotted Whelpes? In the time of Louis XII, a Clerk of his Household (who may have been what the British call a "sporting parson") owned a Bracco (Braque) bitch out of Italy. Of her, other than such designation as she is thereby given, we know nothing, but her mating to a famous Whyte Hound was historically recorded. The resultant strain carried on from this mating became known as "Clerk's Hounds"—"Baux, called Greffiers" as Turberville identifies it. Reasonably, she was of a different sort, but still, all Pointerish types have always been known as Braques in Europe as, for that matter, even the German Shorthair is today (Braque Allemand). If, then, the characteristic of courage lack was so firmly linked with color in the resultant strain, one guesses reasonably it was the legacy of the Italian bitch.

Turberville records that the pure Whytes disappeared as a breed, only the descendants graced with "Spottings" enduring to perpetuate their kind. He tells that those that survived carried always at least a trace of color, even if this proved in some specimens to be no more than a trace of yellow about the head or the ears (which in our times quickly suggests the Clumber!). Pure white as a Pointer color is still the rarest of the rare; many of us have never set eyes on one and, indeed, the approved Standard makes no provision for such. Solid liver and solid black are, however, to be met with, especially in Europe. The pure white, as suggested in photographs of some American field Pointers, is oftenest bracketed with other non-Pointer characteristics. Why the Whyte Hounds, pure for the color, disappeared remains unexplained. Modernly one thinks of some genetical factor, but it is also true that the Whytes were the Boar and Bear fighters, and their courage must have always cost them dear.

Turberville's description of temperament in these dogs has also importance for historians of several breeds. The Fallows, he wrote "yielded pleasure to Kings and Princes and (were) not for meane Gentlemen." The Dunne "did not pleasure Princes . . . are troubled with Crie and Noyse of Huntsmen enough to put themselves out of hearing; they fear Heate, are (good only) for headlong Chace, not for one that twisteth and turneth, casting great Compass when at default, but fear neither Cold nor Water." The Blacke were "commonly all Blacke, yet their Race is so mingled these days we find them all colors. Widely dispersed, mighty of Body, short of Legges, slow with good Scent, they fear neither Water nor Cold . . ." He identifies the Blackes with St. Hubert's Monastery, and the virtues cataloged are recognizable as Bloodhound or as the closely related European scent hounds of which the German Schweisshund remains a modern example.

Only three copies of Turberville are cataloged as being still in existence. The copy in the British Museum provided my material. The Bodleian Library of Oxford University has another, and a third is in the Huntington Library in California. The fragile pages of the British Museum copy are reinforced with silk net, page for page, both sides. This accounts for the "chickenwire" effect in the pictures reproduced. This factor of rarity and virtual unavailability to most dog historians accounts for the scant quotes made from this author. *Hutchinson's Dog Encyclopaedia* is the only one occurring to me offhand as drawing from its richness, retelling most of the "John of Monmouth" manuscript that Turberville preserved for posterity.

Turberville retold the John of Monmouth matter (which reads as legend, but may well be based on Celtic history orally handed down) because in his own search for dog history basics he was frustrated, even as are we in our later time—"because I find not Historie that maketh mention of longer Continuance (of hounds in these parts.) "

The manuscript starts with the settlement of Aeneas in Italy after the end of fighting in Troy. There, the grandson of Aeneas was accidentally killed by his own son, Brutus, by an arrow wound in a hunting accident. Which reminds me, that modern fathers still die of hunting accidents at the hands of sons in Italy! The age-old perpetrator fled into exile with "friends released from captivity since Troy, and with a great number of Hounds and Grey-

166

hounds, sailed by the Straits of Gibraltar, the Ocean Seas, to the Isles of Armorie, presently called Bretagne (Brittany) where he lived for many years peacefully before crossing to make a conquest of certain Giants and to build the chief town of Cornwall. Turnus, the son of Brutus, stayed in Bretagne, went daily hunting in the Great Forest, with the Hounds they had brought. The King of Aquitaine, hearing of these Hounds that never left a Hart till they had brought it down, went to war with the Troyans, and by the Loire, where the city of Tours now is situated, the son of Brutus was slain in battle." The hounds became the loot of war.

This reads like a legendary scrambling of Celtic settlement and Phoenician sea trade routing. Bretagne was Celtic settled, and there was much shuttling across the Channel, mostly in terms of flight before enemies. Celts had fanned out westward over Germany and what was known as Gaul, and one comes upon their influence in the history of many lands, Hungary to Ireland inclusive. Always they are identified with their hounds—and it is interesting to note above how the ancient manuscript discriminates between "Hounds and Greyhounds." The Celtic people, credited with introducing horse drawn chariots into warfare, also used their great hounds in war (German: *Keltenbrache*) which base the great grizzled hounds of today, Irish and Scotch.

From Turberville's time, the gap in knowledge relayed looms wide. We are left looking at that Whyte Hound with his distinctive head that was so at variance with hounds of his time, and not till "Old Spanish" became documented in Britain is there much to grasp at. He came in with his innate instinct to stand to game and that big clunky head of his. He was also a clunky bodied dog, steady as he was slow and stolid. As firearms were improved and it became necessary to liven him, "the lightest and gayest of the Spanish Pointers were judiciously crossed with Foxhound to procure courage and fleetness" (Sydenham Edwards, *Cynographia Britannica*, London, 1800). He was, then, even in 18th century introduction a good worker but still no hero! Edwards thought the foxhound cross ruined steadiness but noted high prices paid. Colonel Thornton sold Dash for "a hundred and sixty pounds worth of Champagne, a Hogshead of Claret, an Elegant Gun and (another) Pointer," retaining the privilege to buy back Dash if he became useless. When Dash broke a leg he was repurchased, much used at stud, but not with success, his crossbreeding no doubt the reason.

Cross-breeding legacy still hinders Pointer production in many parts of the world, and it has not been easy always to prevent a lapse into just ordinary hound. Some peculiar-looking animals have been, over the centuries, identified as Pointers, but the knowledgeably discriminating always knew what the type *should* be, and dedicated people have worked again and again to restore what was lost to bad or adventurous breeding practice. In times past, foxhound cross introduced the desired courage and liveliness, but also foot-

167

American field trial Pointers are too fast to follow afoot. Gallery rides out. Camp Adair, Oregon.—
Dittebrandt.

scenting, giving tongue, high hairy tails and cat feet, uneven coats. Grey-hound cross ruined nose and brains. By 1872 "Idstone" was reporting (p. 119) "whole litters of shivering idiots afraid of the gun," and could see no hope other than more foxhound "suitably diluted." Knowledgeable Pointer breeders always warned against crossing a pointing with a non-pointing breed, explaining that it (to quote Arkwright) "reduced instinct by half and made more work in training. The foxhound cross counteracted the patient character of the old type, the steadiness, the marking of game in silence." His warning fell often on deaf ears, including in the United States, where some of the most eminent of competitive Pointer bloodlines suffered the embar-rassment of dogs that would bark on point.

In the United States, as elsewhere about the world, Pointer type see-sawed to the pressures of fashion. The Americans sought mainly speed and style, but required great endurance. A three-hour stake is no picnic even in good weather, and by no means are all stakes blessed with good weather.

The British also see-sawed in respect of type, though there seems to have been no particular change in work pattern. The British (and Irish) Pointers, like the European, work areas of considerable restriction as compared with the American. The British problem appeared to be to keep out the heavy hound type, but additionally many winners of great distinction carried most un-Pointerlike heads. A useful example is that early 20th century star, Ch. Coronation, pictured in *The Pointer as a Showdog,* by Lola Macdonald Daly, p. i, with a profile that would have given Arkwright fits. From time to time, argument erupts in the interesting columns of English dog papers—what exactly was (is) an Arkwright head? Well, it wasn't the head of Ch. Corona-tion, that's for sure! About the approximate period this one was doing all its winning, William Arkwright presented to the British Natural History Museum the preserved remains of his famous field Pointer bitch, Ch. Sea Breeze. She is still to be seen in the Museum's storage facility at Tring, out-side London, England. By coincidence, about the same time as it was pos-sible to visit and photograph Ch. Sea Breeze, Peter Woodford (Stonethorpe) showed me a Dutch-bred dog he had newly imported, one that in many ways resembled her. Both the living and the dead were lower-stationed than would now be held desirable in the show ring, but they shared many char-acteristics, even to orange-and-white coloring. Maybe the import had picked up something from Arkwright exports to Europe, for many were sent over by him in his fashionable heydey.

It is not generally understood by the modern American field trialler with Pointer interests that the American field trial Pointer is in his origins here based on exactly the same bloodlines as the show Pointer. The "selective breeding" that eventually separated the types is something that remains of course unclarified, merely for guessing. The 19th century importations to

Balance in movement. Pointer, Am. Ch. Heywood's Gay Diamond, owned by Taramar Kennels, Arizona, and handled by Walt Shellenbarger.—*Cammar*.

here came at the high period of English Pointer excellence. This was the same period that the famous Prinz zu Solms-Brauenfels and Herr Julius Mehlich (Hoppenrade) were pioneering experimental types of German Shorthairs, using their fine English Pointer imports to get the desired "high nose." How good their pointer stock actually was is now easily established through the particulars in show catalogs of the 1880s made available to me from the archives of the Kennel Club (England) by the then-Secretary, Mr. C. A. Binney.

In the same exactness, names and descriptions of early basic imports to the United States are available. Writers such as Joseph Graham (1904) and A. F. Hochwald (1920s) provide documentation. Some imports win their praise, some they damn. Thus that familiar cover-boy, Sensation, was described as "disappointing" and the oft-mentioned basic, Croxteth, is recalled unadmiringly as with a "long and lean head" which may have been the equivalent of what Coronation carried if his surviving picture tells the truth. The basic, Croxteth, also had "light eyes and a long body," which no one particularly admired. Hochwald, dedicated field man though he was, has the most praise of all imports he discussed at that period for Graphic (imported 1885). Owned by a show kennel uninterested in trials, Hochwald saw this one as "the best-looking of his breed out of England" and wondered "what the Pointer breed might have developed into today without the type-steadying influence of Graphic" (*Bird Dogs, Their History and Achievements,* p. 22). When that was written (1922), Graphic was still to be identified as the force behind such greats as National Champions Manitoba Rap (1909), Comanche Frank (1914), John Proctor (1916). Through Frank, her sire, he was also behind the greatest of all, the 3-time National winner, Mary Montrose. A lot of "selective breeding" has gone on since her day—and her record is still to be beaten!

Defection from classic Pointer breed type is quite a modern development in the United States. The Old Hands clearly preferred their competitive dogs to look like the breed they were supposed to be. Studs produced both show and field stock. Thus Rip Rap and Jingo are behind as many show dogs as field. Rip Rap's get, often black-and-white, the legacy of his dam Hops, even earned a special name for their high, showy prancing gait in the show rings—"Rip-Rapping," or "Ric-Racking" as it was known to an older generation of judges.

What actually drove field and show interests apart is not clearly documented. However, it is to the breed's discredit that there has never been a Dual Champion made. It could have been done even as late as the early decades of this 20th century. Mary Montrose followed the first of her three Nationals—run in her Derby year!—with a breed win at Westminster Kennel Club show. Her breeding goes doubly back to Graphic, the show dog import.

Her sire was Ch. Comanche Frank. Her dam, Lorna Doone was by Ch. Manitoba Rap out of a famed prepotent, Lady Ferris.

It is interesting to wonder what Mary Montrose might have been if Lorna Doone had been covered instead by Ch. John Proctor, a half-brother to her sire, Comanche Frank. Both were by Fishel's Frank, a Rip-Rap grandson. Their dams, however, stemmed from entirely different sources. Ch. Comanche Frank's dam, Lady Johns, was by Ch. Alford John (whelped 1901). Llewellin breeders of the time would have scorned John's pedigree as proving he "had dirt in his veins," his dam's pedigree petering out in one generation. Actually, he was a hunting dog, chance-seen, acquired, and proved a great performer. His daughters, especially in matings with Fishel's Frank, support much modern Pointer history. The dam of Lady Johns was Lady Woolton, by English import, Woolton Druid. Frank was a tough dog, and all Pointer! He had three tries for the National, was retired to a stud season described as "rugged" and returned (1914) to take the title at last, under handler J. M. Avent, whose favorite horse died next day of the exertions that had been involved.

Ch. John Proctor stemmed differently—and looked different too! Miss Mariutsch, his dam, was ex Blanche Proctor, by Alpine Lad, FDSB 1316 ex Queen Cyrene. Hochwald has written that: "Alpine Lad was a notorious trailer and when put down with a faster dog generally got in behind and went tailing after his more speedy competitor, keeping up an incessant yapping as long as he was in the rear . . . This trait was turned to advantage by the handler. Few high-strung Setters, or Pointers either for that matter, can stand the strain of a yapping bracemate forever at their heels." Hochwald goes on to describe the running of a stake prior to the 1905 National in which Alpine Lad ran the Llewellin, Alambagh, clear out of the country. Lad's handler was happy: "Old Lad run him so far away, he'll never get back in time for the Championship!" (*Makers of Bird Dog History,* pp. 37–8).

Alambagh did get back, and in time to win the National. Our interest here, however, is in Alpine Lad and his noisy, foxhound manner of trailing other dogs. Ch. John Proctor would also give tongue, as did many of his descendants.

Hochwald had to live in his time (as must I also in mine!) and much that he could have said, that was needed to be said, had to be kept out of his publications. Yet, he did his diplomatic best to indicate where "selective breeding" was taking the American Pointer: "Grave faults are beginning to appear in general (American) Pointer stock . . . lack of intensity, of character, general slipshod manner on game, together with a tendency to bark becoming more and more prevalent . . . Two of our so-called 'improved' strains have blood in them that is doubtful. It was good blood that fused well with finer lines, but too much of it may be the element causing (these) faults and is probably the vehicle through which other dangerous qualities are intensified" (*Bird Dogs, Their History and Achievements*, 1922, p. 49) .

As clearly as he could, this respected commentator pinpoints for the thoughtful reader the infiltrating hound characteristics. One wonders, then, what was his *real* opinion, where was parked his tongue, when he wrote a blurb for the breeder's brochure concerning the style of Ch. Seaview Rex, FDSB 73373, of the 1930s. This is the dog that finally and acceptably made fashionable the hound-skied tail. Judges that for years had criticized high tail carriage as a "Llewellin fault" suddenly were hailing it as the epitome of style. One scarcely avoids the thought that it may have been by unspoken consent considered easier to change field trial fashion in style than change the anatomical heritage of the many dogs by then stuck with hound high tail carriage. Hochwald, in that brochure, wrote that Rex "struck a new note in field trials, his superb gestures on game and his extraordinary character on point became the talk of the hour." A new fashion in style had been born, but may have been poor trade for that of Mary Montrose.

The most-used surviving photograph of Ch. Seaview Rex in pose shows him with lumpy shoulders up towards his ears and a long non-Pointer tail flagpoled. This "Dog of Statuesque Poses" label might impress me the more if my own photo files did not include so many color slides taken of field dogs that had been Statuesquely Posed for my camera on handler command— WHOA! Up with the foot, up with the tail, and no bird within miles! If a Poodle can be taught to waltz on his hindlegs, his ancient relative, the Pointer, can be taught to get his forefoot up on command and to lift his tail as months of careful handler-stroking had taught him—provided, that is, he has an anatomical tail-set that permits such an elevation, something that does not exist in pure Pointer inheritance. Often, in lectures, I have used slides of dogs false-pointing for my camera. And not only Pointers. There is that Shorthair whose record includes a National FT placing—dutifully obeying the command to whoa, foot up—and in his embarrassment licking his nose with a long pink tongue! No handler nowadays would likely false-point his dog to make me a pretty picture, but in those days when my camera reaped such a rich harvest, I was an unknown. How could the obliging handlers have guessed that what they thought to be some casual snapshotting galleryite was an international dog journalist, newly from watching the intense natural stylishness of the great modern Pointers of Italy.

So, let's concede that style can be taught, but that does not promise that the scholar will pass along the acquired style to his get other than in the terms of root-basic canine instinct. (My Australian Cattle Dog lifts her forefoot when she "points" garter snakes in my garden!) In the purebred Pointer the instinct was stronger than in other breeds, but still lacking as it would modernly be measured in stylized competitive venues. Earlier generations of judges of performance may have understood better than many moderns that style is not the first measure of competitive dog worth—as witness the crowning of some Llewellin National Champions that actually would at times creep to their game (see English Setter chapter). "Judges," who reach the saddle modernly via committee membership and the ownership of some successful dog someone else trained and handled, tend to stress the minutae of pose and polish unduly, perhaps the measure of the superficiality of their knowledge. A purebred Irish Setter is penalized because he wags his tail, instinctive exuberance that has in a past period been valued, and now, to press this breed into a same mould with all others, is held unfashionably undesirable. That sort of thing, the attempt to reduce every breed's performance to some common denominator, is at least one reason why practical hunting men hold the field trial dog in equal scorn with the show specimen.

Rationalization advances that a high tail is easier seen in cover. One buys that in respect of a Setter flag. When the same requirement is impressed on the dock-tail European breeds the absurdity reaches an apex.

When Hochwald warned in 1922 of undesirable trends it was already too late to change Pointer breed direction. As the old German proverb has it, he who has said A must now also say B. "Selective breeding" is as throwing a can of white paint into a can of black. One has to learn to like grey. Shorthairs, in our time, also became stuck in this mess, when some breeders used Pointer incross—Pointers that inevitably were not themselves pure. Genes are forever.

Ch. Seaview Rex's pedigree, as published, is interesting. His sire, Tarheel John, FDSB 42782, was by Ch. John Proctor (who so often barked on his points). His dam, Rap's May Belle, FDSB 36989, has a background that, as published, is not provided with registration numbers, which may or may not be oversight. Rex's dam, Greycourt, FDSB 79310 is also given without the registration numbers, apart from one, Lad's Doc, 12407, in the fourth generation, which conveys at least a hint that we are back there again with noisy old Alpine Lad. In any case, even if the lack of registration numbers is merely the omission of someone too tired to write them out, Ch. Seaview Rex seems yet to be intriguingly the result of strong noise-making influences.

It is really true, as mentioned above, that practical hunting men have no particular admiration for field trial dogs—this applying to all forms of field dog competition, bird dogs and retrievers, spaniels or whatever.

"If we treated trials as tests of shooting dogs, we might get back to the days when the shooting man did not look upon trial dogs with contempt, as many do today. Somehow, by introducing cut-throat competition, we have lost sight of the fact that we are supposed to be finding dogs with good natural and hereditary ability that can be trained and handled by shooting men themselves . . . Instead, we have produced a specialized dog only suitable

174

to the best trainers and handlers. No one else can handle them, they are too hot" (Mary Roslin-Williams, *The Dual Purpose Labrador,* London, 1969, p. 197). Mrs. Roslin-Williams as breeder, handler, field and show judge, merely spells out here what is conceded everywhere one listens. Cut-throat competition is of course the Name of the Game into which field trial rivalries have always led. However, Europeans have always had safe anchors out to wind'ard so as to maintain the character of their breeds, in terms of appearance, adherence to type, and suitability for practical use. Thus, Europeans customarily do not trial to beat other dogs, but rather to challenge a standard of performance. Any next European trial can provide as many as a dozen First Place dogs that have reached that pride by turning in a first-class performance and getting past the conformation judges as well. The Game that is played when dog is required to beat dog is something else again. It simply must draw the "too hot" dogs and the most capable professional handlers. No reason exists why well-heeled American and English owners should not indulge themselves in such a Game, as readily as do owners of thoroughbred horses. The only protest is that they should not make so many unsuitable, and wholly distasteful, noises to the effect that *only* their kind of running animal has worth, and that all else canine is merely rubbish. It just is not true!

One does beyond question accept that the top quality field-trial American Pointers, which nowadays constitute a breed of their own entirely, are capable of the most breathtaking performances. The great Circuit stars are the magnificent end product of stern processes of elimination, both in the kennel and in the training sphere. And what stars these can modernly count for the record—such as (among many) Muscle Shoals Jake, Rapid Transit, the several Elhews, the great Safari, Satilla Virginia Lady (1967) Riggins White Knight (1968) Redwater Rex (1969).

They have not only search and speed and style, but they have tremendous endurance and fantastic courage. National competition imposing three-hour spans of exertion provide some incredibly wonderful yarns. The Saturday-Sunday afternoon scampers in local field trials rank by comparison as does the flight of the bumble bee with that of the eagle. No ancient charge of small valor could be advanced against top Circuit performers. As, say, Ch. Riggins White Knight in 1967. Weather zero, wind and rain. His thin jacket was coated with vaseline to keep out the wet, and his tail was a ball of ice. He had been out two-and-a-half hours when he missed a jump, fell into a fast stream. Eight years old he was, but no quitter. He struggled out, was dried, massaged by trainer Hoyle Eaton, sent on—to find at the top of the next hill! Veterinary opinion was taken before the next season—was he fit for another year? The green light was given, and he took the National of 1968.

Such performances are something wide as the world from those little field

Dog equipped with the Bringsel strap for the exercise known as *Bringselver-weisen*. A dog hunting off the long line may have to travel long distances to locate his quarry. A deer is too heavy for him to retrieve, so he takes the dangling strap in his mouth as a symbol of success.—*Roberts* (posed by an American dog).

The Bringsel strap is light and short; will not get in the dog's way when tracking. All tracking in this kind of work is done completely free.—*Roberts*.

"Tommy" has found his deer. He returns at the gallop with his Bringsel strap in his mouth—the symbolic retrieve. If his tail looks short, it's because it is "lashing" side to side as he gallops. Owner, Heinz Duy, Wels, Austria, 1968.

176

scamperings to which I once applied the term of "dog ballet." ("Someone will *shoot* you one of these days for saying things like that!" said an outraged owner!) It is of such top Circuit performances that one tends to think when hearing some brave Shorthair owner boast of having "beat the Pointers and Setters last Saturday." No Shorthair born could ever slog it out with the top strata of American Circuit Pointers, not even with an assist from "selective breeding." What of Pointer stock drifts down to multiple breed P/S competition is often enough merely discard material that couldn't make the Big Time grade.

Conceding admiration for the great performers, it still seems to me that time is long past for conceding that the American competitive Pointer is now a *breed of his own*. As American as the Chesapeake Bay Retriever, who also resulted from weldings of various classically-recognized breeds in the past.

Excellent as the American field Pointer is in terms of performance—the best examples of him, that is—he does not however have a monopoly on excellence. The Pointers of France, Scandinavia and Italy (especially) are all rich in performance virtues and, what is more, overall look like the "breed they are supposed to be"——the measure applied by probably the greatest dog judge the world ever knew, the late Leo C. Wilson. That was, he insisted, his first requirement of any dog appearing before him.

The performances of these European Pointers are of course along different lines from those of the American, but that provides no mandate to criticize or downgrade their quality. The Germans and the Austrians have also some good Pointers though disposed rather to lean more towards their own breeds specifically bred for utility hunting skills. Wherever, however, a Pointer *is* in ownership he, like all Teutonic dogs, has to be able to "do it all!" Thus, it was my privilege in Austria to meet a top performed Pointer, name of Tommy. He was possessed of high ratings in Utility, which means versatility. He showed me high style on pheasant in the beet fields; he retrieved enthusiastically from the lake, and most interestingly of all his skills, demonstrated for me an exercise unknown to us in the United States, the *Bringselverweisen,* which may best be described as a symbolic retrieve.

For this, a deerskin had been dragged to make a track through forest for more than a mile and a half. Twelve hours later (and in rain) Tommy was cast off to find this substitute for a wounded deer. He ran completely free of any harness or line other than a short strap that dangled from his collar. Three of us, spectators, had hidden where we could see the "plant." The handler released the handsome black-white Pointer way back at the start of the track. Nose high, and at the gallop, he presently came into view, searched around until he had found the skin hidden under a pile of brush. He pawed there a second or two, then whipped his head around, took the end of the strap that was dangling from his collar, and with this carefully carried in his mouth, streaked back the mile-and-a-half to his waiting handler. The strap, known as the *Bringsel* (The Bring Thing) was his advice to his handler: "Boss, I have found it. I know where it is. Come along and I'll show you!"

This fantastic-to-watch exercise was developed originally by Austrian army dog handlers who sent their German Shepherd Dogs out to search for wounded or dead soldiers. The sporting use of it quickly recommended itself to the hunting fraternity with its strict requirement to seek out and put out of misery any animal that may have been wounded. As a dog cannot retrieve a man, neither can it retrieve a deer. The Bringsel strap is the substitute. Tommy's owner, young Heinz Duy, Austrian field trial judge, told me further that if a trained *Bringselwerweiser* dog should come upon anything he considered needed the attention of his master he will, if not equipped with the strap, pick up a stick or anything else he can find to carry. The thing is, if he comes with something in his mouth he is announcing a find he considers to be important.

If style, but not high-tail style, is held to be the measure of Pointer performance, one place to see it is in Italy. It cannot be mere coincidence that the best of all modern-published Pointer breed books is the Italian-French language work, by G. Solaro, *Il Pointer,* Rome, 1954. It is a pot of gold for a conformation judge to find, but has no application for American field Pointer interests as the entire blueprinting is in terms of classic conformation, the quality of breed-true construction which probably hasn't prevailed in the American competitive scene since the days of Mary Montrose. However, modern Italian competitive Pointers match well-enough the strictness of the Solaro requirements, as the pictures we have been privileged to receive from the distinguished breeder and field trial buff, Signor Luis Zavaterro, adequately prove.

Australia has had some good Pointers, but not for many a year, drawing in past years exclusively on British stock. For a brief period in the 1950s, there was a contribution of American Herewithem bloodlines, brought in by Stonethorpe Swift, from England, a well-performed dog that later gained his Dual Championship in Australia. A daughter of his, representing a welding with some New Zealand bloodlines, came with me to the United States, and eventually died in San Francisco. As her New Zealand dam had also a rich infusion of Herewithem by way of another import, my Aust. Ch. Cruchfield Coo-ee brought back to this country a strong Herewithem inheritance at the same time as Robert Maloney (Herewithem) was advertising his own stock in Pittsburgh with the restriction of None for Sale!

Field trials in Britain are not strongly supported in the numerical sense nowadays, but do attract some notable supporters, of which Lord Rank is doubtless the best known. Well-known Pointer fancier, Mrs. Badenach Nicholson, of Scotland, has at this time of writing one that must be no more than a razor-edge from the Dual Championship. Peter Woodford (Stone-thorpe) places heavy emphasis on working qualities, and equal emphasis on breed type and quality. Some years ago, he took himself across to Europe and searched tirelessly to find stock suited to restoring some of the qualities that British Pointers could use. His imports were subjected to considerable criticism by the local breeders (naturally) but inevitably the type contributions began to show throughout the breed. Now, this knowledgeable breeder (who is also a cattle breeder, by the way) feels it becomes time to re-introduce the old English type to prevent over-exaggeration of Continental type from proliferating. This matches with a reply given by Frank Longmore when I criticized an Australian Pointer as being somewhat heavy: "We do have them all shapes and sizes, but it is always the big strong working Pointer that has to come to the rescue when breeding to exaggerations hurts type."

Importantly, it seems that much grief in field trial breeding over long years has come about from lack of recognition of time "to come to the rescue." If this had not been the case we would still have our Mary Montroses.

Importantly, a Pointer is not just any sound-going dog. He has his classic distinctions. From time to time across the world breeders become engaged in discussion of *Heads*. When reference is to the "Arkwright Head" some will challenge that there was ever such a thing—and claim that Arkwright, a wealthy man, illustrated his book with the help of famous artists, paintings only. However, for those curious to see an actual "Arkwright Head," his famous field trial bitch, *Sea Breeze,* is to see in the Natural History Museum Storage at Tring, England. He presented her in 1905.

The Pointer *body* in classic expression is elegance and curves plus strength. It is deep-chested rather than wide, with a tuck-up under rather than over-emphasized. Backs may not roach or dip. Hindquarters are powerful propulsive engines, and thighs must be wide to house muscle. A narrow-thighed Pointer is not to admire. Angulation should be adequate.

Feet are vital. A thousand years ago, the codified Welsh Law of Howell the Good placed the same cash value on the feet and the life of the Hawk, the Horse, the Greyhound. All depended on their feet. Modernly, too, a Pointer or any sporting dog is no better than his feet. A wonderful tale in a Donn Byrne novel of some years ago describes a horse buying. The hunting man would see the availables first completely robed, ears to tail, so that only feet and pasterns showed. His reason was that if he saw the entire horse some aspect of style or beauty might catch his interest and he might be likely to miss a fault in feet. When the poor-footeds were rejected, the robes came off. It is a procedure that some judges in the dog rings might emulate. In my own case I promptly discard any bad-footed dog, in any breed, no matter how glamorous.

Of the Pointer *tail* Arkwright wrote: "The head is the seat of character,

179

but for the certificate of blue blood, apply at the other end." The classic Pointer tail, thick at base, short, bee-sting tipped, falls victim of crossbreeding. An American judge should not hold his breath till he sees one, but from time to time his interest will be rewarded. The 1968-revised AKC-approved Pointer standard includes now the new and interesting requirement that a *"docked tail shall be penalized."* Clearly this is response to the situation from time to time encountered in the judging of Sporting Group when some off-type liver-and-white suspect "Shorthair," that should never in any case have reached the eminence of Group, stands next to the Pointer and the gallery has to check length of tail to decide which breed is which. While Shorthair governing interests lag in providing protection for their breed in terms of Standard revision, the Pointer folk have jumped right in to protect theirs.

Gait: There is nothing special about Pointer gait except that it is easier to assess in a smooth-coat. It should be reachy, sound-going, high-headed, with lashing tail and free of hackney prance.

Color: One is back with Turberville's "spotted Whelpes," plus the solids, black and liver. Scandinavians still keep solid blacks, and some have been introduced to America years ago. However, none have ever crossed my path. The only solid liver known to me is the one in a painting of Mr. Ogden Mills driving his showy team of black matched hackneys, an unbelievably elegant, classic type of solid-colored Pointer running ahead. England has had solid blacks, Arkwright especially liking these, and exporting many to Europe which provided the basis for the color in those countries. One sees plenty of black-whites in the English show rings still. They do tend to be of a somewhat different type, and it is interesting to see how everywhere Pointers of this color tend to the showy action linked here in the United States with the famous Rip Rap, whose dam, imported Hops, was described by Hochwald as "colored like a well-used sheet of blotting paper."

The AKC-Standard replaced in 1968 was blessed with a piece of composition most admirable re *"Balance and all-over symmetry (which) is much more important in the Pointer than size. It is just as vital in a dog bred for field work as it is in an athlete or racehorse, and for the same reasons; it indicates muscular co-ordination, endurance, and an equilibrium of power. Whether large or small, a well-put-together Pointer, 'smooth all over' is to be preferred to an uneven one with contrasting good and bad points. Provided there is balance, considerable variation in size and weight is permissible."* This may never have anywhere within Sporting dog description been better said, and deserves to be preserved, a privilege it has been my pleasure to seize.

Temperament: An authority of the 19th century wrote: "Many Pointers have a ferocity of temper which will not submit to discipline and correction unless taken in hand very young." This translates as that when faced with

180

sadistic or over-heavy punishment a Pointer would fight back (as does an Irish Setter and some of the Continental breeds). Historically, life has been rock hard for Pointers. Sir Walter Scott ("St. Ronan's Well"), in a famous quote, described the Setter as fitter for a place on the hearth-rug, "not from any deficiency of intellect on the part of the Pointer, but because he is so generally abused while in the management of brutal breakers and grooms that he loses all excepting his professional accomplishments of finding and standing steady to game."

As late as the 1930s, *Hutchinson's Dog Encyclopedia* (p. 1372), claimed that "there is no record of a Pointer being kept as a housedog." Actually, in the years intervening, especially since England veered away from bird-dog use in favor of human beaters of driven game, many Pointers have been given companion status. A pleasant Pointer is actually a charming dog to have in such capacity. My own Ch. Cruchfield Coo-ee (almost all "Herewithem" bred) spent all her life in the belief that the world was full of people who meant well by Pointers and responded accordingly.

One does wonder why the American Pointer scene has not been blessed with wealthy patrons interested to make Dual Champions, as in the other Sporting breeds. Stock was available. Not only such as Mary Montrose, but also Ch. Becky Broom Hill, who won three Nationals, a very likely candidate had she been so-campaigned. Her sire, Broom Hill Dan, English import, was a good-looker that no one would use in America until Becky made him famous, after which, and in his old age, his services were sought for all the puny, undersized bitches of his time. Another famous field trial bitch, Ch. Great Island Ringing Bells, was also by an English import, Tom Speedy, whose dam, Her Majesty, was at that time the outstanding producer of champion English show stock. Hochwald wrote of this Tom Speedy that "he had great intensity on game, a world of character, a nose that was almost uncanny." He too might have had a breeder's rush after the phenomenal success of Ringing Bells, but by then he was dead.

Even distinguished breeders with an interest in breed type retention seem never to have bestirred themselves in the interest to make Dual Champions. Robert Wehle (Elhew) could have done it; so could Robert Maloney (Herewithem). Wehle wrote (*Wing and Shot*):

> Breeding for a single, or a few factors, is always a short-sighted policy. Dog breeders are here but a short time when compared with the age of their breeds, which in some cases will continue long after the present breeders are dead. Today's breeders are merely temporary custodians of breeds handed down to them, entrusted to their care . . . I wonder if we have the authority or inherent right substantially to alter (them). Short-sighted breeding has changed breeds substantially, destroying the work of previous generations.

181

With such belief, it is not surprising that the best of the Elhews do retain a fair share of authentic breed type.

Herewithem was interested in shows, but Mr. Maloney would retain no dog that could not serve him as a shooting dog. My file includes a remarkable pedigree compilation sent me by Mr. Maloney, his comments scribbled all over with comments on the individual dogs, as from his Ch. Governor Moscow, a Westminster Best in Show to Herewithem Brown Bomber, against whose name is scribbled: "Tougher than Joe!"

AKC registrations in show stock plummet sadly. Field trial breeding, as recorded in American Field week by week is prolific, but wastage must be enormous, by evidence of what survives to show up in competition.

It seems reasonable to believe that the world will never lack Pointers, and while not all countries agree as to type, the ancient heritage remains. A Pointer is a Pointer.

RIGGINS WHITE KNIGHT

National F.T. Ch. Riggins White Knight (1968). The American field trial Pointer has over the years developed by specialized breeding into a completely distinct type. Required is fantastic speed and endurance to survive gruelling rigors of three-hour heats ahead of a horse. This champion, whose record is impressive, kept his performance quality into advanced age. Owner, Dr. Nicholas E. Palumbo, Hawaii. Breeder-handler, D. Hoyle Eaton, Mississippi.

182

Reach and thrust at speed (seen from side-on). German Shorthaired Pointer, Pat. v. Hanstein (Germany).—*photo lent by Herr Gustav Machetanz, Dortmund.*

The Great Rough Water Dogge, from *The Sketch Book of Jean de Tournes,* pub. Lyons, France, 1556. "... the general features of his (the Water Dogge's) Countenance big, united together should be Lyonlike as might be for that shewes fierceness and goodnesse ..."—*Gervase Markham,* 1621.

This sketch, from a publication of more than 400 years ago, cannot fail to have interest for historians, not only in connection with the retrieving breeds, but also in its establishment of proof that a type that would become later accepted as "Newfoundland" was actually in existence in France in the Middle Ages.—*Reproduction and courtesy of permission to use from The British Museum, London.*

The Retrievers

IT does seem that the British, even centuries ago, favored the ideal of a specialist dog. While European sporting dogs were expected to cope with all chores—as they still are—even as far back as Elizabethan time, Johannes Caius was identifying curl-coated Water Dogges by the name of *Aquaticus feu Inquisitor,* The Water Spaniel or Fynder. He was alone of his time to call the Water Dogge a Spaniel, and it would be a century before anyone else did so. He is more generous than usual in describing this Dogge: "somewhat Bigge, and of a measurable Greatnesse . . . with long curled hair not obtainable by extraordinary trades, but given by nature's appointment . . . poivide and notted in front of the Shoulders to the hindermost Legges and to the end of his Tayle, which I did for custom rause, that being somewhat bare and naked by shearing . . . they might achieve lightness and swiftness . . . so troublesome and needless a burden being shaken off . . ."

Caius conceded also "a certain difference in this kind of Dogge, either for something which is in their Voyce to be marked, or for something which is in their Qualities to be considered." The Dogge was efficient, playful, "bringing our Boultes and Arrowes out of the Water, which otherwise we could hardly recover, and often they restore to us our Shaftes which we thought never to see, touch, or handle again."

Caius does not mention a rough or long-coated Water Dogge, but tells of a puzzlement concerning reports reaching him of "a Dogge which seeketh Fishe by smelling among Rocks and Stones . . . and I have been diligent and busie in demaunding question of Fishermen and also of Huntsmen (for) assuredly I know of none of that kind in England, neither have I received by

Captain Cartwright with his hunting Greyhound in Labrador. Frontispiece of his "Journal of the Transactions and Events during a residence of nearly 16 years on the coast of Labrador." Published Newark, England, 1792.

THE FOURTH VOYAGE.

This was a terrible, bad day. The ground is greatly flooded, and I fear the rivers will overflow. If any fhips are on this coaft now, God help them! unlefs they are piratical privateers, coming to plunder innocent people again ; for fuch, I recommend to their friend the D—l.

This morning, all the ice, both in this harbour and White Cove, was gone. One of my people having a large boil on his belly, and fome more appearing, I applied a poultice to each of them, took feventeen ounces of blood from him, and gave him a dofe of jallap.

A thick, wet fog all day.

After dinner I went to the people's houfe, where I took the fhallop's fails out of the bark, and fpread them to dry. I then went to Mr. Seydes' boat, which I found left in a fhameful fituation ; being liable to be carried away by a high tide : I made faft the end of a rope to her, which was all I could do. I hid

away three traps, alfo killed a pair of eider-ducks ; the feafon is fo backward, that they were not yet with egg.

This morning was very foggy with fmall rain ; at ten o'clock it fnowed, and the remainder was mifty, dark, and cold ; very fuitable for December in England.

At noon I walked to Mr. Seydes' boat, and hid away another trap. I got a fhot at about forty eider-ducks, pretty well doubled up, and killed three ; alfo crippled five or fix more, but got only one : for both the weather and water were fo cold, that my greyhound, who has learnt from the Newfoundland dogs to fetch birds out of the water, would go in but once ; they were a very fine fhot for a large gun, but my double-barrel has fo fmall a bore, that it carries only fifty-two grains of B. B. fhot.

Report that there is any such kind of Dogge which followeth Fishe to apprehend and take it."

Caius, who published in 1550, first in Latin, the English translation appearing after his death, was a credulous man of his time. He guessed at Otter, even at Beaver which in the Middle Ages was still common in the Old World, and he believed the Beaver to be a flesh-eater: "It doth participate this property with the Dogge, namely that when Fishe be scarce, they leave the Water and raunge up and down the Land, making an insatiable slaughter of young Lambes."

How close Caius did come to the reality. His error was in confining his thought to his own country. From years earlier—tales travelled slowly in those times—since Jan Cabot had come back from his trans-Atlantic voyaging to Bristol, England, to tell of having reached the western lands, sailors' yarns would involve the big black dogs used by the natives for haulage purposes. Maybe these were the descendants of the big blacks described in the sagas as having been taken to Vinland by Leif Eriksen. Maybe tales told by sailors at innside fires had drifted eventually to the ears of Caius, of dogs hunting fish along bleak and rocky shores, of turning from the water "when Fishe be scarce, making an insatiable slaughter of young Lambes."

The tales match with the realities of dog management in those regions, Labrador, Newfoundland, that lasted right into the 19th century. When they were busy with the fishing, the fisherfolk turned their big haulage dogs loose to forage for themselves. The practice may have been learned from the natives, and would have fitted in well with the frugal instincts of the dominantly French—Breton, Basque—peoples who pioneered the fishing industry there.

By the turn of the 19th century the practice had become scandalous. It was dealt with by the law. The Grand Jurors of St. Johns made Report and Recommendation to the Court of Session, 1815: "Such dogs become not only dangerous and troublesome by starvation and disease, public nuisances in the streets, but goaded by hunger, in natural desperation, assemble like wolves in packs to destroy poultry, sheep, anything eatable within reach" (Capt. Thomas Brown, *Biographical Sketches and Anecdotes of Dogs, Edinburgh, 1829, p. 200*). A law passed—and deeply resented by owners—directed the destruction of all dogs roaming publicly. Away from the settlements, trappers, sealers, hunters, also abandoned their dogs to forage whenever these were not actively in use. May one not guess that the natives Cabot had seen had the same habit, and that over intervening centuries passed it on as a practice?

One school of thought believes the big black dogs were spontaneously engendered in those regions. Another school quotes the sagas to provide proof that Leif Eriksen brought them to Vinland, but does not stress the obvious—that Eriksen brought them *from Europe*.

A most informative and scholarly book, published 1970 by the Natural History Press, *The Natural History of Dogs* by Richard & Alice Fiennes, identifies two likely sources of trans-Atlantic dog origin. Fiennes classifies the Newfoundland in the Mastiff bracketing, holds it "introduced from the Pyrenees by Basque fishermen, and developed as an independent breed there," and quotes Edward Ash as believing it to have been "introduced by Norwegians in the 16–17th century, and developed by selection and crossing with other introduced strains." Ash had stated that such dogs resembling the Newfoundland had been kept by Norwegian peasants for hunting wolves and bears in the mountains." Such a theory provides at least a possible source from which Eriksen could have drawn. Fiennes quotes also that further introductions were "made to Labrador in the 17th century by Breton cod fishermen, probably derived from the French braques" (*p. 120*).

Always there has lacked a true, early-time contemporary picture to establish that big shaggy blacks actually existed in Europe. The picture worth the proverbial thousand words came under my notice in the British Museum, a bonanza from a little work entitled *The Sketch Book of Jean de Tournes*, pub. Lyons, France, 1556. As artists of the period favored exact reportage and not impressionism, one is compelled to accept de Tournes' Water Dogge of the great size, noble profile, shaggy coat as exactly represented. It is a picture that Newfie historians cannot afford to ignore.

My beloved Gervase Markham (1621) describes Water Dogges in Britain as being both curled and rough-coated. If the Curled Coats, as Caius identified his, were British, and the Rough Shaggies, as per Markham, were French, as per the pencil of de Tournes, then Markham's prejudice in favor of curl is understandable. The British have ever inclined to their own breeds.

Most Labrador Retriever historians have drawn upon the paragraph that even earlier historians have culled from Markham. It is a description so much used as not to merit reproduction here in full; merely one desires to draw attention to the particular reference made to "general countenance, united together as a Lyon might be, for that shows Fierceness and Goodness." The "Lyon-like" fits exactly the profile of the de Tournes dog.

A great many myths and speculations, and even a fair percentage of nonsense, has over the years been written about dogs drawn from the Atlantic sea-coast regions. Thus in 1968, a lady resident of Newfoundland writing to Frank Warner Hill, who republished her letter in *Dog World* (Eng.) —August 2, 1968—advanced as gospel that "centuries of isolation in a rugged, seagirt land determined the development of a distinctive Newfoundland breed, undiluted by the whimsy of man, or contact with more cosmopolitan canines."

Lady! Lady!

Craft from half of Europe visited the fishery areas as from centuries past and "contact with cosmopolitan canines" was a local fact of life, documented by entries in journals and even in the sacred logs of ships as from earliest times. No space here to retell all those Go-Ashore shenanigans of doggy sailors, but for a taste let us look at a very early one. In 1620, Sir Richard Whitmore, over to Newfoundland for the fishing, logged his Mastiff jumping ship: "running off into the woods with the beasts of the country, continuing nine or ten days, and did return to us without hurt." A normal heat period! As Fiennes establishes all drop-eared breeds within the "Mastiff Group"— including Newfs, Pyrs, Bloodhounds, Spaniels, Setters, Retrievers, mini-Spaniels—the activity of Sir Richard Whitmore's AWOL crew member must be viewed as acceptable.

This thought was much reinforced recently as my camera collected some shots of a superb Mastiff male out of Canada, shown at the upstate New York show, the Kanadasaga Kennel Club, where he went to second in the Group. The Fiennes' work so newly read, the Mastiff presented fresh interest as I assessed his bodily structure, the shape and proportioning of this beautiful specimen. One need have little difficulty to transpose his qualities of length in relation to height, his general outline into a retrieverish setting. In the same way the nobility of the Mastiff head lends ease to the exercise of visualizing it contributing, ages ago, to the formation of the classic Pointer head, even while recognizing the endless modifications that the passage of time inevitably imposed. Continually, in the pursuance of dog history research one is brought to face with such involved inheritances suggested, the See-Shells-Guess-Eggs sequence that makes sense when linked to the scientific delvings of the qualified anatomical experts.

As to the color inheritance that could have come in with the introduction of such a "cosmopolitan canine" (and the Mastiff breed was not alone in such a conveyance, as later notes will show) it is well-documented that both yellow and brindle endowment came to England with the earliest introduction of trans-Atlantic dogs and that such can awkwardly even present themselves in modern litters.

Sydenham Edwards (*Cynographia Britannica,* London, 1800) provides a color picture that should undermine for all time the naive belief that the Newfoundland came to England in other than a variety of shapes, jacketings, colors. There existed no such cookie-cutter type conformity as modernly recognized, those handsome blacks that however, in specimens of lesser quality, can at times suggest over-size Labradors. The 1800 A.D. brace provides a classic Landseer coloring (black-and-white) but also, and startlingly to our modern sight, *a bright yellow patch* that proves the presence of the yellow factor in original trans-Atlantics. One coat is curled. One dog has cropped ears, not shaped as on our Danes and Dobermans, but merely lopped, severe half-length truncation which suggests that part of his employment was as a fighter. The half-way lopping seems to have been a very old French style. The bear and boar fighting hounds on the Devonshire Tapestries (15th century) are so cut and, for goodness sake, in French Somaliland, in Djibouti, I photographed *donkeys* with the same mutilation. Somaliland donkeys don't fight, merely haul great loads. Many trans-Atlantic dogs had to haul heavy loads *and* fight.

This brace from *Cynographia Britannica* establish how wide are the variants present in the breed inheritance. If it bothers us to identify them, be sure researchers closer in time fared no better. Captain Brown (1829) presumes the crossing of Newfoundlands and Setters (correctly, these base the Flat-coateds) and the "further crossings with the Water Dog or Poodle, of Water Dog shape but with thick curled silky hair, generally white or white-patched, popular in France where it is taught curious tricks and excels on water fowl."

Always and *always* the route markers point us to France!

Later authorities also passed the buck. "Water Dogs here in Britain are so crossed with other breeds as to have lost their identity." (*Vero Shaw,* 1890). Contemporaries did not contradict this. Mr. Charles Eley, early Labrador Club president, also conceded the "impossibility of elucidating satisfactorily the stories of Labrador origin." With all the multiples of inheritance factors involved, one must respect those that stabilized these breeds for us.

Mr. August Belmont's black Labrador, Super Chief, National Retriever Field Champion of 1968 and National Amateur Retriever Field Champion of 1967–68.

The Labrador Retriever

WITH no intent to re-hash the contents of the many competent Labrador Retriever breed books, let us start here with examination of a work not commonly brought to the attention of those with interest in trans-Atlantic dogs, the *Journal of the Transactions and Events during a Residence of Nearly 16 Years on the Coast of Labrador,* by George Cartwright, Esq., published Newark, England, 3 vols., 1793. Reprinted in the 1930s, the work still seems to have failed to catch dog-interested eyes. The sole reference so far come under my own notice appeared in *Daniel's Rural Sports,* 1801, where a most important piece of matter received mention, as will presently appear here as well.

Cartwright's name is still lettered on maps of the Labrador coast, by my thumb-measure (being no nautical expert!) on a school atlas about 53° North. He left England May 1770, in the 50-ton schooner, *Nimrod,* taking a servant, a "housekeeper," a brace each of Foxhounds and Bloodhounds, a Greyhound, a Spaniel, a Pointer—"cosmopolitan canines" if ever. He took chickens, a pair of rabbits, a goat. The goat came first of them all to grief, drank "a gallon of rum from a bucket left on deck, continuing in such a state of intoxication as to be unable to get up on her legs for days." The "housekeeper" was caught in *flagrante delicto* with a sealer and was banished. The Greyhound killed the buck rabbit. The servant shot his dog instead of a bird—whether this was the Spaniel or the Pointer is not clarified, but neither was ever mentioned again in the Journal. The Foxhounds survived the wolves after a kennel-break in "weather so cold the combs and feet of the chickens froze stiff, so they had to be taken into the house," but their eventual fate was sorrier. His boat far out in heavy seas that hindered return to the camp he was leaving, Cartwright remembered having left the Fox-hounds "tied to the tilt." The Bloodhounds flourished, multiplied, and when seal meat was short, provided the sealers with a fat whelp or so.

The Greyhound was king. Hooded like a falcon he rode the sled, and when game was sighted he was slipped (as Greyhounds are for the chase) to run in that cruel terrain. He harried otters; he chased wolves, "which he would not tackle alone, but ran them hard till the Bloodhound bitch, off her second litter, came to help." The cold eventually destroyed him: "over-come by the severity of the December weather he was unable to travel further. We made him a bed in the woods with my greatcoat, but when we returned he was dead."

When Cartwright went back to England with his furs, he picked up more Greyhounds and a terrier. He reported finding, on his return, the Newfound-land bitch he had left behind, still alive at the camp. He wondered how she had managed to survive. "Smelling for Fishe among the Rocks and Stones," old Caius would have guessed. He had no uneasiness about having left her—it was the custom.

"*March, 1776:* Slipped the Greyhound from the sled on a Polar bear. He would not chase till the two Newfoundlands came up. Then we had a fine battle. I closed to shoot, but the ice was rotten. When I had extricated myself, the bear had bit all the dogs and made his escape."

The mauled dogs were unable to haul, and the traces were then taken by two Eskimo boys. On another occasion, when the Greyhound was slipped from his lead to take after a deer, "the Bloodhound and the Newfoundland that were in the traces followed after, sled and all, tumbling everything into the snow in the glorious melee."

The Journal is full of interesting references, including one that mentions the acquisition of an Eskimo dog "but the cur would not hunt." It did not seem to be known to Cartwright that hunting was not necessarily the prov-ince of this breed. He mentions the interest he took in finding this dog's tail curled over its back, whereas wolves carried theirs straight out.

The quote that made *Daniel's Rural Sports* was dated February, 1779: "I got a shot at about 40 eider ducks, killed three, also crippled five or six more, but only got one. The weather and the water was so cold that my Greyhound *who had learned from the Newfoundlands to fetch birds out of the water, would go in but once*" (The italics are mine, CBM).

"Cosmopolitan canines" anyone? The toughness of the Cartwright Grey-hounds is astonishing. He mentions one that "struck so deep in through light snow and ice as to cut his legs so much he had to desist." He also mentions a Newfoundland bitch that stayed with her trapper master and froze to death because she would not leave him. The way in which these several breeds

194

Field Ch. Anzac of Zenith, Labrador Retriever, owned by Carnation Farms Kennels, 1968.

Ch. Shamrock Acres Light Brigade, top Sporting Dog at American shows for 1968. Owner, Mrs. Sally B. McCarthy, Wisconsin.—*Tauskey.*

lived and worked together is thoroughly established. Cartwright was not the only trapper working these coastal lands and fringes south and north of Belle Isle Strait during his 16 years that the Journal covers. So, is it surprising that a sheaf of travellers' notes of the 19th century mention "good dogs kept by settlers on the coast, with smooth and short coats, able to stay free of ice," and of "sharp-nosed ones on the south shore of the mainland on the Straits of Belle Isle." Several such references are well and exactly documented in Helen Warwick's definitive work, *The Complete Labrador Retriever*, 1965. She includes also an interesting question raised in *The Encyclopaedia of Rural Sport*, 1840, by a gentleman who noted that "black Pointers might have been used on Newfoundlands, because when Labradors are inbred, the result is often a light-made dog, long on leg, light of bone, with a thin tail and Pointer-like ears." Give or take the ears (which could have come even from the braques out of France!) the other characteristics described go well with the king dog that rode the sleds with Cartwright decades earlier.

There is also that matter of brindling. "Stonehenge" (editor of *The Field* and the most distinguished of 19th century dog writers) in the now very rare first edition of his work (1860), commenting on retrieving breeds, wrote:

> Many well-known sportsmen now possess their own breed of dogs, used for retrieving on land and water, but there is no established breed. Good retrievers are to be found in all breeds. Thirty years ago, William Evans, now head keeper to Lord Fitzwilliam, had a famous retriever by a Bloodhound of the late Lord Ducie's out of a Mastiff.

This would not surprise modern authority Fiennes at all, as he includes these breeds, along with Newfs, etc., in a single grouping. "Stonehenge" further quotes Craven (*The Young Sportsman's Manual*) describing a celebrated land and water retriever bred "between a Bulldog and a smooth terrier," and added that an "English retriever, smooth or curly-haired, should be black and tan or black with tabby or brindled legs, *the brindled legs being indicative of the Labrador*" (again my italics, CBM).

It was a work of Hugh Dalziel's (*British Dogs*, 1881) that first drew my attention to this "Stonehenge" quote, and a fine time it took to run it down, as first editions of "Stonehenge" just *weren't*. The British Museum's earliest appeared to be the third. It was my friend, Herm David, who eventually provided me with the photostat from a copy in his possession, lacking which it would have been difficult to discuss with confidence brindled legs in Labradors as an early-recognized indicative feature. Dalziel had commented that "a black-and-tan, or a brindled dog, however good, would stand no chance in competition, because self-colored dogs have been brought to such

196

Dual Ch. Knaith Banjo. This famous English dual champion yellow is a must in any Labrador Retriever survey. He was one of the greatest of all time, and lasted forever into old age.

Foxhanger Mascot, a Dual Ch. Knaith Banjo descendant, could possibly be described as England's best-known Sporting dog, he's been around so long. His owner, Lady Simpson, handled him at 1968 Crufts, when he was aged eleven—which is when it was my luck to see him. His Working Dog awards, and Police Dog awards, are many, which befits the circumstance that the late Sir Joseph Simpson was Commissioner of Scotland Yard.

a pitch of perfection that they equal, if they do not excel, the marked ones in all points, and possess the desired jet-black color in addition."

How the world turns in dog fashion. Now it is the black Labrador that is fighting for his life all over the world. The triumph of the yellows is all but complete in British countries, and the same take-over promises in America, though not yet fully accomplished. In a 222-entry of a Labrador Retriever Specialty that I judged in Australia at the end of 1969, the blacks could have been counted on one person's hands. In England, so few blacks showed that in one of my critiques I raised the question—was the classic dog on the way to extinction? One hopes not, for it does become apparent in so many dog breeds that there are distinct linkages between color and qualities, and the classic black dog, generally the most honest of fellows, has too much goodness to let lapse. In American field (retrieving) competition the black is still king, a position one hopes he will maintain. Famous Labrador breeder in England, president of the breed club, Mr. Maurice C. V. Gilliat, of the black Holton strain, has told me that it seems to be the favor of the ladies that has taken the yellow Labrador to the top, most strongly of all in terms of those bought for pets.

The discussion of trans-Atlantics being introduced to southern England via the fishing fleets, strongly through Poole, Dorset, has been well-covered in many breed books, so no need to recap here where space is restricted. It seems perhaps more useful to raise the question of an other somewhat neglected source of introduction, the officers of British naval vessels working the long-maintained Labrador Fisheries Patrol, that deadly-dull, uncomfortable sea-service. Logs of many such vessels give clues to dog interest; naval men took with them hunting dogs, as did army personnel (already discussed in Setter chapters) in those more leisurely services of earlier centuries. An interesting example (of far too many to quote here) is that from the log of *H. M. S. Rose,* Aug. 16, 1830. Captain Dewar had landed to stretch his legs on an uninhabited island in the mouth of the St. Lawrence, taking his first lieutenant and his own Newfoundland dog for company. He sent the dog "into a creek to catch some ducks swimming there," and went in himself to "encourage the dog." Taking cramp, he was swept away and drowned. It was his lieutenant's melancholy duty to take the body back to Halifax, Nova Scotia, where this service was based. Not only did naval men bring dogs *to* Nova Scotia from England (as historically they did Clumbers, for example) but also they took various dogs of local origin back to England. As traditionally British naval officers were drawn from aristocratic families, such imports would have lived useful lives in the service of huntin'-shootin' folk on great estates, and inevitably have added their services towards increasing the breeds' numbers.

The circumstance that many of the retrieving dogs were so privately kept

Eng. Ch. Damson of Mansergh (Reanacre Sandylands Tarmac ex Ch. Bumblikite of Mansergh), a splendid contemporary example of that most admirable of dogs, a true-type black Labrador. That the foible of fashion could ever endanger the continuance of such is not to be even endured as a thought. Her competitive show record is excellent, and included among her several CCs is one under Mrs. Helen Warwick (USA) at the Labrador Club of Scotland show, 1968. Several BIS awards, plus Qualifier and field performances that make her a "full" champion, round out a distinguished record. Owner, M. Roslin-Williams, Yorkshire, England.—photo, *Anne Roslin-Williams*.

Field Ch. Sandhurst Sweep, Labrador Retriever, wins the English Retriever Championship of 1968 at Sutton Scotney. Owner, R. S. Wilkins. Handler, R. Male.—*Cooke*.

may be one reason why the Labrador breed in England did not receive separate Kennel Club status until as late as 1902. The reigning retrieving breed was the Wavy (Flat) Coated that as late as 1911 was registering 400 to the Labrador's 146. Nor was there any particular interest in the United States. The National Geographic Society's *Book of Dogs* (1919, p. 36) grants one paragraph and no picture while describing the Labrador color as being "generally some shade of brown that must not show more than a trace of white on the chest."

American recognition of true type in Labradors came but slowly. Until quite recently show interest was minimal. A few exceptional ownerships finished Dual Champions, oftenest dogs of a great distinction in performance as well as type. However, as late as 1960 an American-published book on Sporting breeds tells us "that show judges prefer the small English Labrador that is pretty, but which lacks the power to win Field Trials, or take on heavy water work." The author's opportunities for observation must of course have been restricted to what he has seen in some sections of this country where, in truth, many Labradors in competition have been big, tall, high-tailed fellows whose breed type is no more than coincidental. Apart from the fact that many of the Field Trial greats in America (I think now of such as have come under my personal observation, National Ch. Massie's Sassy Boots, etc.) have been true-type dogs of great breed elegance and handy size, it becomes necessary to take issue on the subject of "power." It has been my privilege to watch Labradors of famous English strains, imported to New Zealand, working those wild-running, icy, snow-fed rivers, such as the Ruamahaga, wide and turbulent, fighting their way, and it has also been my interest to think of such drastic testings while standing beside the puddly little sloughs and the unexciting creeks where retrieving trials appear oftenest to be promoted in America. What is more, those English-breds and their descendants, worked on their own initiative, not to automatic handler direction. It would be a brave observer that would dare to downgrade the performances they provided, though their legs were not overlong, nor their type suspect. Pretty? No—I wouldn't claim that they were pretty. No true-bred Labrador typey dog is actually "pretty." What he is is *functional*—very!

There undoubtedly developed here for working competition a longer-legged, lighter-framed, plumy-tailed dog that sorely troubled experienced international judges to see under the designation of "Labrador Retriever." It was Leo C. Wilson who said he accepted the explanation that such dogs suited American working conditions, if that was the case. "But then," he added, "don't call them Labrador Retrievers—which they just don't happen to be. Find them a name for themselves." The bald fact is that though the dog had its origins on this Continent, it was shaped to a separately-recognized breed in England, and it is the dog as there crystallized in type that the world (including present-day American) standards have accepted.

How modern the breed recognition is, is also emphasized by Joseph Graham's seeming unawareness of retrieving breeds other than Chesapeake Bay and Irish Water Spaniels. Correctly, he forecast that their fortunes were linked with the numbers of ducks. Certainly, the market shooters of the 19th century, who made the most general use of retrievers, appear to have had no equivalent of the Labrador. Also, it would seem that while American retrieving trials are modernly blessed with many stout and loyal supporters, and the entries at the shows are increasing magnificently (type as well as numbers!), the game clubs show no interest worth mentioning in retrieving dogs. A man with a boat is considered sufficient to fish out dead ducks, and cripples—who bothers? There is nowhere in America an equivalent for the Germanic Hunting Code of Honor which obligates a hunter to search out game he has wounded.

In the United States retrieving trial competition is Non-Slip. A dog retrieves to direction, having memorized what he sees fall. He has no real need for a nose. In blind retrieves he is the equivalent of a chess-piece moved across a board. There is little spectator value so far as other than participants in the game are concerned, and certainly no equivalent of the exciting European retrieving processes whereby an unshackled duck has crossed a stream and hidden itself and provides a dog with the task of locating it, shepherding it back to the stream and—using his own initiative placing it handily on the water for the guns. However, the peak of excellence to which the trained American retrieving dog is shaped is also remarkable to see in terms of pace and obedience, and the value of such in the blinds is beyond dispute. Other lands, other aims—in dog performance as in all else. Performance is tailored to need and to fashion, a reasonable arrangement.

The first Labrador Retriever Field Champion, Blind of Arden, was finished in 1935. At that time, numbers were still small and no one could have guessed that this breed would eventually top the registration table of Sporting Breeds as compiled by the American Kennel Club. The latest count available to me reported 19 Dual Champions, among which Dual Ch. Shed of Arden is distinguished in that he also carried off the honors in no less than three National Championships (1942–1943–1946). National Champion of 1947, Bracken Sweep, is also a Dual Championship holder. To the mid-1960s, the British reported nine Duals, one of which at least it has been my privilege to see, the great Dual Ch. Knaith Banjo.

Apart from his superb retrieving abilities, the Labrador Retriever is provenly versatile. He is a favored guide dog for the blind; he serves the army; and he serves the police in England especially as a sniffer-out of drugs. The best-known of him modernly in England may have been Foxhanger

In Australia, where Labrador Retriever strength is considerable and quality high, the 1968 Specialty of the Labrador Retriever Club of N.S.W. drew 222 individual dogs. This was the Baby Puppy Bitch Class (under 6 months). The win went to Brangus Moray, just under 4 months, a beautiful baby, putting all in.—*C. Bede Maxwell* (judge).

The day was hot, and it took time to sort out so many. Brangus Moray decides enough is enough. Time for a nap, 1st place peg, blue ribbon and all notwithstanding. Owned by Gunnislake Kennels.

202

Mascot (a Knaith Banjo grandson) in the ownership of Lady Simpson, whose late husband, Sir Joseph Simpson, was Chief Commissioner of Scotland Yard. By the time my luck was to see this dog he was quite old, basking in a string of police-dog, utility dog, obedience dog titles and a tally of get that probably set an all-time record for a stud in the breed.

A breed quality has been characterized as "an untiring zeal to please," a quality delightfully described in a *Dog World* (England) column that, within my view, should not be lost to us. Emma, the Labrador, lived in the house with Poodles. She studied their ways, and the success they had with her humans. Her owner wrote that Emma's persistence in copying took on "the character of the Pantomime Dame dancing pas-de-deux with the Fairy Queen" as she whirled around in her heavy way with the Poodles. "Her jumbo cavortings reflect every trait that endears, maddens, disarms, in the Poodle. Her ballet steps lack finish, but she practices assiduously, and never does a bounce without attempting a pirouette . . ."

The report appeared in the Poodle column and the writer hoped no Labrador person would chance to read it!

The Labrador in the show ring should be a standout for type and outline. A leggy, shallow, light-boned, snipey, thin-or-feather-tailed dog is still not a Labrador, nor is a tall heavy-boned moose. No judge willingly places un-sound or off-type dogs, but eternally one hears the silly argument of Type-vs-Soundness that each new wave of novice owners discovers with delight. That type has improved so generally and so magnificently in the Labrador Re-triever rings must provide great relief to conscientious judges who had to cope with that problem when making placings.

Some judges worry over Labrador toplines. Many good Labradors do show a *slight* depression behind well-placed shoulders and possess strong driving rears, but such assemblage is not to be assessed as a swampy or weak back. *Skulls* can be as from broad-broad (especially when a handler hauls the lead up there behind the ears and brings up folds of neck flesh) to Minnie Mouse snipiness. The ideal is something along the lines of Baby Bear's por-ridge, medium. *Tails?* In this breed *very important*. As with the Pointer, the Afghan Hound, the Irish Water Spaniel, etc. etc., a Labrador tail is a badge of race and purity. That it is not to be held up *a la* Airedale in the show ring is now generally accepted. Few pros do that any more, and the one (very) distinguished one that still does will likely get the message eventually.

Mr. Charles Eley, already quoted, wrote that the Labrador's tail, along with "webbed feet and the water impervious coat, the short thick tail" were "proofs of maritime existence prolonged through countless ages." "Short and thick" isn't quite a right description for a correct Labrador tail. Mary Scott, distinguished international judge of Sporting breeds, discussing this with me, points out that such a tail would seriously unbalance a Labrador's outline.

She quotes the gist of the English and American Standards which agree on "very thick towards the base, gradually tapering to the tip; of medium length, practically free of feathering, but *clothed all round with the Labrador's short thick dense coat, thus giving that peculiar 'rounded' appearance"* (my italics, CBM).

So, it is the *hair* that must be short and thick, not the actual tail. The thing to wonder about the Labrador tail that has become a breed badge under the designation of "otter" is how and where it originated. The Newfoundland wasn't blessed with it. Nineteenth century books, such as Hawker's, "Stonehenge" etc. show pictures that certainly don't fit the modern conception. There are as many high tails and long tails and plumed tails as ever one would see at an American field trial, even years ago. And one reads descriptions such as: "the very high and curled tail carriage of the Labrador, which was much less evident in the St. John's dog." And one leafs back to those Newfoundlands in the Sydenham Edwards book, for goodness sake.

Mr. Eley's theory of the tail (which he may have thought of as in terms of beaver type and employment) simply won't hold water. Nor do webbed feet prove out "maritime existence prolonged through countless ages." More than a hundred years ago "Stonehenge" was pointing out that all dogs' toes are joined by membrane, and that Water Dogs merely show it more because their feet are bigger.

And that brings us to the water-impervious coat, concerning which, we who judge in America find ourselves up against a strange condition. The Labrador Retriever Standard (1957) presently approved by the American Kennel Club—and which by our undertaking, judges are required to honor and observe—does not require a Labrador to have a water-impervious coat. Both Standards, English and American, require the coat to be short, dense and without wave and that it should give a hard feeling to the hand. The English Standard adds the requirement for a "weather-resisting undercoat." It is difficult to imagine how the weather-resistant undercoat requirement was overlooked in compiling the American Standard. Was it possibly because at the time of compilation (1957), Labrador type was still somewhat mixed and dogs in the public eye lacked such a feature? But surely, someone should have noticed the omission. Water-repellent jacketing, by the way, is not either, as Mr. Eley believed, a proof of "maritime existence, etc. etc." My Australian Cattle Dog bitch has a magnificent, thick, water-repellent undercoat and her breed has not been connected with the maritime at any time since foundation. Hers is likely the legacy of generations of hard living and exposure to all weathers, the common lot of hard-worked farm dogs.

Temperament is important in this, as in all breeds. The Labrador needs to be good-humored, intelligent, never dull. Most are eminently sensible, though the occasional bad actor can crop up. Yellows have at times been

This lovely head study is of the Labrador Retriever, Ch. Jagersbo Dana. Owner, Erik Bergishagen, Jr., Michigan.

Eng. Ch. Artistry Laffah faces with composure suited to his breed a dire threat of violence. Owned by the late Colonel Morris, Stafford, England.

205

criticized for temperament, perhaps in the early days of building up the strains in this color. My recollection dredges up one, a horror, imported to Australia. Very good type, much used at stud, he bestowed his aggressiveness perhaps too generously, though by now, no doubt, the breeders have screened it from their strains. No Labrador of questionable temperament, however good otherwise, would do any winning under me.

Color has long been stabilized. That the Sydenham Edwards' color plate establishes yellow as a legitimate factor within the Newfoundland inheritance may help fend away criticism of yellows in terms of breed purity. Beyond doubt, the color is a recessive. Of course, what may have been added subsequently to strengthen the inheritance may be something else again, and beyond my province here to explore. The documented, well-known instance of the yellow dog, Nous, cropping up in a litter of black Wavy-coats to become the taproot of the Golden Retriever is elsewhere discussed. Yellows in Labradors can range from fox-red to lightest cream. Chocolates, that in other breeds might be called liver, are permissible in range from light sedge to chocolate per se. Particolor black-tans and even brindles are not unknown, even in the purest litters, but are probably disposed of at birth. They are not eligible to show.

An unmistakable tendency in the breed is to run to flesh even to the extent of ponderousness. My experience of judging the breed includes seeing some literally as broad as they are long—fat, useless slugs. "Cow whales" is my name for them. In this respect it was interesting to have seen Munden Single as preserved in the Natural History Museum storage annex at Tring, near London, England. She has been preserved in a comfortable, coiled-down position and remains in first class state of preservation, though she had been donated to the Museum by her owner, then the Hon. A. H. Holland-Hibbert, in 1909. Her place in history is very secure, not only as a member of a famous family of three, but as the first of her breed to place in an English field trial (1904).

She was beyond doubt a far cry away from the "cow whales," neat as a pin, not very big, certainly a world of difference away, too, from the famous Dual Champions that set the style from the Banchory kennel of the late Lorna, Countess Howe. However, her name is one to conjure in terms of the support she won for her breed in the early years. We carried her over to a window to be able to photograph her down there in the basement where her neighbours included a Spanish fighting bull and a boa constrictor that was 23 feet long. Of the many great dogs of the past, in so many breeds, preserved down in that basement, she was by no means the least interesting, and possibly even the most appealing. However, that she would appear physically inadequate in terms of size to most modern owners is beyond question. In her time,

206

breed divergence in size as well as in type, may well have been as wide as it has been for a great many years here.

It is also true that nature abhors, in dog-breeding as in all else, man's attempts to standardize, and fashions in dog shapes and sizes tend to fluctuate as do all other form of living flesh—which is why breed standards require from time to time to become subject to revision. When the Labrador Retriever Standard comes next under scrutiny for AKC approval, let us hope it includes a requirement for that "weather-resistant" coat.

Ch. High Legh Blarney, as represented in a famous Maud Earl painting, is the classic example of what a Flatcoated Retriever should be. Apart from his excellencies as a competitor in shows and field trials, this magnificent dog proved his prepotency in the establishment of more than one strain that has endured into our time.

The Flat-Coated Retriever

THE pride and comfort of the Flat-Coated Retriever ownerships in Britain is that the breed has been spared what Mr. Wilson Stephens,
editor of *The Field* and a dedicated Flat-Coat owner, describes as "a major
access of popularity." There is agreement that theirs is "a gundog for the
minority whose tastes and circumstances enable them to understand and appreciate him, but not—emphatically not!—just for the majority." (Foreword:
A Review of the Flat-Coated Retriever, Dr. Nancy Laughton, 1968). If that
sounds a bit on the undemocratic side, one still feels inclined to concede
that the ownerships have reason on their side. Who ever knew a breed to
benefit from "a major access of popularity?"

The fortunes of the breed have always been a matter of ups and downs, so
far as popularity and numerical strength is concerned. Breed registrations in
Britain, as Dr. Laughton charted them, resemble contour maps of Alpine
chains, deep valleys between the sharp peaks. The apex of 440 (1924) contrasts with the valley of less than 100 (1963). In America, figures are even
more modest. 32 were registered in 1965; 47 in 1966; 65 in 1967; down to 46
in 1968 and 26 in 1969; and back up to 69 in 1970. One could not call the
success of the breed here to be of such a character as to disturb Mr. Wilson
Stephens or, for that matter, any other British owner.

No one ever explains why one breed catches public fancy and another does
not. There was a time when the breed had a tremendous popularity in
Britain, but its fortunes fell with the other retrieving breeds as the Labradors
took over. However, one can still find a surprising strength in terms of
entries at the great British championship shows, and it takes very little prob-

ing to discover how rich the percentage of practical working dogs among the Flat-Coated entry. In this respect, it leaves the other retrieving breeds whole streets behind it. A measure to confirm this is in terms of the number of "full", (i.e. field qualified) champions to find in major show entries. For example, Crufts of 1969 drew 59 Flat-Coateds, individual dogs. Of these seven were "full" champions, most of whom were backed in their pedigree particulars by "full" champion forbears. Labradors also counted seven "full" champions, but drew them from an entry of 212. Golden Retrievers scored higher than the Labradors in that they had entered 13 "full" champions, but drew them from among 226 entered. Further, among those fully titled Labradors and Goldens, there were respectively two and three Irish-bred dogs. While an outsider cannot place these statistics in accurate relationship to the status of the three breeds mentioned, it is still apparent that the Flat-Coateds run away with the honors, percentage-wise.

Even more importantly, the "full" champions dominated the placings. Ch. Woodpoppy and Ch. Fenriver's Golden Rod were Best of Breed and Best Opposite Sex respectively. Reserves were Ch. Heronsflight Black Bell of Yarlaw and Ch. Donovan. Third in the magnificent Open Bitch class to the two (above) was Ch. Ryshot Velvet that had been Best of Breed at that show in 1967. Ch. Fenrivers Golden Rod had taken that honor in 1968. Ch. Woodpoppy has been Best in Show at the United Retriever Specialty that caters for all the Retrieving breeds. Ch. Ryshot Velvet was Best in Show at the famous Windsor show, as well as First in Group at W.E.L.K.S., where the entries always count to thousands.

So, let one probe a little deeper. Chs. Woodpoppy, F. Golden Rod, and Donovan are all by Ch. Woodlark. Ch. Ryshot Velvet's kennelmate, Ch. Ryshot Copper Ablaze (liver), qualified the same year as she did. Ryshots, that it was my privilege to visit, are all working dogs, champions and all, regularly engaged at practical "picking-up" at the shoots under the handling of Dennis Izzard and his wife Margaret.

Breed history is even patchier than that of the Labrador. That the Flat-Coated was formed by crossings of British Setters with trans-Atlantic imports is known but not well-documented, originally contrived decades before the formation of a Kennel Club and the imposition of registration requirements. Since return to the United States it has come to my attention that the 3rd Earl of Malmesbury, who was so active in Labrador sponsorship, also discussed Flat (or as in his day it was known, Wavy-Coated) Retrievers, in a work believed to be titled something like *The Sporting Breeds of Hampshire*. Maybe some enthusiast who has time and geography on his side may care to try to locate that in the British Museum catalog.

Otherwise, even in the highest tide of breed popularity stud books tended to be private and eventually to become lost. Closely concerned with this

Ch. Bramcroft Dandy, U.D., a beautiful headed, accomplished Flatcoated Retriever. Owner, Mrs. Sally Terroux, Colorado.

Flatcoated Retrievers. Eleven-year-old Ryshot Copper Beau (right) musters his relatives in a famous English kennel. These are all professional working Retrievers as well as good show dogs. Owners, Ryshot Gundogs, Hampshire (1968).

breed was the late Mr. S. E. Shirley, who was also associated with Kennel Club early history. His name is perpetuated in a Trophy awarded to the Best of Breed Flat-Coated each year at Crufts.

Of early studs one stumbles oftenest over the name of Wyndham, eventually to learn there were two of him, Older and Younger. The Older is believed to have produced the "wave in the coat that became a ripple, a surge over the hips." When attempts were made to flatten and straighten such coats, the alternatives most often proved *too* close, too straight. Golden Retriever breeders can be at times troubled in the same way. Modern Flat-Coated coat requirement has become stabilized along the lines of "flat as possible." Of the many dogs one sees in show competition in the breed in England, most carry coats matching such description.

Though the owners give strong support to many major shows, this is not to be described as primarily a "show" breed. Virtually all Flat-Coateds are in the hands of owners that use them in a practical way, most of all as hunting dogs rather than as field trial competitors, though many Flat-Coateds do compete also in the trials. Gamekeepers incline strongly to this breed. They always have done so, so much so that there was a time decades ago when the breed was designated (a little snobbily perhaps?) as The Keeper's Dog. That it was in such professional hands does however ensure that working qualities are maintained.

It has never been my fortune to see a Flat-Coated Retriever in competition in America. The breed strength may be considered now as concentrated in Colorado, where Mrs. Sally Terroux breeds blacks and livers in a very strong breed-evenness of type. She has based her breeding primarily on a most excellent black dog it was my luck to see there, Am. Ch. Bramcroft Dandy, U.D., an English-bred import. However, Mrs. Terroux, in Colorado, is out of the mainstream of field trial competition, and most of her dogs go locally as hunting or companion sales.

Assessed along the benching at major English shows (1967/68) it was apparent that there is still wide variation of type in the breed, heads especially. As along the Golden Retriever benching, one sees in the Flat-Coateds all the shapes of head there are, from stopless wedges to rounded high domes with strong stops. Yet the ideal Flat-Coated head is individual and recognizable, exquisitely in balance, a stop slight but discernible. It is not a Labrador head, nor a Golden, even if the variant and undesirable heads do tend to favor one breed or the other. Nor, as importantly, is it a Setter head, something a judge might also file in memory. Eye is very important, the "small sunken eye of the Newfoundland" especially to be avoided. Slanted eyes that hint of Collie influence are also undesirable. Ears are "small, well-set, carried close" and also not Setterish. Balance and soundness of running gear are mandatory, and the handsome flag is required to be active. *How* active was demonstrated

The dogs of the famous Ryshot Flatcoated Retriever establishment in Hampshire, England, are all practical workers. Even the distinguished show champions, including BOB winner at Crufts, work at "picking up" at the shoots. Mrs. Margaret Izzard of the Ryshots, handling one of her dogs.—*Coe.*

Flatcoated Retriever, Pewcroft Prefect, U.D.T., imported. Owner, Homer Downing, Ohio.

213

at 1968 Crufts when my attempts to photograph Ch. Fenrivers Golden Rod (black, by the way) were frustrated by the liveliness of his tail. Every picture shows him tailless, so busily did he whip it flank to flank! Mrs. Izzard tells me that old-timer judges have a habit of feeling for the last joint of a Flat-Coated's tail, it having been a practice to shorten tails that were considered overlong.

While some commentators are cautious as to authenticity of the solid liver color in this breed, it is established by such as "Idstone" (writing in 1872) that the color has been long-recognized in this breed. "Idstone" didn't care for it, because "in fading it tends to take on the shade of a rusty nail," a disability common to dog coats in the color as many fanciers in other breeds well know. One breed columnist who seems to have some possible reservations about the liver color wrote in *Dog World* (England) that "whatever the English in their sophistication think of liver Flat-Coats they really matter in the United States." Well, if one goes back a long way and quotes "Idstone's" comments, it is true that the classic writer noted "the preference of American duck-hunters for dogs colored red or brown," but that's a long time ago, and in any case doesn't seem to apply much any more. There was a time when hunters wouldn't take a black dog into a blind, holding it scared away the ducks. Once upon a time . . .

It is most interesting to read through Dr. Laughton's most informative breed book. Her own strain of Claverdon has been greatly distinguished over many years, and her knowledge is wide and intriguingly presented. Reading cannot fail to stir up interest in her breed, and who knows, resuscitation may in time attend Flat-Coats here. But the *Dog World* columnist has been sadly misinformed if he entertains the belief that there is any particular interest in the breed here, whether color is liver or whether it is black. As it is such a pleasant breed it would be nice if the wheel of fashion, always unpredictable in dogs, would bring the Flat-Coated to fashion again. As of the moment it seems unlikely, but one would be brave to say it could not happen. If dog history here teaches anything it teaches that once a fashion in a dog breed becomes accepted, the interest runs off and away faster than fire.

214

The Golden Retriever

IT is impossible to overlook the world-wide popularity of the Golden Retriever. As in the case of the Labrador, the public interest in the Golden is not exclusively related to the circumstance that the dog is a superb practical working retriever. For every Labrador and Golden that competes, say, in Field Trials, count dozens that have never set foot on a trial area in their lives. Even those that are actually acquired for the purpose of practical hunting purposes can be matched numerically with those acquired merely because ownerships were inclined to want a nice dog around the place. There are, of course, Dual champions in both breeds—not many, as say in the case of Shorthairs and Brittanys, but at least sufficient to indicate that the breeds have dual potential that could be developed where owners happened to have the interest (and the means!) to do so.

Not all the retrieving breeds, tipped out of a greater part of their useful employment by the dwindling of the numerical tally of the ducks, season by season, have been so lucky as to find acceptance as wide as the interest of the general public has provided for the Labrador and the Golden in most countries across the world. The Irish Water Spaniel and the Curly-Coated Retriever have taken a bad battering, and there seemed for a time little hope for the Chesapeake Bay who, strangely enough, has in recent years made a strong and very successful bid for public support though the number of patrons likely to use him extensively for actual practical duck-hunting chores has also declined. Who can forecast where the fashionable interest of dog purchasers will tend, decade by decade?

Breeders of the Golden Retriever have not modernly shown any particular concern to follow the aim of the Flat-Coated Retriever interests that wish to keep theirs as "a dog for the minority." In Britain already for long enough, and in the United States increasingly, this very beautiful breed becomes rather "the pet dog for the majority." Variation of type is increasingly evident, and the various physical disabilities that attach to the ever-widening commercial breeding are not lacking. One would wish that a breed so handsome, and so charming of disposition, could be spared the over-exposure that historically does no breed good. But, of course, where a demand is raised, the supply of any commodity will always be raised in better than exact proportioning.

The Golden Retriever has so much going for him. He is not only good-looking and well-dispositioned in the main, he is blessed also with a jacketing that needs no professional trimming. A bath and a brush will take him anywhere, and for the housepet, it is a gratifying circumstance to observe what wonderful "self-cleaning" qualities the Golden Retriever coat does have. Then, if an owner's interest is in practical matters, given the chance the Golden can handle waterfowl superbly and upland game extremely well. The breed is eye-catching in the show-ring and in the Obedience ring has stacked up a phenomenal record over the decades.

There needs to be no apology for the good looks. Dog history does not support the theory that good looks cancel out working qualities. Good looks in the dog, as in all creatures (including man) is a matter of working parts in harmony. Disproportion wrecks appearance and hinders work. That disproportion serves but poorly the force of inheritance has long enough been clear to all disposed to see, rather than merely to close their eyes.

Hard work went into the task of shaping the Golden into the style in which one presently recognizes him. This is one more of the many dog breeds that were shaped during the last half of the 19th century—a period in time that the Germans have named the *Kynological* for the richness of its yield. Further, the Golden Retriever has been blessed with dedicated modern historians, the names of Mrs. Emma Stonex (England) and Mrs. Rachel Elliott (U.S.) coming perhaps most readily to mind. Additionally in the United States, the breed is blessed with some of the most comprehensive statistical compilation in respect of all spheres of breed activity: field, show, obedience.

Within my view, considerable clarification is still required to establish the origin of this breed. Most ownerships, in all breeds, of course, take little interest in what lies back of their breed, having concern only for wins to be secured in immediate, contemporary competition in whatever venue it happens to please them to compete. However, the Golden Retriever, as many other breeds, has inspired its proportion of dedicates to undertake the task of delving, of disentangling, and a fine task such have set themselves. But at least they have something more stable to work with—if stable is the word!—

216

Eng. Ch. Camrose Nicholas of Westley (Ch. William of Westley ex Ch. Camrose Jessica). This distinguished and prepotent English champion Golden Retriever was bred by Mrs. J. Tudor (Camrose), and was owned and handled by Miss Joan Gill (Westley). He had, then, everything of the best going for him. Whelped 1957, in 1968 he was still looking forward to next shooting season, to serve as in all the shooting seasons of his life so far. Nicholas presents everything admirable in the breed, with quality, prowess, personality, poise, a gentle disposition. He is not dark, but he *is* golden.—*Fall.*

Ch. Cragmont's Hi-Lo, at Westminster K.C., 1967. Owner, Mrs. Charles W. Engelhard, New Jersey.—*Shafer.*

217

than the historians of breeds whose origins are frankly lost in the mist of centuries past. For the Golden Retriever is beyond all doubt a creature of the *Kynological* time, and there exist many scraps of evidence in the form of documentation as well as tradition, to help those who are interested to discover his beginnings. Most "histories" tread the well-worn path of the repetitious, but not all . . . Let us look at some of the better-researched.

Everyone, of course, must go back to Sir Dudley Majoribanks of the 1850s, later to become Lord Tweedmouth. This was a time when the then Wavy-Coated (later to be known as the Flat-Coated) was the fashionable dog for use in retrieving work, he being a derivative of trans-Atlantic breeds crossed on British Setters. He was fashionably black, as by then all types of retrievers tended to be. That these descendants of trans-Atlantic imports to Britain carried the yellow factor had been forgotten by dog folk, for it was by then likely the best part of half-a-century since yellow-marked Newfoundlands had been seen, the fashionable black serving to screen the color from sight. Only, now and then, in the manner of recessives, a yellow pup would erupt in a litter of blacks. Perhaps it was usual to put it away, as solid reds are modernly put away from Gordon Setters and whites from Boxers, and so on. Perhaps, though, there were also those who, knowing of the occasional yellow pup in black litters, had a thought to acquire one and breed experimentally against the tide of fashion. Maybe, such a motive animated Sir Dudley. He seems to have left no record of it, but it is possible that he may have known of the yellow-marked Newfoundlands through, say, the possession of *Cynographia Britannica*. By the 1850s, it was already a collectors' item but let us suppose he owned a copy. May one guess that in that case he could have conceived an intention to resuscitate the color?

Could such a concern account for his immediate interest in the yellow retriever, Nous, that the breed historians tell us he met while strolling a street in Brighton (England's South Coast resort). Could it be such an interest that inspired him to acquire it and see what he could breed from it. Mere speculation, of course—but then what but speculation is dog history in all breeds, anyway?

The historians tell us that he bred four yellows from Nous and a bitch named Belle, identified as a Tweed Water Spaniel from the Border country—whatever that may have been. What the historians fail (so far) to emphasize, however, is that His Lordship had Nous in ownership for four years before he hit that jackpot. Might one not suppose he had tried other experimental matings before he had the success he sought, securing his four from Belle, described (on what authority is not known to me) as "a bitch of a similar color to Nous."

Tweed Water Spaniels have given Golden Retriever historians a great deal of trouble. The only reference we all manage to locate is that provided

Golden Retriever, Bonnie Island Lass, U.D.T., and with G.R.C.A. Working Certificate and show points. Owners, John B. and Roberta Anderson, Washington.—*Roberts*.

Bonnie Island Ladd, U.D.T., son of Bonnie Island Lass, U.D.T., also has his G.R.C.A. Working Certificate. The breed is very versatile, as good on upland game as on waterfowl. Owner, John Roberts, Washington.—*Lee*.

219

by an Irish Water Spaniel breeder, a Mr. Skidmore, a brief description which appeared first in Vero Shaw's famous *Book of the Dog* and was subsequently re-used in the classic Phillips & Cane work, *The Sporting Spaniel*, pub. Our Dogs, England. "From their appearance, close coat, sparseness of feather and style of head, I always thought there was a dash of Bloodhound in their veins, which was strengthened by the fact that when I have bred from them with dogs of the McCarthy type (i.e. Irish Water Spaniels, CBM) they have often thrown pups with tan feet, cheeks, and vents. Their heads were conical, lips heavily flewed, ears set in Bloodhound like, whilst they were all light in colour." In the Vero Shaw quote, from which the authors of *The Sporting Spaniel* culled their quote, there was also mentioned by Mr. Skidmore the observation that the closeness of their light-liver-colored coat, which he described as curled, was such as led him to guess that they owed to some smooth.

The search for a pictured dog that could in any way match the description provided by Mr. Skidmore has been tirelessly pursued by Golden Retriever historians. My own efforts were no more successful. But visiting Montreal in October 1970, improving the occasion to visit the local art gallery as is always my custom, knowing what richness can at times be so discovered, my astonishment was considerable to find a Gobelin Tapestry of 1550 A.D. simply seething with Spaniels that in many ways fitted the Skidmore description. These are fully discussed in the Irish Water Spaniel chapter of this present work.

Cane & Phillips visualized from the Skidmore description something along the lines of an Otterhound, and only they knew what, in their time, an Otterhound really resembled. Well, it is a free world (more or less!) and if they were privileged to guess, so am I. My inclination is to stay with the Spaniels.

Taplin in his *Sporting Dictionary and Rural Repository,* 1803, writes of a "small yellow-pied springing spaniel," and there exists among the multiplicity of Spaniel colors a superbly beautiful light *golden* liver which is uniquely carried by one Spaniel breed only, and that breed in many features parallels the description Mr. Skidmore provides in respect of the Tweed.

During the earlier half of the 19th century the aristocratically fashionable Spaniel was the whole-color Sussex, specifically described by his original sponsor as a Spaniel designated for the Use of Gentlemen. He has a head and an ear, especially, that match well with Mr. Skidmore's description and support a possibility of original Bloodhound inheritance. He does not have a curled coat, but one beautifully, sleekly close, and his feathering is sparse. The golden sheen of an authentic specimen of this breed, now regrettably so rare in purebred status in England, is unmistakable. The designation of "light liver" gives no indication of his color unless one specifically includes the word "golden." Might the Sussex of then-fashionable favor, have been the "smooth" that tightened the curl in the "close" coat of the Tweed? Certainly, the Sussex has a tremendous prepotency for that golden color. It has over the decades survived drastic crossings made necessary by the dwindling of strains in Sussex due to various misadventures, from distemper to rabies. Yet, cross the Sussex with what one will, he remains a light liver dog. Only the cross of the black Field Spaniel has ever, additionally, succeeded in robbing of his gold, imposing a dullish brown such as, by the way, one may see modernly in the English show rings where the Sussex, fighting for his breed existence, is often cruelly caricatured by specimens carrying his breed name.

If Belle, the Tweed Spaniel, carried Sussex inheritance within her gift, the gold of the fashionable Sussex coat, and the texture of it, may well have dominated her shade of liver color, as well as the curl texture. In a breeding to yellow Nous, the Wavy-coated Retriever, the curl would have been still more decisively sidelined.

It is not my intention to claim that the above represents more than my personal speculation, but as already confessed, speculation is all we have while exact documentation continues to elude us—in *all* breeds!

The four yellow whelps from Belle and Nous were spread around. Ada went to the Marjoribanks relatives, the Ilchesters. Cowslip worked hard at home, and doubtless Crocus and Primrose provided their share in helping to form a retrieving breed that was pale when all other retrievers were black. A few years ago—the 1950s—the Golden Retriever fanciers were provided by Majoribanks stud books, belatedly found, that charted some of the breeding activities of Sir Dudley almost a century earlier. Mrs. Stonex has carefully reproduced and analyzed the information from these books. There are recorded weavings and interweavings of black Wavy-coateds, yet another Tweed Spaniel in addition to Belle, a Labrador or two. The compilation comes to an end with the produce of Queenie (1887), one of ten black pups that in her turn whelped two yellows to a yellow stud directly descended from the original Nous (and also named Nous). These records cover a period of about 20 years.

The discovery of the stud books has been hailed generally throughout the Golden Retriever breed as documentary refutation of the theory that had long been entertained, that the Golden Retriever breed stemmed from the descendants of a batch of "Russian circus dogs" acquired by Sir Dudley. This story, published by the then well-known dog journalist, A. Croxton Smith, gained wide dispersal throughout dogdom, Smith claiming that the story was originally provided by a then-breeder of Goldens, Colonel the Hon. W. le Poer Trench, who published poetry and bred famous Irish Water Spaniels.

No one would surely be inclined to dispute that the modernly-discovered stud books authenticate at least *one* strain of Majoribanks breeding. However, they do not, within my view, cancel out the possibility that *other* experimental strains were furthered under the same family sponsorship. My firmest belief has always been that wherever in dog history curls smoke, there one may reasonably presume fire. So, let us here give Colonel le Poer Trench a little space.

He wanted the Kennel Club to classify his retrievers, secured from the family as "Majoribanks and Ilchester breed of Russian Retrievers." And a contemporary report describes these dogs he proposed to exhibit as "large, pale, heavy-boned, thick-coated, coarsely-bred throwbacks to early antecedents."

What early antecedents?

The period of Majoribank's interest to produce a new breed was the period of the Crimean war. Soldiers have always brought back local dogs from "foreign parts"—as they still do wherever quarantine regulations permit. That dogs from the Crimean-Asia Minor area actually *were* in England at that time is established by the reliable "Idstone" (*The Dog*, 1872). He describes "Russian Retrievers" as "large leggy dogs, blind from quantities of hair overshadowing their eyes and nearly deaf from the same cause. Their coats required the greatest care or they became felted and unpleasant, and on a wet day they were wretched objects. I recall seeing one at a battue, which attempted to fetch a hare out of a thick brake, and became so entangled with thorns and burrs that the beaters had to cut away a quantity of his coat to liberate him, and in the confusion the hare was lost. Further comment on 'Russian Retrievers' for this country is needless" (*p. 136*).

Any next dog-informed person will cry Komondor! As "Idstone" employed the plural, clearly there was more than one around. This writer customarily named ownerships, but maybe this time he was being tactful. However, a serious historian cannot overlook that such dogs were in Britain and that Colonel Trench had "large pale thick-coated, coarsely-bred throwbacks to early antecedents" that he insisted on having identified as "Majoribanks and Ilchester breed of Russian Retrievers."

Mrs. Rachel Elliott, a serious Golden Retriever historian, concedes that some actual Russian infusion would seem to be supported by a British show registry covering 1859–73, in which "the retriever, Sultan, bred by Lord Tweedmouth's son, E. Marjoribanks, is identified as by Moscow ex a Tweed Water Spaniel." Mrs. Elliott adds that as this breeding is not seemingly elsewhere mentioned, it may have no historical significance in terms of Golden Retriever history. Maybe yes. Maybe no. What may be as reasonable a belief as any, is that what needs to be discovered is some more stud books, not merely the 20-year record of one strain. After all, Colonel le Poer Trench involved more than one branch of the Marjoribanks family in the interest.

So, now we cross over to look at an interesting discussion from the work

222

of the famous Theo Marples, published in *Our Dogs* (England) March 1, 1912, and later in a book which had wide world circulation at the time. He tells of the hassle over the Crufts entry of the "Majoribanks and Ilchester breed of yellow Russian Retrievers and Trackers" and how, with "much inbreeding the strain had petered out, and how efforts were made to get more of these dogs out of Russia, without success. In consequence, a cross was made with a Bloodhound, as being of the same habit of work, i.e., Tracking."

This seems to support Mrs. Elliott's belief that the strain has no longer historical significance EXCEPT for the fact that individual specimens probably survived, and influences lingered strong enough to produce Colonel le Poer Trench's "large, pale, coarse" ones and likely enough lie close-hidden behind the increasing proliferation of the "large pale coarse types" my camera kept finding in the English show rings in 1967/68. Those of the British breeders who don't admire such know them derisively as "Chalkies." Those stuck with them, defend them valiantly. They are not handsome and they are not Golden.

Let's go back to Theo Marples:

> Early in the '80s, Colonel Trench (to whom we are indebted for the resuscitated breed shown at Crufts) became possessed of one of these dogs bred by the Earl of Ilchester, a beautiful specimen of the breed. This dog was seen by the late Lord Tweedmouth (who had lost his true breed by the introduction of the cross) who was greatly pleased with it, and after a careful inspection pronounced him to be a perfect type of the dogs acquired by him in 1858.
>
> Colonel Trench then tried *his* hand at getting a bitch to breed with this dog, out of Russia, but was also unsuccessful.
>
> A little later, through the influence of Colonel Trench (who was subsequently elected to the Committee of the Kennel Club for the second time) Russian Yellow Retrievers were placed upon the Club's register, and Mr. Harding Cox drew up a standard description and code of points, of which the following is a copy.
>
> Drawn up by Major Harding Cox with the concurrence of Lord Tweedmouth, the Earl of Ilchester, and Colonel le Poer Trench: DESCRIPTION OF THE YELLOW RUSSIAN RETRIEVER AND TRACKER: (Descended from the Caucasian Yellow Sheepdog. First imported to this country by Dudley Majoribanks Esq. in 1858, and since known as the Majoribanks & Ilchester Breed:

There follows a Standard, as drawn up by the four gentlemen named, from which, in the interests of space pressure, we here take only the reference to Color:

Rich tawny yellow tinge, darkening on the back and showing lighter creamy tints on the flanks, legs, and belly. Any mixture of pure white is to be deprecated, but very often the color shades off in the feet to a very light tint. The warmer red shadings which are observable in dogs where the cross of Irish Setter or Bloodhound has been admitted are detrimental as a clear indication of such a cross having been resorted to.

So—doesn't it seem entirely clear that there is still a lot of homework for Golden Retriever historians to do? That Colonel le Poer Trench worked together with Lord Tweedmouth and the Earl of Ilchester to draft the breed Standard for the Kennel Club establishes that at least a degree of rapport existed among these gentlemen. Clearly, the Nous-Belle strain was *one* strain, and probably the best, but it would be beyond reason to discard the reasonable belief that the legacy of what was clearly very extensive experimentation undertaken by this family did not survive within the inheritance of others that have come down into our time. And one feels less than confident that the "Russian" inheritance, whether pale or whether yellow, can be entirely discarded.

There has always been frantic anxiety within the Golden Retriever interest to avoid the red of the Irish Setter, but those who have had to compound with the inheritance of pale bleachings passionately defend this, within my view, equally undesirable jacketing for a breed obligated by its very name to be *golden!*

While we think nowadays of the Komondor always in terms of white, it is also true that breeds from trans-Caucasian and Asia Minor area run to yellows and reds (Hungarian Vizsla, Yellow Turkish Hunting Dog, ancient German Scent hounds, etc.) and one does regret that "Idstone" in his report did not mention the color of the dog he described.

That much hard work was done to stabilize the breed (in England, from which, of course, it had eventually found its way to the United States) is clear from an interesting judge's critique (Ladies Kennel Club, England) published in *Dog World:*

> For years, the old hands tried to get rid of the over-sized, long-legged, long-bodied, slab-sided dog that originally existed. Those who remember the improvements of the 1930s–50s, see the good work done in turning the Golden Retriever into the neat, short-bodied, deep-chested, good-boned, sturdy animal of today. Now comes the cry for longer legs, sometimes for bigger dogs, made by the newer breeders, and comes creeping in again those over-sized, long-legged, slab-sided, etc . . .

My camera supports such criticism, and it occurs to me to wonder if those "newer breeders" were finding themselves needing to opt for dogs such as the judge described. It is historical truth that in many breeds standards have

224

had to be revised in the wake of breed changes, rather than breeds changed to conform to existing standards. A glimpse at historical pictures quite often makes this clear.

In the main, the Golden Retriever in the United States, while providing plenty of type variation, remains well within the requirements of his Standard. The disqualification clause that applies to height restriction may have helped, and judges have in the main adhered to the exact Standard description of the coat color, that it shall be "lustrous golden of various shades." There is no provision for cream, as in the English Standard, a provision that is certainly very liberally interpreted by some breeders, and seemingly without protest from the judges. Of course, in England the majority of judges who officiate at the Championship shows (all breeds) are breeders which, one feels, may at times operate against the hindering of trends. The all-rounders have likely less tolerance of trends, but find it difficult to make their intolerances stick. Thus Frank Warner Hill:

> I have always felt the rather beautiful name should describe the color of dogs registered as Golden Retrievers. In times gone by it was described as that of a freshly-minted sovereign. However, as I imagine the greater part of the present-day owners have never seen such a coin, there is every excuse that, just as in yellow Labradors, any color shades between the extremes is acceptable. Bowing to a majority opinion always when judging the breed, I sink my personal preference.

An American judge has no need to "bow to majority opinion" if "majority opinion" inclines to pale chalky Golden Retrievers. The Standard is the support for requiring "lustrous golden of various shades." But *golden*. The best definition of breed color here seems to be that of Marcia Schlehr in her fine booklet on the breed:

> The brilliance in coloring with definitive golden (yellow or yellow-orange). Too dark colorings approaching Setter red or mahogany are not desired, neither is a pale creamy overall, nor a dull tan or brown. Lighter shading (to silvery cream) on underparts and feathering are quite allowable, and often add to striking appearance. Light shadings should not be confused with white markings. Greying or paling of the coat, especially on face or muzzle, due to age, or white hairs on scars, are to be recognized but not penalized.

And then there was that visiting English breeder-judge, a distinguished one who reported herself happy to notice that "American judges, who used to discard the light-colored ones now seem to be getting used to them." If the breed club charged with parental responsibilities, notes any such tendencies, it would seem to have an obligation to fulfill. If height can be protected by a disqualification clause, the all-important breed definitive of color could be given like protection.

Work qualities in the American Golden are well proved. There is a fine muster of Dual Champions and might well be more if the numerical strength in Labradors were less overwhelming. The parent club, by the way, honors one "honorary Dual"—Ch. and Am. Fld. Ch. Lorelei's Golden Rockbottom, U.D. The Am. Fld. title does not contribute to AKC recognition of a Dual Champion, but this dog's magnificent record is further studded with a Best in Show and 5 Group Firsts plus 38 Group placings.

British interests have also finished several Dual Champions and "qualified" several show champions. The British Qualifier is something akin to the Working Test for retrieving breeds sponsored by American Clubs. This serves owners uninterested, or unable, to engage in the expense and travel involved in field trialling. It requires testing of dogs "in the retrieving of two birds on land (doubles) in moderate cover, with birds approximately 40–50 yards from the line and not less than 90° apart, and (2) the retrieving of two ducks in swimming water, as back-to-back singles in light cover, with ducks approximately 25–30 yards from the line." Dogs completing the test satisfactorily receive a Working Certificate, a copy of which goes to the Club Historian to become a permanent part of the dog's record.

The length of the list of Obedience-titled Golden Retrievers in Club records is astonishing. Only the Irish Setter, within the Sporting Group, can produce a record as eye-catching. One would wish to highlight much detail but space sadly lacks. It is only possible to draw on a representative dog whose accumulation of titles is emphasized by his prepotency for the factor of trainability. He is not actually exceptional in these regards; many good Goldens stud the records. However, Ch. Indian Knoll's Roc Cloud, U.D., compiled 25 Highest Score and 6 Perfect. His son (ex Ch. Sidram Shining Star, U.D.) Am.-Can. Ch. Sun Dance's Rusticana, U.D.T., compiled 135 Highest Scores, 36 Perfect, plus the Working Certificate. The dam (above) had two other U.D.s by different sires.

In all, Roc Cloud sired 16 Obedience-titled Goldens including, at the last count available to me, 7 U.D. and a U.D.T., a "batting average" further supported in that one, Ch. Sidram Shady Lady, C.D.X. also enjoyed field trial success. Still with Roc Cloud, we look at Ch. Ben's Major of Sun Dance, U.D., with 37 Highest Scores and 14 Perfect, and at Sun Dance's Bronze, C.D., a show Specialty Best of Breed. Skip a generation or so and still find the magic: Sun Dance's Hardbottom Express, U.D., is a double great-grandson of Roc Cloud, and the last time his record came under my eye it was already studded with Perfect Scores and he was still compiling more to astonish us all.

Such a look-see is merely skipping, not recording. Those who wish to examine the amazing breed record within this sphere may draw upon Year

Newborn! Owners, Ironstreams Kennels, Ontario, N.Y.

Golden Retriever puppy, Ironstreams Sharwilada Chief. Owners, Mr. and Mrs. Johns, Ontario, N.Y.

Book compilations that are scarcely to be bettered, a parent club production. It is when such compilations as these come under my eye that anger surges within me against those who mouth praise so faint as only to be held insulting in respect of any dog activities other than those which happen to hold their own interest, field or show. A well-performed dog in any sphere is a good dog! It cannot be said too often.

Trainability presumes good temperament. Generations of Obedience-titled forbears should be reasonably a guarantee. Most Goldens are affectionate and reliable and those discovered to be otherwise should be eliminated from breeding programs.

In judging Golden Retrievers, as in Flat-Coateds, heads can give one pause. There are so many varied types. In any large benched entry one strolls along and takes note that, again as in Flat-Coateds, heads can vary from heavily-domed to flattened stopless wedges. It always seems to me that when a completely flattened head comes under my notice it tends also to have small and rather piggy, "foreign" kind of eyes. In general, too, one noticed that the big coarse head invariably sits for'ard on the big coarse body.

One hears one's share of bad news about Golden Retriever rear-ends, but then that is to hear nowadays about all the breeds there are. Many doubtless stem from bad kennel and pup management, but many, alas, also from congenital abnormalities. Too many dogs lapse into disability from sheer lack of normal exercise; from unsuitable restriction, though this may happen perhaps less in Golden Retrievers than in some other breeds. It is always my thought that the charge of rear-end abnormality is too-readily clapped against too many dogs. Competent radiographing is the only proof. And there is also in this connection the sobering thought voiced recently by Newfoundland breeder, Kitty Drury: "Some of these experts would have people so concerned with breeding X-rays they'll never be able to breed *dogs!*" That far too much abnormality exists is sadly true, but a fair proportion must be blamed to mismanagement, for dogs are not canary birds to live in cages—not even Chihuahuas.

The Golden Retriever Standard avoids the boo-boo of the Labrador Standard where the requirement of a water-repellent coat is omitted. A dense, repellent, good undercoat is specifically demanded. Texture should be neither hard nor silky. Breeders of Goldens take especial umbrage when writers of hunting-breed books, "experts" often totally unfamiliar with the breed, refer to the Golden Retriever's "silky coat" as a feature affecting his popularity in the working sphere. There never was an easier coat to manage than a Golden's. It has to be lived with to discover how easy. Our Jody digs in our red Oregon clay for gophers, preferably in wet weather. She comes in plastered all over. Ten minutes rolling around in her kennel-house straw and she emerges appearing bright and shining as that "freshly-minted sovereign" Warner Hill talked of so nostalgically.

Nor is this a difficult coat in show preparation terms. The desired outline of the breed favors more, not less, hair in front of the throat and chest, so there is no incentive to shear outrageously as is too often done in the case of some other Sporting breeds. The Standards of both the English and American governing bodies permit a coat to be flat or wavy. Many breeders express a preference for a slight-wave over a coat that is glassily-smooth.

One does have to consider the American Standard a very good one, and easy to follow in judging. However, there will always be judges that will give a well-promoted dog the advantage in placings, and a great deal of harm can be wrought by allowing off-type, or off-color dogs to compile big show records. As of the present, the working Golden and the show Golden are one in type, their activities interchangeable, venue to venue, a position as unique as it is satisfactory within the Sporting breeds classification.

Curly-Coat, English Sh. Ch Banworth Sunflower of Siccawei, one of the all-time greats in Sporting breeds. Her record number of Challenge Certificates in her breed may never be matched. Three times BOB at Crufts, 1966, '68, '69. BIS, Windsor Gundog Show, 1968. Owner, Mrs. C. M. Halford, Surrey.—*Fall*.

The Curly-Coated Retriever

THE Elizabethans clearly established the presence of their curled-coat retrieving dogs and even aired some problems they proposed. Johannes Caius described his manner of trimming to relieve the dog of weight in the water. Gervase Markham, a century later explained that: "In Sommer by Heate of the Sonne and the greatness of the Dogge's Labour, he becomes very noysesome and troublesome, and the dog by over-heating may also take the Maungie (Mange)." He added that in shearing the dog must not be stripped all over, and his patterning was clearly the same as that of Caius.

Wet retrievers do stink. It's no particular secret. It was also one of the things I learned early-on. The local parish priest kept a Curly-Coated, the first of the breed to come under my notice—this in Australia where the Curly-Coated has always been in good repute, if in no great numerical strength. Bombo was a liver, obese, a playmate to successive waves of kindergarteners. Most of us thought of him in terms of another presbytery dog that had attained a contemporary popularity in verse, "John O'Brien's" amusing *The Presbyt'ry Dog:*

> His rotundity now to absurdity runs
> Like an abo gone to the grog,
> For the knowing old shaver the Presbyt'ry shuns
> When it's time for a meal, and goes off to the nuns,
> Who're deceived in the Presbyt'ry Dog.

> —*Round The Boree Log*, Sydney, 1943.

Sister Mary Joachim was the one that coped with his major problem. Black skirt pinned high, she dunked him regularly in the convent's laundry tub.

231

Australia has always liked a good Curly-Coat. This is Aust. Ch. Pamika Gypsy Moth. Only five months when this picture was taken, she showed later under the author as a champion in 1969.—*Green*.

Ch. Black Rod of Siccawei (imp. England), first Curly-Coated Retriever to attain the American championship title in many years. Sparsely shown, but has several Group Firsts. Owner, N. D. Detweiler, Pennsylvania.—*Gilbert*.

232

It is wholly unfair to quote such a characteristic first in discussing such a good breed but it does serve as at least one reason, additionally to the decline in ducks, to account for lesser popularity. There are many active dog-folk in America who have never seen a Curly-Coated Retriever, and so have no conception of how magnificently the best specimens are constructed. In the last few years a superb fellow has been showing on the East Coast, Ch. Black Rod of Siccawei, owned in Pennsylvania. He really had it rough to secure his title; being without breed competition meant he had to make it through Group wins. His title achieved (1969) was the first secured to his breed in the United States for more than two decades. That this dog, "Limey" to his friends, is as good as he is need astonish no one. His dam is one of England's all-time greats in any breed, Show Ch. Banworth Sunflower of Siccawei. Her record to date includes four Bests of Breed at Crufts to 1969, and in this breed, as in the Flat-coated, while entries do not compare with those of Labradors and Gordons, competition at Crufts is fierce. Twenty-one entered at 1969 Crufts included likely some of the very best and soundest of dogs to be found within the Sporting Group, for this is no "fancier's breed" to be exploited. It is highly individual, not only in terms of the beautiful tight-curled astrakhanish coat, but in terms of basic construction—that is balance of parts, freedom from exaggerations, adherence to type. My own inclination is to consider Sunflower one of the very best dogs I saw in a year in England (1967/68) and her Best in Show at the United Retriever Specialty over all retrieving breeds helps support the belief.

As have the Vizsla and the Weimaraner, the Curled-Coat Retriever has an inbuilt protection against "selective breeding," i.e. mongrelization. It can't be masked. He is unique among retrieving breeds in respect both of outline and height. He is the tallest of the retrievers, and indeed one of the tallest in the Group. The American Standard does not quote permissible height. The English allows him to 26″. The American suggests his legs should "be of moderate length" which actually doesn't help much—moderate in relation to what? His body is shortish, and so is his tail. In fact, that his tail is along Pointerish lines (apart from the curled covering, which is obligatory) may suggest something about his original formation, the circumstance that while his background is strong in trans-Atlantic breed influence, and even his curled-coat can be matched among such, his shape and make is not in tune with the other breeds so derived. He should not (maybe could not) look like a Labrador in outline, nor a Golden, nor a Flat-Coated. He is all his own dog!

He is a sober customer in the main, sometimes dour, and with a mind of his own, but a magnificent dog to own. More than a century ago "Stone-henge" was complaining that no one knew how the Curly-Coat was formed because breeders were unwilling to lead others to like success. "Experience does not lead me to place much reliance on the worth of secrecy," he added.

Dalziel, some years later made like complaint, adding: "Curled-coat retrievers do not breed true, and the further we get from the different sources originally resorted to, the sooner we will be able to rely on securing good level litters" (1888).

The good level litters came into being, the breed reproduced truly. That Pointer influence may have been strong is suggested by "Stonehenge's" description of it as "clever, but unsuited to the work of a retriever." "Idstone" (1872) made a provocative if surprising comment that it was "gay and cheerful, without which (temperament) no dog can be tortured into a retriever." All such contradictions emphasize the diversity of the basic, formative factors that made the breed. However, from the mill of 19th century experimentation emerged a distinct breed and a distinct temperament in which courage is strongly evident. Australia has always valued the Curly-Coat, and though one sees them rarely in the show rings, they have always had rural support down the generations. As early in 1897, Walter Beilby (*The Dog in Australasia*) could publish long-drawn-out pedigrees. In his time only three retrievers were recognized, the Wavy (Flat) Coated, and the black and the "red" Curled-Coats which he treated as separate breeds. His published Standard matches with what we have today everywhere, including penalty for the "saddleback patch of uncurled hair behind the shoulders" still operative.

The Curly in Australia was always required to be versatile, not only a duck dog, but a guard for remote homesteads, which his temperament suited. As a hunting dog nothing discourages him. The dog in our marvelous kangaroo-fight picture serves as an example: "Nothing overawes him," writes the owner. "He tackles boar pigs, Old Man kangaroos or packs of strange dogs with equal enthusiasm when necessary. His confidence in himself is such that by comparison Cassius Clay is an introvert!"

"Limey's" success in American show rings has served somewhat to re-awaken interest in the breed. Curly-Coats have been bred, a few campaigned. It is likely that with his quality, had he been in the hands of promotion-minded ownership that spent good money to tell the judges how good he is, he might even have started a fashion.

The strong "Old Man" Kangaroos of Australia will, if hard hunted, take to water, to the peril of hunting dogs. Greyhounds and Cattle Dogs are oftenest ripped and drowned. Not Timmy, the Curly-Coat! Every time the kangaroo pushed him down, the active, aggressive water dog twisted, dodged the lethal hind-leg ripping toe, and bit the kangaroo in the soft of the belly—hard! The fight, which yielded a series of remarkable pictures, was eventually declared a draw, and the dog called out.—Photo, *Donald A. J. Macara*, N.S.W. Australia, owner of the dog.

Irish Water Spaniel, English Sh. Ch. Jakes of Tarbay (Sh. Ch. Shamus of Seedhill ex Mistletoe of Annagh), BOB at Crufts, 1968, '69. Owner, George Rickard.

Irish-bred Irish Water Spaniel, Eng. Sh. Ch. Colleen of Seedhill (Int. Ch. Shotwick Bruin ex Strangford Brownie). Note throat pattern of the coat. Owner, Mrs. V. C. Yates, Lancashire.

Lineup of competitors at the National Specialty of the Irish Water Spaniel Club of America, held at Bremerton, Washington, March 1970.—*Roberts.*

236

The Irish Water Spaniel

EXERCISING the author's privilege, the Irish Water Spaniel is here classified with the Retrievers. Long ears he does have, but his occupational leanings are not Spaniel. Nor is his temperament. Nor is his coat pattern, he with his topknot and the all-round clothing of his forelegs. His tail is not Spaniel. He does not cross successfully with any breed in the Sporting Group, as his original promoter, Justin McCarthy, warned in an article more than a century ago in *The Field*. The sole proposal of a cross likely to be borne, he wrote, was the Bloodhound. All else would destroy the unique coat, ears, tail, symmetry. McCarthy was one of the close-mouthed type of Irishman, and those, where they exist, are not to be matched for keeping secrets to themselves. So, actually, no one ever knew how he formed his breed, whether he resuscitated something ancient in Ireland, or whether he implemented some radical cross and if so, with what.

All contemporary references confirm that the dog appeared with suddenness and that, extraordinarily different as its type was, it bred true. It still does, and Justin McCarthy a century and more gone to his rest with his secret close kept. Writing in 1890, the reliable Vero Shaw was emphatic: "In the earlier part of the 19th century the Irish Water Spaniel was unknown as a breed as he now exists." Sure, there were Water Spaniels of various types in Ireland, north and south. None carried characteristics other than a coat that curled in any way matched to the characteristics of the McCarthy dog. From centuries earlier, Caius recorded curled-coat Water Dogges, and down the centuries artists and commentators did the same. Reinagle painted curled coats on Spaniels, and Sydenham Edwards (*Cynographia Britannica*) curled coats on Newfoundlands, and down the years ambitious modern researchers have seized upon every minutest reference to a dog that could even be guessed at being a contributor to this puzzling, so-unique creature. What such have turned up in the main have been words—only words. What has always lacked has been a *picture*—something depicted that looked to have even the hint of characteristics to match those that Justin McCarthy's dog reproduced so faithfully and in such firm resistance to cross-breeding.

Often quoted, but still important enough to repeat, is the Phillips & Cane paragraph (*The Sporting Spaniel*, pp. 17–18) :

> Whether Mr McCarthy really originated the Irish Water Spaniel, in the sense of manufacturing a new variety by dint of crossing two or more existing ones, or whether he merely rescued a moribund breed from its impending fate and resuscitated it, is hard to say, and we have no data to go upon. If he "created" the breed, his success in fixing a type was phenomenal. . . . No existing breed of dogs has a more marked individuality of type, and from the earliest days since they became generally known, no breed has shown less inclination to diverge from it . . . It has been suggested more than once that the origin of the breed was a cross between a Poodle and some other dog but . . . the only points of resemblance between a Poodle and a Water Spaniel are that both have good noses and make good sporting dogs when trained, and that the coat of both shows a tendency to mat together or cord if neglected. The curls of the Irishman, however, are much longer and of altogether different texture . . . and his bare face and tail are peculiarities which are all his own, and quite unlike those of the Poodle . . .

Indivisibly, McCarthy's name was linked with the breed, even into Europe: "*C'est là (Ireland) une race l'on appele 'McCarthy' et est apprecie dans tout de continent Anglais.*" (Benedict Henri Revoil, *Histoire Physiologique et Anecdotique des Chiens*, Paris, 1867.)

By his written admission, McCarthy "gave the breed" to Mr. Joliffe Tufnell, of Dublin, "a gentleman who justified the gift." Included was that original founding father, the stud Boatswain (1834–52) who is properly identified in the stud book as "McCarthy's Boatswain" amid all the multiple Boatswains that serve otherwise to confuse.

That distinguished modern breeder, the late Trench ("Terry") O'Rorke confessed long since that "many weird theories have been aired as to the breed genesis," a statement with which no serious researcher will quarrel. The breed is unique, the characteristics as peculiar as they are tenacious in inheritance. There lack not those who, compiling "history," seize on any mention of the word "spaniel" as belonging to this breed that shows such diverse endowment from all spaniels otherwise familiar to us nowadays.

As in the case of the Irish Setter, documentation as originating from the Green Isle is lacking print and picture. Yet here and there erupts a source

238

A faultless retrieve. Irish Water Spaniel, Eng. Ch. Seamus of Seedhill at work. Bred by Mrs. V. C. Yates (Lancashire) and owned by Miss J. Long of Norfolk.

"Cleopatra," the five-months-old daughter of Phil the Fluter, demonstrates all the Irish Water Spaniel characteristics, including impish play. Owner, Mrs. Harvey-Kelly, England.—Photo lent by *Mrs. Frances Squarey.*

239

A Meenah of Jajurh with Afghan Hound. From *"Letters Written in a Nahratta Camp during the year 1809,"* by Thomas D. Broughton.—Picture, courtesy *Gerald Massey*, London.

A famous 19th century Irish Water Spaniel winner, Ch. Harp, KCSB 22518. Harp, in the ownership of the distinguished breeder, Col. the Hon. le Poer Trench, in the 1880s, was first of the breed to be brought into competition with all dead hair combed out, and shape defined. The circumstance establishes the several characteristics of shape and make—evident in the late Trench O'Rorke (possibly a relative), described as the breed ideal in the 1930s—which continue to intrigue many dog historians, with their tantalizing likeness to Afghan construction, coat oddities (apart from curl, of course) and of course, that tail!

of provocative interest—away from Ireland. Such as the 1809 published picture in Thomas D. Broughton's *Letters Written in a Mahratta Camp*. This picture has already been used in the Miller & Gilbert work, *The Complete Afghan Hound*, New York, 1965. Featured on page 21 of that work, the "Meenah of Jajurh's" dog can only startle Irish Water Spaniel interests. It was first made available for the Afghan Hound book by the distinguished London collector, Mr. Gerald Massey. Mrs. Miller, a long-term friend, writes me: "I have long noted similarities in conformation, stance and, from what I have read, temperament in Irish Water Spaniels to the mountain-type Afghan, even apart from the coat pattern oddities. The relationship may however prove complicated and far-reaching. I do believe, as do the Germans, that all Spaniel forms originated in the East and were subsequently and elsewhere crossed on the local stocks. The Irish Water Spaniel may not have gone through the same influences as the others, but arose independently from different Middle East mixtures. He could be more closely related to the Puli and such." (*Letter*, 1968).

"Puli and such" brings to our consideration those oddly-coated dogs of Asia Minor herding breed types, including not only the Puli and the Komondor with their round-covered legs, their topknots, but also of course the Poodle. No person could possibly undertake to assert that these owe in terms of literal generation one from the other, only that quite reasonably they may share some remotely ancient common ancestor.

This manuscript was already with my publisher when in later 1970 chance took me into the Museum at Montreal, Canada. There came under my astonished sight what so many searches in European museums had denied me, smallish liver-colored spaniels with roughish coats on a medieval tapestry! The Gobelin, dated 1550 A.D., entitled the *Hunt of Maximilian*, includes in addition to one magnificent huge, smooth hound, several spaniels of a type no tapestry of the uncounted numbers I examined across Europe ever showed me. One could link them up at the instant with the several spaniels of odd (and liver) characteristics which have long seemed so unsponsored in the historical sense. These seem to me to have exceptional interest for the Irish Water Spaniel interests, for the American Water Spaniel interests, and just as a venture, drawing perhaps a longer bow, for the Golden Retriever interests who have been constantly searching for clues to that elusive liver, curly-coated Tweed Water Spaniel that figures in the original formation of their breed. At least, the Gobelin established beyond any possible argument that these dogs with their coat color and patterning did exist more than 400 years ago in Europe. Their tails are bare and tufted, but could have been shorn. Also, the startling view of one busily engaged in a bowel evacuation whilst his handler, holding the lead, remains unaware, suggests that if dogs have changed in appearance, the inattention of handlers to their charges was always a constant.

That dogs of the Gobelin-woven type could be placed in France so long ago brings to mind the circumstances that Justin McCarthy, of the original Irish Water Spaniel development, was a traveller and may well have had always a warm welcome in France. An earlier Justin McCarthy of Mountcashel led 5,000 Irishmen to France just before the Battle of the Boyne and they served Louis XII against the common enemy of France and Ireland— England. Louis made that Justin McCarthy his first ever commander of his Irish Brigade. So, if spaniels of the highly individual sort *were* in France, and Justin McCarthy travelled to there, it is at least possible to accept that in this breed, as in so very many other Sporting dog breeds, the world is indebted much to France.

Of course, the British people long cherished a belief that if a dog breed could not be believed to have been shaped within the British Isles, it was not worth bothering about anyway, an opinion that has suffered severe shocks since World War II. However, French dog books, more than any other European publications, come up with spaniel types of various lengths of coat and even with such long thighs and short hocks as Justin McCarthy's breed acquired.

McCarthy always refused to share the secret of his breeding, but the tremendous tenacity of type inheritance in his spaniel, operative still into this our day, thoroughly scouts any theory that he made up his dog from outcrossings in his own time. There may well be the weight of centuries even back of those little liver fellows on the Gobelin, and McCarthy merely polished a little what had come interestingly to his hand in whatever ultimate shaping the years between the 16th and the 19th century may have imposed. Some *very* Afghanish spaniels turn up in such books as *Les Chiens Celebre*, Paris, 1796.

If we must deal—as all dog-curious historians must—in possibles and probables concerning origin, there is no lack of a word-perfect description of a McCarthy spaniel of the 1870s. "Idstone" writes that he had been "searching for some retrievers to send to some Americans, who prefer red, fallow, or liver for duck-shooting." Unable to find them purebreds, he settled for "three crossbreds by an Irish Water Spaniel of McCarthy's genuine breed with all the points insisted on as being those of his class. 21″ high, with a large and capital topknot, smooth face, curls on his head coming down to a sharp point, beautifully shaped muzzle, bold forehead, in which Mr. Lindoe's Rake also excels, while his tail, naturally short, which I like in any dog, was large at the body,' tapering to a fine and sudden point. His legs were coated *all round* (Idstone's italics). His eye was a trifle full, but inquisitive, penetrating, what in a woman would be called arch. As he held his head a trifle on one side and looked up at his master, one would not have wondered to hear him address him in that rich brogue to which his ear in infancy had been well accustomed. In water he was of course proficient, more in his element than on land, working among the rushes and sedges with a resolution and daring which could not be superseded. He is willing in covert, but his coat prevented him getting through brambles. In partridge shooting few could equal him." (*The Dog*, p. 139).

Fifty years later, O'Rorke described his breed ideal, maybe as he saw his own Ch. Breifny Count of 1920: "Standing out unique, unmistakable for anything else . . . the topknot of long loose ringlets, the face peculiarly long and perfectly smooth, ears very large, lowset, far-back, lobe-shaped, close to the cheeks, nearly 30″ tip to tip. His long arched neck carries his head above the level of his back, *higher than in other breeds* (my italics, CBM) doubtless indicating a clear conscience, merry heart, a frankness of nature to look the whole world in the face . . . *Long, long rakish thighs, short hocks, set lower than in any other breed of dog* (again my italics, CBM) . . . Feet large, spreading, well-covered with hair."

Unmistakably, leaving out the "ringlets" such a description can apply to the nearest show Afghan Hound. So, we need a picture of what the words convey, and so are happy to have been handed that of Ch. Harp, KCSB 22518, by Blair ex Widgeon, owned Col. the Hon. W. le Poer Trench met in our Golden Retriever chapter. Ch. Harp was first IWS to be shown with dead hair combed out, so permitting her hound heritage of long thighs and short hocks to be seen. Instinctively, one knows what her movement must have been—just as O'Rorke spelt out ideal IWS gait: "All quaintness, strength, power, active as a steeplechaser, yet withal peculiar, suggesting he is walking on hot coals."

How important the "peculiar" aspect of the breed gait is to be gathered from the opening of the English Kennel Club breed Standard: "*Characteristics: The gait of the IWS is peculiar to the breed, differs from that of any other variety of Spaniel.*" End of characteristics.

The American Kennel Club Standard imposes no such necessity for a judge to assess IWS gait as "peculiar," merely that it be seen "*square, true, precise, not slurring.*" Which is fine—for by and large that is what one will see nowadays. But while that takes care of the responsibility of a licensed judge it should not take care of the responsibilities of breeders—and of historians—to recognize that herein one deals with no ordinary breed. In our showrings it is rare indeed to see an IWS who goes with head and tail high. Most I see run with head low, often straight carried in a manner that in my agricultural livestock reporter days I identified as the gait of a sick pig. However, many IWS are less than happy in the show ring. I think of watching Am. Ch. Tir-na-nog Kerley O'Padolil who stayed here with me in Oregon for a while, striding out here with head and tail up, extending himself in play to a looping gallop with my pup.

When Kerley went with me to a retrieving trial here, galleryside, several middle-aged men came to rumple his rich, dark topknot: "Used to hunt with these years ago, wonder where they all got to?" was the comment from each man.

An Irish Water Spaniel is not a dog to forget.

Registrations now are few, any country. Yet fans are loyal. Since Mrs. Violet Yates ceased to breed her "Seedhills," her time being taken up as a most distinguished judge in Sporting breeds especially, one may still find the echo of her influence. Mrs. Yates is another of the long-term breeders who is much aware of possible Eastern hound linkage: "There is only one breed, and that a very ancient one, with a Standard in so many respects identical with that of the IWS—forelegs, hindquarters, topknot, somewhat similar ears, differing principally in coat texture—the Afghan hound" (*Letter to me*, 1969).

A tremendous excitement of 1970 in the Pacific Northwest was the National Specialty of the IWS Club, the Parent body, held at Bremerton, Wash. Thirteen was an amazing number of this breed to find in a present-day show ring.

In England, so I heard, it was "Terry" O'Rorke that did much to kill show interest in the breed. His dogs were so good, and he was always *there*. No one else could get a chance at major wins. No greater misfortune can overtake a breed, numerically small especially. Human nature being what human nature is, people just won't hold on without some rags of encouragement. No such misfortune so far befalls IWS in this country, perhaps mainly because no great winner has appeared. There have been two that topped the Group at Westminster, in New York, Ch. Mahoney's O'Toole in 1943, and Ch. Kalibanks Water Gate Wanderer in 1959.

Mr. C. A. Binney, past secretary of the English Kennel Club has a good Irish Water Spaniel yarn to tell, of being at Belfast (Ireland) in the capacity of onlooker, when famous breeder, the late Mrs. Barrington, thrust a fistful of dog leads into his hand and said: "Hold these a minute!" before haring off to her rings. "The ten Irishers decided to follow her," he laughed, "and anyone can guess they took me along with them!"

One takes it on trust that there will always be dedicates to keep from becoming extinct those unique characteristics of this breed—and to argue interminably whence it may have stemmed, and whether or not Justin McCarthy deserved all the credit his contemporaries never presumed to deny him.

The American Water Spaniel

THE increasing popularity of the little American Water Spaniel may astonish show-oriented folk, most of whom have failed so far to set eyes on even one. By now as solidly "American-made" as the Boston Terrier, the American Cocker, or the Chesapeake Bay Retriever, superficially he will remind some——when at last they catch up with him——of an Irish Water Spaniel. But actually he is poles apart from the bigger fellow in all but color and a curled coat. He is all Spaniel, has no oddities of build or coat-pattern. His registrations continue to mount, so one has no notion as to how far his present increase of popularity will take him. Though comparisons are always odious, one has to note that he solidly out-registers the IWS. This is how the figures run:

    1965: Am. W. Spaniels; 164. IWS; 71.
    1966: Am. W. Spaniels; 246. IWS; 47.
    1967: Am. W. Spaniels; 241. IWS; 82.
    1968: Am. W. Spaniels; 236. IWS; 68.
    1969: Am. W. Spaniels; 324. IWS; 80.
    1970: Am. W. Spaniels; 324. IWS; 80.

His main sponsorship has always been in the Midwest where, for that matter, so many Sporting breeds received their early bolsterings. No one gave him any particular attention, merely there he was. His type was not always exactly constant, but the predominant features survived the generations, his size sometimes variable, but never was he a big dog. His work pattern of useful versatility was greatly valued, and the tight marcel-effect of his brownish-liver jacketing was recognized as his badge.

"Breed history" is a matter of tradition. He has no real written history. Perhaps the best descriptive run-down he ever received was from the pen of the distinguished David Michael Duffy of *Outdoor Life*. Duffy credits Dr. F. J. Pfeiffer with having rescued the grand little worker from threats of extinction, and securing for it eventual AKC recognition as a breed. Argument to establish the status was in terms of consistent reproduction of identifying characteristics. The doctor's own Curly Pfeiffer was the first American Water Spaniel registered.

If it does not derive from the IWS—even though it seems likely an occasion cross could have been made way back—whence did it stem? Dare one guess it to have been from the now vanished English Water Spaniel? Or, had it some linkage with that curled-coat light liver that was known last century as the Tweed Water Spaniel (see Golden Retriever chapter)? It is entirely possible that settlers of earlier centuries brought such curled coat Spaniels with them, and carried them West as the country beckoned. Distances and transportation difficulties of the times would have led to local inbreedings that indelibly fixed characteristics, much as the same forces helped to fix Laverack and Arkwright 19th century type Setters and Pointers in New Zealand. Sheer speculation of course, but as it is necessary to keep saying, sheer speculation, examination of the possible where documentation lacks, is the whole story of dog history research.

This must be one of the rarest breeds to see in the show ring. Ownerships appear in many cases to have what amounts to pathological fear of exposure in the show ring; that it might in some way destroy their good little working Spaniel. The only outstanding show record, in terms of heights scaled, seems to have been that of Ch. Happy Hiram of Ty-Grim, fourth in Group at Westminster Kennel Club show some years ago. Caramel Candy, with two Bests of Breed at Chicago International and an Obedience degree, and Americana Wahoo, with 199½ of a possible 200 in three straight Obedience outings, Highest Score on each occasion, are so far somewhat lonely in their eminences.

The breed character is fully Spaniel in its charm, and the breed trainability is so developed that Mr. Duffy tells of his nine-year-old daughter successfully training her own. Importantly, such a pocket-size dog, whose earliest working value included the minimal space he took up in a skiff, and the minimal amount of commotion he caused when he dived from a skiff after a downed duck, could win much favor in our ever-shrinking world. Is this perhaps one explanation for the consistency of the registration figures? It may also be true that ownerships are not overly anxious to court popularity to any degree. But that the breed is being spread across the country away from the previously-prevailing tight location in the Midwest is a fact. My own introduction to actual living specimens was delightfully provided by a breeder in El Sobrante, California in 1969. He seemed receptive to my suggestions that he enter some of his pretty little fellows in local California shows, but if he has done so it has not been at any shows which I have attended. That they would find friends and purchasers following show exposure seems certain. As certain as that seems not to be what the owners want for their breed . . .

A judge astonished with the eruption of one in his ring might remember that the Standard's requirement for *"not too compactly coupled"* doesn't mean to suggest Basset Hound length. Legs are of medium length but not short as related to body height which runs 15″ to 18″. For the purpose of handily estimating this in an emergency a judge would recall that an American Cocker tops out at 15½″. Coats must not be too straight nor *too* tightly kinked, not too soft or too fine. Marcel wave is quoted as being desirable, but one wonders what the now-generation would know of Marcel.

There is only one disqualification included in the Standard—for yellow eyes. The liver-coated breeds, in and out of the Sporting group, do have a problem with light eyes, and desirably they should be kept out as, once infiltrated they are usually in a strain to stay.

If the steady registration figures can be taken as indication, the American Water Spaniel has a solid base of his own in the American dog world. His qualities—and his size!—could win him a host of friends and supporters if he were but given exposure out in public where people could get to see him. Maybe, that is why he is so carefully kept under wraps—his supporters don't want him to become popular. Who knows, they may have good sense and reason on their side.

Chesapeake Bay Retriever, Field Ch., American Field Ch., Canadian Field Ch. Nelgard's Baron, C. D. Owner, Mrs. Walter Heller, California.

The Chesapeake Bay Retriever

WHILE the other curled-coat breeds saw their popular support completely lost as the ducks dwindled, the Chesapeake Bay Retriever has clearly by-passed most of the hindrances to continued enjoyment of approval. Several factors seem to have contributed to this distinction. He has friends. He has dedicated breeders to produce him. He tends to attract moneyed patrons, always useful to a dog breed. He has adaptability. He is a topnotch retriever but he is also possessed of temperamental qualities which, along with a certain reputation for combativeness, discourages any who might otherwise take liberties where he guards. He is good in retriever competition. He is good in Obedience, and by and large he is improving his looks to suit the requirements of the show ring. There are modernly to see some very handsome Chesapeake Bays, and no one so far tells me that they are any the worse in the practical sense on that account.

For those who register some surprise when faced with statistical records of Chesapeake Bay success in Obedience, the observations of knowledgeable Mrs. Daniel Horn (Eastern Waters) are instructive. She feels that the breed attracts people who "like to do things with their dogs . . . Obedience activity in Chesapeakes is the result of owner initiative, not necessarily formalized Club policy, though the Club does approve thoroughly any activity likely to bring Chesapeakes before the public."

The operative words within this assessment are "owner initiative." Development of a dog in any breed to the extent of its capacities always must be the result of owner initiative.

It has been demonstrated to me that many people are wildly surprised

249

when faced with the figures of Chesapeake Bay Retriever's modern registrations with AKC. In 1970, while Curly-Coateds registered 59 and Irish Water Spaniels 80, the Chesapeake Bay Retriever registered 1,611, which maintained him in 49th place in the all-breed tally. The absolute impact may be the better felt by adding that English Setters in 54th place registered 1,275, and Pointers, in 77th, registered 396.

It has to be the sum of his virtues that gains him ever-increasing support. Truthfully, his handsomeness is in terms linked with his own type, something that prevails in many other dog breeds besides. His beauty rests where does beauty traditionally—in the eye of the beholder. Even 70 years ago, Joseph Graham described the breed as "common looking (but) not so peculiar as the Irish Water Spaniel. Stout and strong, but no beauty." (*The Sporting Dog*, New York, 1904). Contemporary owners nowadays will merely shrug, maybe add that 'Andsome is wot 'Andsome Does. Chesapeake Bays with dogs carrying titles in all three venues of American competition, field, show, obedience, lend weight to the claim.

Breed formation appears to have been casual and extended over almost two centuries so far as tradition records, and likely centuries further back beyond even the reach of tradition. There would always have been dogs used in the Chesapeake by the hunters, and in the casual way of such ownerships, they would have bred anything that appeared likely to sharpen the dog as a tool. It should be more generally understood by those dedicated historians (in every breed) who possess the laudable, but unreachable, aim of documenting The Dog (every breed) back to the Garden of Eden, that throughout historical time, cross-weldings have been made, none of which are documented by other than the varying characteristics that the breeds exhibit. One picks up the hint of what went on here and there among the French, German, English medieval writers. The process that went into the shaping of many a dog breed that in our time reproduces truly and to type may have been best suggested by a delightful quote from James Bridie's *Storm in a Teacup,* a play that had considerable vogue a couple of decades ago. The scene is a courtroom, where the dialogue concerns the description of the dog, Patsy. The veterinarian is testifying:

> "Have you examined this dog, Mr. Cassidy?"
> "Well, Sir, he's a proper bonanza, that dog is. If you think a dog's only a dog and that is all there is to it, there's the living answer for you, sitting up here by me like patience on a monument smiling at grief. I have niver in all my experience beheld a specimen comprising in his own person such a variety of characteristics of so many different breeds. From his rump to his shoulders you'd say he was a sheepdog, but he has the mizzle of a setter and ears that are a wee bit reminescent of a Cocker Spaniel. He's got the serious

Dual and Am. Field Ch. Baron's Tule Tiger, C.D. is the son of Nelgard's Baron. A very distinguished competitor who carried the honors for his breed during much of the 1960s. Owner, Mrs. Walter Heller, California.

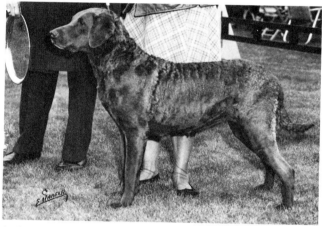

A classic example of Chesapeake Bay Retriever type, Ch. Eastern Waters Baronessa, winner of the National Specialty 1964, '65, and '66. Owners, Dr. and Mrs. Daniel Horn, Maryland.—*Shafer*.

look of an Irish Terrier and the fine soldierlike tail on him of a Pomeranian, and the coat of a Retriever and sad noble eyes of a Poodle. In short, me Lord, he is not so much a dog as the epitome of all the dogs that ever ran round the world on four legs."

Heaven forbid anyone should jump to the conclusion that I am offering Patsy as an equivalent for Chesapeake Bay Retriever inheritance factors. Merely the wish is to somewhat lighten the discussion and to provide a lead-in for the documented fact that an extremely wide variety of characteristics and qualities were drawn upon, and magnificently and even cleverly combined to fix the very distinctive breed type as it is recognized now in its true-breeding productive status.

Every Chesapeake Bay historian inclines to start with Canton and Sailor, the waifs plucked from a sinking vessel off the Eastern Shore. This may be because the story of the rescue gained publicity in the press and became so preserved. It does not establish that these two waifs were Adam and Eve of the breed. They seem never to have bred together, and in appearance they were reported to share only "short, very thick coats and conspicuous dew-claws." Sailor was "dingy red with some white on face and breast, of fine size, lofty in carriage, built for strength and activity, remarkably broad across hips and breast, head large but not out of proportion, muzzle rather longer than common in *that breed of dogs* (my italics, CBM). His coat was uncommonly thick, more coarse fur than hair, tail full, long-haired, always carried high. Eyes bright as to appear unnatural, which he carried on (in his get) and it was held good for swimming dogs."

Sailor's dingy red and what may have been a yellow eye are still features in the modern breed, but his reported progeny seems always to have been black. Much of the description given would fit a Newfoundland of the time, the coat especially.

Canton was black. No one seems to have worried about her looks, but her character may have been her legacy to the breed, as persistent as Sailor's color patterning and pigmentation. "Her patience and endurance (were) almost incredible. She would fight wounded swans after pursuing them for miles, and retrieved ducks over rotten and floating ice in fogs and darkness." Her best son, Drake, was described as "sorrel-colored with yellow eyes." Interesting, while Sailor could throw blacks, she could throw reddish, which makes clear that they shared such a like endowment as the Curly-coated Retriever still does modernly, factors for both black and liver. Leo (1840), described as a direct Sailor descendant was "black, with a small white spot, some white on each foot, yellow eyes. Form like a Setter, lacking the feathery tail or the smooth tail of the Pointer. Not so deep in chest as a Setter, but rounder in body, longer in neck, ear smaller, more set up, tips turned down. Hair not

252

so long, but far from short. Woolly undercoat. He could swim as far, dive as deep, stay down as long, come up as dry, as any dog in Newfoundland."

As to the weldings achieved . . . In 1877, Chesapeake Bay Ducking Dogs' owners came together after a Baltimore show (*Chicago Field* report). The aim was to clarify *what* was a Chesapeake Bay Ducking Dog. A Capt. Taylor described: "black dogs, smooth of hair, fierce, powerful, sagacious, with two skins, one hair, one fur, an india-rubber dog, smooth as glass." Members howled that black dogs would be shot on sight in the Chesapeake, ducks would not come to a blind. No one seems to have mentioned Canton.

A next speaker identified two strains: "the larger, a reddish, longhaired Newfoundland-Labrador Water Dog type. The smaller, compact, shorthaired, with an underfur coat and otter paws, a dog with a coat bright as sedge, darkening in winter. A great retriever, able to endure bleak conditions and unlikely to benefit by foreign crossings. Even the best retrieving dogs from England cannot endure Chesapeake chill and ice."

A Mr. Foulks stood to say his people kept dogs in the Chesapeake area from the later 18th to the early 19th centuries, and had known them as "Red Winchesters." Imported from Ireland, he held these "the best water dogs in the world, noble, fearless, guarding the interests of their masters on the bleakest shores, the iciest nights."

How one longs to know more of the Red Winchesters that may have been a link with Irish Water Spaniel history. Was it something of the sort that Justin McCarthy of Mountcashel used to base his breed experimentation? It teases me so to recall, from another interest of mine, that H. M. S. Winchester was the flagship of the British Navy's Labrador Fisheries Patrol, based on Halifax, Nova Scotia, and active up and down the American East Coast and the Chesapeake even still as late as the aftermath of the 1812 War. Vessels on this dreary service, in fact British naval vessels generally, tended to clear from Cork (Cobh) in those times, taking their last sight of land from Southern Ireland's shore and the area where Justin McCarthy lived. And, as elsewhere in these pages noted, officers brought along their dogs on sea-service so often.

Of such threads, tangled beyond any hope of unravelling, is woven the web of dog history. And, within my experience, beyond all doubt, the most exciting clues are to be found in reading other than specialized dog writings.

The Baltimore folk finally settled to recognize three types; the Otter, the Curly-hair, the Straight. The two latter were red-browns, white chest spot permissible. All emphasis was on males. Bitches were required only to "show color and approximate to general points of the class to which they belong."

Dogs were measured, weighed, averaged. Turk, 18 months, 80 lbs. Monday, 5 years, 89 lbs. Rob, 6 years, 90 lbs. Height average 25″, providing mid-mark

Where it's right for Chessies to be . . . Owners, Eastern Waters Kennels, Maryland.—*C. Bede Maxwell.*

Ch. Eastern Waters Tobyhanna, Chesapeake Bay Retriever with exceptionally good breed-true coat. Owners, Dr. and Mrs. Daniel Horn, Maryland.—*C. Bede Maxwell.*

in moderns 23–26″, but a heavier dog. Top weight is presently given for males at 75 lbs.

Nine years later another committee sat in Baltimore. Type had become more even. Another Monday was introduced: "of color dead-grass or sedge, reddish-brown or brownish red. ¾″ long, dense, wavy, not curly, a filling coat that protects skin from contact with water. A shake or two dried it. The 'filling' quality could be detected by taking a coat-clip and looking at the butt end. No other dog's coat acts so in water."

That ounce of seeing that is worth all the hearing (or reading) was my privilege when the beautiful modern Ch. Eastern Waters Tobyhanna permitted me to part her coat as one parts the fleece of a sheep and photograph deep down to demonstrate the qualities above described. "Toby" also posed Coat Wet and Coat Dry for me, my photographs showing the way a shake threw away the water from the peaking of tiny coat clumps all over.

"Dead grass" is still within the approved color range of shades. Liver is a disqualification, a circumstance that would seem to require some very exact color discrimination abilities on the part of a judge. When does brown lapse into "liver." Liver, in sporting breeds, can vary from the light gold sheen of a Sussex to the puce of an Irish Water Spaniel. A lay person would describe every darn one of them as "brown." Interestingly, in Baron v. Bylandt's famous world-wide survey of dog breeds (1905) he describes the Chesapeake coat color as "nearly resembling sedge grass or the discolored coat of a buffalo." Living for years so handily to Golden Gate Park, San Francisco, it is well-known to me that new buffalo calves, each season, were rust-reddish, much indeed the color of Tobyhanna.

Eastern Waters also provided the privilege of photographing three litter-mates that were dead-grass, reddish, brown, the permissible gamut.

Monday, examined by the 1886 Committee, was described as "having all his life worked an average of five days of every seven, for when ducks come in September till they leave, ever since he was old enough to work, his owner has averaged a thousand ducks each Fall."

Hence, in good time—duck limits!

"Such as Monday," continued the demonstration, "are not sight hunters, nor likely to chase all over the marsh in hope to run into a duck. They use their noses; through ice and mud they will get there following a cripple."

This is exactly what German Shorthairs do in Germany. However, modernly the question is raised—of what use is a nose to a dog in non-slip retriever competition where the primary virtue is held to be the following of handler signals.

Strength and endurance are still virtues inherent in the Chesapeake Bay. *Heads* are broad of skull, with a medium stop, a muzzle somewhat shortish by comparison with the skull, the muzzle, though very slightly run-off, not to be pointed. Yellowish eyes are still required. The increasing breed support in other than work venues may eventually propose a darkened eye "for cosmetic reasons" as has happened in connection with the Welsh Springer Spaniel in England, whose original pigmentation was light (as the Brittany's) and whose Standard still permits such—but concerning which breed authorities tell one that giving a win to a light-pigmented Welshie would be poorly received. Maybe, if the yellowish eye is held important to the Chesapeake, such change may be forestalled. It is certainly true that where fashion drifts, Standards eventually follow. A check back at original Pointer Standard eye requirements in American show competition may make the matter clear.

Shoulder assemblage requires "front-end flexibility" indispensable for a retrieving dog. Rounded ribs give width and strength to a chest that must house a brave heart. Outline, seen from the side, includes a visible rise behind, powerful back quarters provide swimming drive. Feet are webbed. Hind dewclaws are a disqualification. Tails are medium length, moderate feather permissible, but most of the best that have come under my notice have a thick wavy cover.

Temperament is the more important now the breed carves itself a new niche, moving away from the kennel caging endured by generations of retrievers used seasonally. The breed still inclines not "to use its strength foolishly, going after it didn't know what, and sometimes nothing, as some hotheads incline to do." Maybe the reputation for dourness (and worse!) was resultant on harsh training methods. The Chesapeake is not a dog to wilt passively under severity. However, usage in different venues discovers for owners what modern behaviorists tell dog owners in terms as of new discovery. The best dog writers have been telling us the like for centuries. Gervase Markham (1621), for one, warned that in dog-training "to words of reprehension you must also joyne words of Cheerishing so (to) encourage and comfort the Dogge as he doth your Pleasure."

Competitively, the Chessie does well in those several spheres to which he has become introduced. We note titles such as Dual & Am. Fld. Ch. Baron's Tule Tiger, C. D.; Dual & Am. Fld. Ch. Meg's Timothy, C. D. X.; Can. Fld. Ch. & Am. Fld. Ch. Nelgard's Baron, C. D.; Dual Ch. Sodak's Gypsy Prince; Dual Ch. Mount Joy's Mallard. Show competition has honored some great bitches, Ch. West River Ripple, Best of Breed, Specialties of 1959/60/61; Ch. Eastern Waters Baronessa T. D. (Specialties of 1964/65/66). Ch. Cherokee South Bay, C. D. is reported as being near Dual Ch. status, and present-day competition is enlivened with two fine ones in Ch. Lady Ginger of Hampton Court and Ch. Eastern Waters Brown Charger, C. D., while from the West Coast, Mrs. Eloise Heller newly reports her Ch. & A. F. C. Tiger's Cub as gaining his final field points, making him the third in direct line

(Nelgard's Baron and Baron's Tule Tiger are his sire and grandsire) to nudge into distinction.

This is not a book of *names,* nor was ever intended to be. Yet, in all breeds, certain names *will in,* do what one may to hold them at bay. It would delight me if it were possible to highlight the magnificent Obedience records, but once launched in that direction, quick restriction of space would be obvious. In conclusion, however, it has to be said that the Chesapeake Bay's adaptation to changing fashions in competition has been not only radical but most admirable—not to mention worthy of emulation by ownerships in some other breeds.

Keltenbrache (Celtic Hounds). On the neck of a vase of 600 B.C. in the National Museum, Athens, Greece.

European Sporting Utility Breeds

THE first thing to say of the European sporting utility breeds that have enriched the world over the past few decades is that they were originally and *specifically* formed, developed and stabilized by their breeders to be able to discharge all aspects of hunting dog activity. In other words, they were to be completely versatile, land and water, and in tracking. They were not formed to be specialists in any one venue. Yet it has been often their misfortune, worst of all in America because longest-enduring there in unsuitable classification, that when they left their homeland they fell often into the hands of owners completely without understanding of what they were. Such could visualize and work only towards turning them back to specialists, even to the extent of completely reversing the processes that formed them in the first place. Even to mongrelization when nothing else served.

It has been the tragedy of the sporting utility breeds introduced to the United States that there lacked here, and still lacks, any slot in which to file them. There were Bird-Dogs here, there were Spaniels and there were Retrievers. The European dog was none of these, and yet paradoxically he was all of them. He *was* a Bird Dog, though never an horizon-runner. He *was* a Retriever, though non-slip work was not his accustomed style. The awkward truth was (and is) that he was exactly what European breeders HAVE for a century sweat blood, time, treasure to make him—a dog of all skills for a hunting man to use and value.

It has been a worse misfortune for many dogs of such inheritance that many men in America entertain a hopeless aspiration towards the phantom ideal of the Great Going Dog, the Big-Running Bird Dog as A. F. Hochwald best defined this, "the dog for the man on horseback hunting big open country of the south, etc." Truly, it seems likely that many who acquire a field trial dog picture themselves in the southern gentleman's saddle. Impediments spell out in terms of money and geography. A man that can buy a dog cannot always acquire additionally the horse to work it, and "big open country" available for hunting in our time (and around the world!) dwindles astonishingly. Yet the veneration of the big-running dog lives on, possibly helped somewhat by professionals who in some cases have elected themselves to be trainers by grace of but sketchy credentials. (There is no licensing of field trial trainers as operates in respect of show handlers who MUST be competent.) The less competent among field trial trainers probably discovered long since that it is easier to haze a dog into running wide and fast than to train him in versatile hunting skills. Many Sporting writers, often also meshed in narrowed breed interest, fell for and promoted the brainwash. Capable, dedicated Bird Dog men wrote the "How To" books.

Every European sporting utility breed, then, that came here was pressured into the same classic fantasy shape, all effort brought to bear to change it to Bird Dog status (see Wirehaired Pointing Griffon chapter importantly for documentation!) back to the specialized performance the Europeans had managed to widen. The Germans especially had engaged with dedication to develop utility qualities, the versatile dog, and succeeded to perfection. If such versatile accomplishments imposed difficulties of classification, this was quickly found in other lands to yield to common sense re-ordering of priorities. Thus, already many years ago, the English governing body instituted a completely new classification for what were described as "Dogs Working the Pointing-Retrieving Schedule," removing Shorthairs, Wirehairs, Weimaraners, Vizslas out of Pointer/Setter competition to trials of their own.

This matches German (European) usage. Specialized breeds are not valued in Europe.

Though the mid-19th century aim was to produce a dog to serve persons who could not afford to maintain specialist kennels, the work of forming such fell upon those financially able to afford it. So, one finds within the histories the names of such as Altmeister von Zedlitz ("Hegewald"), the tireless Prinz zu Solms-Brauenfels; Herr Julius Mehlich (Hoppenrade) and E. K. Korthals (Korthalsgriffon), to name a few of the most eminent and successful.

What did they use? Why, what came handiest! There was that old German *Brack* (Braque, Bracco, depending what language one spoke) tending to variation of size, temperament, but in the main steady and slow, with flop ears and nose to the ground. He was a tracking dog but was called a bird dog by those who could put up with his exasperating slowness. He was, after all, the one choice available. The *Schweisshund* is his heir, direct inheritor of the scent hound virtues of steadiness and a magnificent nose, albeit low carried.

When compiling my German Shorthair breed book, the Schweisshund came to my attention, and made it necessary to go into considerable documentation to prove that this basic to the Shorthair was NOT a Bloodhound, as an error in translation of German to English had designated him. At that time my belief was that the Schweisshund had vanished as a separate breed, absorbed in the new-made sporting utility types. The documentation in the Bylandt compilation of 1905 was for long all I could find, pictures therein matching so exactly the earliest basic and experimental Shorthairs that they went into the second edition of my breed book as historical discoveries. However, not until attending European shows in 1967/68 was it possible to learn that the breed still exists, the dog of the foresters, the gamekeepers, of Europe. Austria, Czechoslovakia, as well as Germany, still keep them, and some beautiful specimens were benched in Budapest (Hungary) in 1968. Both types, the *Hannoveraner* (the large one that is meshed in Shorthair background) and the smaller, the *Bäyrischer Gebirgsschweisshund* (Bavarian Mountain Schweisshund), that was formed by breeding down from the larger for smaller legs better suited to the Bavarian mountain hunting venues. Both types are used for tracking and are called upon to take over when a hunter's own Shorthair or such becomes unable to complete a search that becomes inordinately difficult or protracted over days. Such searches for an ambulatory wounded animal are for the expert. No search for such is ever abandoned until the creature is found, dead or alive.

Benched Schweisshunde in Budapest fascinated me. A casual remark of mine, how nice such a dog could be to own, provoked angry protests raised in several languages. A Czech owner waved his right hand in front of my face: "Does a man sell his own right hand?" A forester needs his Schweisshund in his work and takes years to train it to his exact personal requirements. A pup is started young but may not reach perfection in work until about age five. Fortunately the Schweisshund is a long-living breed.

Further, a note of scorn crept in over the top of polite intention not to embarrass me: "What work could there be in America for a Schweisshund where there is no honorable obligation imposed on a hunter to care whether a wounded creature lived or died?" American wastage of resources, animal, vegetable, mineral, is understood and unadmired in Europe. My response that a new generation promised to be more conservation-minded was received politely but, as expressions betrayed, no one seemed inclined to bet on it. The Czech owner placed that right hand of his protectively on the head of the glorious red, black-masked bitch . . .

My agreement is total. America is no place for a Schweisshund. The mis-

261

The C. F. Decker painting of the German Pointer of the 1860s shows us still a tremendous strength of hound influence. He even retains still his full length of hound tail with his heavy body. Breeders had managed to get his head up from the ground, and for that they named him the High-Running German Bird Dog. He was an early stage of utility dog development, and interesting to compare with our pictures of Hector Foedersdorf and the Schweisshund.

Hector Foedersdorf, described as a "German Pointer," has been for decades of the British Natural History Museum, England. His likeness to the Schwe head and expression, and his endowment of long hound ears, is unmista interesting link between the Scent Hound basis and the eventual German type development.—*C. Bede Maxwell.*

The Hannoveraner Schweisshund. This is the famous German Scent Hound breed, so often confused by translators with the Bloodhound. It contributed to the development of the various Sporting utility breeds. It is impressive, docile, clever, a great tracking dog. Note the huge functional nose with the "double" groove. Colors are always in the red-yellow range, with black masks and shadings about the ears, German Hound endowment, out of Asia Minor centuries ago.—*C. Bede Maxwell, 1968.*

Bäyrischer Gebirgsschweisshund. Sportsmen in the Bavarian mountain country found the big Hannoveraner unsuited to their rough terrain, but were also under the Hunting Code obligation to find and put out of misery any creature they wounded. The Hannoveraner was crossed with Dachs-Brache (a lower-stationed breed, reminiscent of the dog we know as the Dachshund). The resultant Bäyrischer Gebirgsschweisshund (The Bavarian Mountain Scent Hound) is a keen tracker, too, rather sharper of temperament than his larger forbear. Note the same magnificent nose and the dewclaws on all four legs. This one photographed in Vienna, Austria, 1968.—*C. Bede Maxwell.*

handling of the sporting utility breeds is the proof of it. Before one could turn around twice someone would be recommending "selective breeding" to make the heavy dog run faster, his hound status completely ignored, as most cruelly of all in the case of the Weimaraner, who may well be nominated with the Wirehaired Pointing Griffon, as the most unlikely candidate for American Pointer/Setter trial competition ever to reach these shores. Including those that made their titles! Against odds!

Mr. C. A. Binney, of the English Kennel Club, lent me some German show catalogs of 1880–1883 that establish interestingly that the distinguished Schweisshunde pictured in the Bylandt were in the ownership of—guess?! Prinz zu Solms. That he owned also the very best of contemporary English Pointer breeding establishes just how good was the foundation material used in original formation of the versatile Shorthair that so many present-day American owners single-mindedly aspire to tear to sheds as a utility breed.

Now, from the Schweisshunde in Europe, the next step was in being able to photograph in England what may be the only representative of the early stages of Shorthair development still to be found above ground. His name was Hector Foedersdorf, owned by the Natural History Museum in England. Hector, who may have lived a long life before the taxidermists caught him, was merely labelled "German Pointer," which was how the British catalogued the breed at its only showing in the 19th century in English competition. The characteristics he shares with a modern Schweisshund are startling. Beyond Hector, we can reach back to the C. F. Decker painting of the 1860s of der Hochlaüfige Deutsche Hühnerhund (The High-Running German Bird Dog) which represents the first success breeders had in Germany, getting the hound nose up from the ground. Decker's dog was a hound in body, ears, tail, profile, but he *was* a first stage in the process of developing *Hohe Nase* (high nose).

The breeders, separated in the geographical sense, undoubtedly came up with different types some of which merited perseverance, some of which were for discard. No one seems to have recorded the boo-boos. A first success was the *Stichelhaar* (Stitched-hair). Rudolf Freis, a distinguished modern German Sporting breeds writer (*Unsere Jagdhunde,* Germany, 1960) is a best authority on this emergent, his family owning such, possibly being foresters, as he is himself identified on the title page of his magnificent book. He describes this experimental dog as versatile, useful, good on birds and in water, but very sharp. It would fight any predator, even strangle wild dogs, a quality valuable to the foresters but not for ordinary hunting men. He records that it became a victim to breeder-feuding, some aiming to produce a smooth-coated dog with a beard, characteristics that do not go together genetically. Stichelhaar, then, became absorbed in the developing Shorthair

264

and later the Wirehair. The occasional tough customer that can crop up in these breeds may well be in debt to Stichelhaar. Genes are forever!

The Europeans don't seem to worry as much about sharpness in dogs as we reasonably do. Those German catalogs Mr. Binney lent me included the direction: *"Gegen Mensch bissige Hunde müssen bereits in der Anmeldung und nachher auf der Addresse bestimmt bezeichnet sein."* ("Dogs that bite people must be clearly identified on the entry form and on signs subsequently used.") Dogs that Bite People were especially in evidence on the benching in Budapest in 1968. Many were muzzled, including Dobermans, Boxers, Komondor, Kuvasz, German Shepherd Dogs. Some that were not, lunged at passers-by while owners stood by and smirked in pride. One walked warily. One presumed to touch *nothing!* There were however no warning signs in any language of any acquaintance, though the catalog was printed in Hungarian, French, German.

Freis thinks crossing the Stichelhaar with the Korthalsgriffon might have been good, but breeder feuding cancelled that too. He added that the rough jacketing added to developing sporting utility breeds a great practical aid for waterwork. He identified this as originally from Asiatic herding breeds. The smooth-coated old German Brack, he wrote, was not exactly water-shy, but less than keen when weather and water were cold.

Dirk v. Doenitz, an example of excellent present-day Wirehaired Pointing Griffon type, with the correct jacketing. Owner, Mrs. Donna Lusthoff, Oregon.

Attila D'Argent, All-Age winner at the first Field Trial of the Wirehaired Pointing Griffon Club of America, held in California, May, 1968. Owners, Dr. and Mrs. Clifford B. Trott, California.

266

The Wirehaired Pointing Griffon

IT is important that those interested in the various European breeds should at least skim through this chapter, even if they own no Griffons. It was first of the breeds to be brought to the United States as a registerable breed. M. Korthals, early in the interest to produce a sporting utility dog, was a Belgian who went to Germany to pursue his aim.

Korthals always said he introduced no foreign breed, used only Griffons. The reasonable question raised—what is (was) a Griffon? Reminds me of my son, Colin, then aged eight, told to go outside and play, that he was at the moment superfluous, asking: "Who was the *first* Sir Perfluous?" In the same enquiring spirit one asks what was the *first* Griffon.

Webster provides: "*Grfoun, Grifo, Gryphus, Grypo*—a mythical monster, half lion, half eagle, also a wiryhaired dog of European breed, so called because of its resemblance to a Griffin." So, who is wiser? The German word *grif* connotes all variations on the English word *grip*, but still fails in help to visualize the dog M. Korthals first drew upon to make his breed.

"Idstone" (*The Dog*, 1872) drew on matching word pictures, describing a dog he had seen in England, "a veritable griffin or heraldic dog, not excepting tags of hair depending from hocks, elbows, chest, the pointed imperial on the chin, and 14″ or so of tongue, which seems to be the 'points' of attraction on dogs *passant* and *rampant*. Rampant he was all day, seemingly his first time out (in the field). He was, I believe, a first prize winner at Birmingham."

As German breeders liked to show their achievements in England in those pre-quarantine times, this dog "Idstone" described was almost certainly an early Korthals. The famous writer did not condemn it as he did the "Russian Retriever" (see Golden Retriever Chapter). Which reminds me, an officer of the American Kennel Club, who has been in so many ways helpful to my work, advises that Zolette, first Wirehaired Pointing Griffon registered by that body was classed originally as a "Russian Setter." Her pedigree is visibly Korthals, including Guerre, grandson of Donna, the foundation bitch Korthals took to Germany, and Zampa the dam of Tambour.

These basics crop up also in catalogs of the 1880s filed in the archives of the English Kennel Club that include entries in this breed made by the tireless Prinz zu Solms-Brauenfels. Was there ever a Sporting breed of the time in which this dedicate was not concerned? Pedigrees given illustrate how inbred the Korthals stock was in the formative years. Chasseur Moustache, KCSB 26001, wh. Jan. 16, 1882, was by Moustache II ex his Clairette; she by Moustache I (ex Donna, above). Moustache II, also by Moustache I, was ex Zampa, dam of Tabour (above) Zampa was by Satan ex Madame Angot, Korthals' very first brood bitch—which brings us back to his described "only Griffons." All the entries in the English catalogs owned by Prinz zu Solms were identified as "late the property of M. Korthals," which may suggest that the Prinz had taken over Korthals' interest.

Europe has never discarded the Korthals breed, and it was interesting to see at the 1968 show in Brussels the many *Griffons d'arrêt à poil dur* that contrived to tangle leads around our legs. French-Canadians imported many to Quebec especially, and indeed the Wirehaired Pointing Griffon Club of America is currently served by a secretary resident in Ontario (Canada). The Club Bulletin rays out from there, a well-produced publication that periodically brightens my mail here.

Undoubtedly, this was the first *recognized* of European sporting utility breeds introduced into the United States. The proper breed name quickly became a catch-all designation for foreign breeds the bird-dog men could not identify. As late as 1922, A. F. Hochwald, the most distinguished Sporting dog writer of the time, gave a chapter to the Wirehaired Pointing Griffon linking the name with "varieties differing in some extent in coat and outward appearance, but all possessing practically the same characteristics. Nearly all strains are represented in this country, but they all come under the head of Wirehaired Pointing Griffons." (*Bird Dogs, Their History and Achievements*, p. 53).

As there exists now much evidence that Shorthairs were in America before Dr. Thornton brought his to Montana, one may say confidently that Hochwald would have seen such here, unregistered practical hunting dogs, brought perhaps with new settlers. The fashionable interest in the Wirehaired Pointing Griffon amazed him, not least the price paid for pups. He conceded that such dogs served hunters well enough on foot and their water-work was good,

Wirehaired Pointing Griffon, Gretel von Friedrichtal, at 12 weeks.

Gretel von Friedrichtal at 7½ months, retrieving a Chukar from the opposite side of the river.

Gretel at 9 months, a grown-up gal now, on point.—All photos by owner Tomie La Fon, Idaho.

but if a man wanted a retriever there were already Labradors and Chesapeake Bays. He and his contemporaries could not conceive an idea in terms of non-specialist dog performance. The Wirehaired Pointing Griffon was damned with faint praise, for "it would never please the man who has hunted the big open country of the south on horseback (or) the lordly prairie chicken on the wide plains" (p. 60).

Each breed of sporting utility dog as it came from Europe was subjected to the same assessment; held in like poor regard by competitive bird-dog men for lack of pace, but snatched at joyously and made supremely popular by the buying public. Many dedicated Pointer-Setter breeders switched breeds as the public approval became the plainer. But with the switch went stubborn refusal to adapt to the character of the new breed, and instead a stonewall insistence on changing the breed to the only measure by which they could assess performance. Pointer-Setter judges rode the saddles. "The Wirehaired Pointing Griffon is not suited to field trial competition," continued Hochwald (p. 60), "unless it can be improved by selection and mating to the best and fastest and most stylish of the field dogs." It is to laugh were one not the more disposed to cry. Who *wanted* the versatility bred into the European? Practical hunting men did, all skills in one dog to feed. Field trial pressure towards specialization, turning back the clock, narrowed aims, so that nowadays judges complain (in print) (*Kurzhaar Punkte,* GSHP Club of America) that many dogs under judgment do not swerve to hunt cover; pressure of whip, shot, electronic jolts in training condition them only to keep going, avoid search in likely places where birds may be, finding virtually only those they fall over or blunder into at the gallop.

Griffons were acquired by men who *wanted* a dog they could follow afoot, that would find them birds and retrieve them from land or water, men who probably shrugged indifferently when shown the Hochwald advice that they "selectively breed." In any case, how does one mongrelize a Wirehaired Pointing Griffon? The shaggy beast couldn't stand a cross of Pointer, Foxhound, Greyhound, or even Llewellin Setter, to liven him, bless his coat and whiskers! If M. Louis Thebaud and his friends and relations, who originally sponsored the Griffon (as they did later the Brittany), had *wanted* Bird Dog performance and specialist skills, they were financially in a position to acquire Bird Dogs of which, Heaven knows, there was no lack in the country. But what they wanted was what the Griffon could give, a dog to have fun with in *their* way of having fun; to follow afoot. Theirs was the right the field trial man still advances in defense against charges that he ruins breeds; he *will* have the dog that performs in the manner he wants, seeing he pays the bills. Sure, fair enough! Then why, and for decades, has he and his like so bitterly downgraded the interests of dog ownerships whose inclinations march to the beat of a different drum?

270

One unlucky strike against European imports was that American official-dom had no slot to offer for a dog that could do it all. Only now, modernly, does it become plain that provision should have been made early-on to protect the European sporting utility dog's unique qualities. Now, and belatedly along the lines of "better late than never," have come recognitions leading to suggestions for better management. But alas, now has also to be combatted the organized strength of those whose indoctrination has been only in terms of Bird Dog performance, and the spanners they heft to throw in to proposed works are very heavy. Such will hinder every proposal to re-store versatile inheritances.

Inability to mongrelize a Griffon may account for his never achieving great popularity here but he has loyal friends. The Club works to educate members in terms of work quality, soundness, rejecting dysplastics from advertising columns in the Journal, stressing coat quality that must be hard-textured, thick, short, water-repellent in terms of undercoat, advising that a soft-coated pup is not to command as good a price as a hard-textured.

Though few Griffons see the show ring, there is wide dispersal across the country, and those who favor them do so with enthusiasm. The dog still has something of his original curious appearance, a clownish suggestion, but he is no clown in his work.

Unanswerable proof that there were Shorthairs in this country long before the Thornton imports of the 1920s. This unidentified picture was picked up in an empty house in Dallas, Pennsylvania some years ago. The sole clue it offers is the name of the photographer on the back—Cobb, Binghamton, N.Y. Enquiry at the City Hall in Binghamton proved that Cobb was in business there from the 1890s to the early 1900s. The elegant quality of the dog is apparent, and one reflects that he was a near-enough contemporary of the Hoppenrades.—*Photo lent by Richard S. Johns, Pennsylvania.*

The German Shorthaired Pointer

I T has been the unvarying record of the German Shorthaired Pointer that he has gone quickly ahead in terms of public favor wherever he has been introduced. Even the insular British have conceded his qualities, and nowadays it is by no means uncommon to find in British championship shows that the Shorthair entry is larger than the Pointer—though Pointer support at such fixtures is extremely good, especially by American entry numerical standards.

Though breed historians must date their work as from the original importations of Dr. Charles Thornton of Montana in the late 1920s, many clues (including the reference made by Hochwald, as quoted in the survey of the Wirehaired Pointing Griffon), indicate that Shorthairs were here much earlier than that, family dogs perhaps, that came with settlers. Snapshots have occasionally been sent me in belief that they depicted Shorthairs of earlier vintage, but none of a quality suited to reproduction. Then Richard S. Johns (Grabenbruch) came up with one that was so suited. He tells me it was picked up in an empty house in Dallas, Pa., and brought to Dick because "he owned those kind of dogs." The people are unknown. The only identification to help date the picture was the stamp on the back: Cobb, Photographer, Binghamton, N.Y. So off to there. City Hall was nice to me, searched old directories that proved Cobb operated there, early 1890s to mid-1900s.

What a beautiful dog it is, strapping and strong. One must also remember that the period was but a couple of decades or so removed from the time of actual breed fixation. The Shorthair breed had gone through many changes before stabilizing in such a dog as this. The various stages have for the most

By the 1880s, heavy hound had yielded to elegance of streamlined construction. Hound profile and high earset remained the badge of origin. Morell Hoppenrade, a rare picture by the famous German artist, Sperling.—*Picture sent by Major and Mrs. Godsol, California.*

The Shorthair I would have liked to bring home with me from Germany. Caesar v. Bomberg, D.I.; S.I.; V.G.P.I.: J.K.P.I.; Verzuglich. A beautiful liver dog typifying the qualities sought for modernly in the breed in Germany. A prepotent, successful sire. Photographed for this book in late 1969, at age of eleven. Owner, Herr Hansjörg Huggenberg, Germany.

274

part survived to be easily identified in present-day dogs. They are in pure status importantly three; the solid liver, often tending to be on the light-substance side; the somewhat heavier, thicker-substanced that are often seen with very handsome light coloring, tick-patch; and the rangier, elegant, tick-and-patch type, often somewhat darker. A judge may be faced with all three in the show rings and, knowing all three are authentic Shorthair types, make his placings in accordance, something that gets him no credit from the gallery as a rule. That the breed also legitimately produces a tiny percentage of white-liver "Pointer-patterned" is true, but one does not see them in Germanic countries, though doubtless they crop up there in the litters, maybe become dumped at birth. Scandinavian import influence to the United States is particularly strong in "Pointerish" types.

It is not proposed in the restricted space available in this work to rehash breeding statistics already in my Shorthair breed book (*The New German Shorthaired Pointer*, N.Y., 1963–6). Rather we mean to examine gleanings gained in a year spent in Europe (1967–8) in which it was my privilege to attend all major German Shorthair trials, and to follow as well practical hunting dogs in several countries, as well as see the breed in show rings, including the 184–entry Specialty it was my privilege to judge in England (1968).

My abiding impression, carried home, was of sorrow that we ask so little of the Shorthairs competitively here in America when it is their ability to give so much. It isn't even necessary to go to Europe to find that out. In 1968, also, it was my privilege to follow, on a Scottish moor and high land, the property of Lord Ferrier, the Shorthair brace, Hie-on Clyde and Hie-on Tweed. Mr. George Richmond worked the dogs, Mr. Geoffrey Sterne, president of the German Shorthaired Pointer Club did the explaining: "We use our Shorthairs always to save our own legs. We don't propose to climb up there unless we have to. That's for the dogs. If a dog doesn't come back into sight we presume it is on point up there. *Then* we climb." That was the way it was. If Clyde went out of sight up there, didn't come back, we followed him up and there he'd be, on point! Tweed, the bitch too.

This was no territory for a mere horizon-runner, the sheer hills slashed deeply by what my hosts called a "wee burrrn!" Both dogs went at a good pace, searched all the right places, ignored all distractions, such as the large numbers of sheep spread over the landscape. Even when silly ewes jumped up in their faces, blatting to their lambs to follow, the Shorthairs gave no sign of being aware. That is the same indifference one saw in Germany, the Rhineland, where Shorthairs work between old ladies swinging hoes, tractors (men drive!) and chain-bridled, curious cows grazing free. It occurred to me in the Rhineland that this could eventually, in a shrinking America, also become a hunting pattern, using farmland, the rows of standing crops, so rich in birds. That however, must await a new generation of hunting folk, won free of fantasy and impatient of restriction of skills. These Europeans do have fun!

That same thought was lively in my mind on the Scottish moor where the dogs, thorough as they were, and fast, were yet always within control, doing the manner of work for which their breed was designed. Their work provided not only good hunting, but good gallery. Spectator interest in American Shorthair trials can be difficult at times to generate for other than owners actually with a dog working. A few dedicates hire horses and join the riding judges for many braces, but the majority of those attending tend to stay by the chuck wagon or the autos where their dogs are resting. There is no resting in crates or autos for European trial dogs. They start out early in the morning, tramp with their handlers, judges, gallery, through a multiplicity of exercises, all the livelong day. Every so often comes a dog's turn at a required exericse in performance, fur or feather, track or water retrieve. There are no planted birds. Wild ones are plentiful or scarce as the day's luck dictates. At the Internationale of 1967, at Kehl-am-Rhein, the strutting gaudy Chinese pheasant cocks were everywhere to see. In the Shorthair Derby in Austria, 1968, young dogs had a lean day, had to work hard to find their birds, imposing long tramps on judges, handlers, and gallery.

The German judges cannot be fobbed off with any skimping. Once I saw three judges tramp a field criss-cross from three directions when a dog had failed to find a bird (Kleeman trial). They raised one—and that dog was out! Post-performance critiques are devastatingly frank, of an order that would likely provoke resentment if applied here to an American dog. However, Europeans trial to have a dog assessed, learn its worth. There is no dog-against-dog competition as we know it, but against a standard of performance. A European owner wants to *know*—aspires for a mark of *Alles Vier* for his dog, four for each exercise, right across the board.

Waterwork is entirely dependent on dog initiative, skill, nose, tenacity. A strong duck is set in a flowing stream, minus his main flight feathers but otherwise unshackled. He paddles off for the opposite shore, chosen streams being always rich in bordering cover. The dog is brought when the duck is out of sight, given the scent where it was launched. It is wonderful to watch a dog working out scent on top of moving water. As the stream is flowing, he lands lower than did the duck, the scent having drifted somewhat downstream, and his job is then to find that duck and shepherd it back to the stream. His location of his quarry is always signalled by an indignant quacking and the eruption of the duck from the reeds onto the stream. The dog's task is then to work it under the eyes of the judges, swimming after, never quite able to grab it, as it paddles frantically and hooks back desperately from time to time. What the exercise demonstrates is the Shorthair's require-

All three are individually finished as Dual Champions in both Canada and U.S. They are: Arrak v. Heisterholz (German import) ; Gert's Dena v. Greif; Gert's Duro v. Greif. Deno and Duro are littermates, ex the first dog to hold the Dual title in two countries, Can. and Am. Ch. Gretchen v. Greif, a phenomnenally prepotent dam as well as a fine performer. Ralph A. Park, Sr. of Seattle, who was first president of the German Shorthaired Club of America, may also be counted unique in the ownership of four two-country Duals, a proud record indeed.

A fireball in training. German Shorthaired Pointer, Dual Ch. Al-Ru's Eric, with Richard S. Johns, Pennsylvania.

Adam, Scandinavian-bred German Shorthaired Pointer.

German Shorthaired Pointer, Ch. Adam v. Fuehrerheim, son of imported Scandinavian-bred Adam, has proved to be decisively prepotent, with many good ones to his credit. Owner, R. McKowan, Pennsylvania.

ment to find and shepherd a duck from the cover for his boss to shoot. When the judges are satisfied as to his ability to do this, the duck is shot on the water ahead of him and he brings it ashore just as he would if this had been a day out with his owner for sport. He is then put on the down. The dead duck is thrown out into deep water where he can see it, sitting quivering in eagerness the while, and at the word of command (only) he makes a spectacular spring and re-retrieves it, this part of the exercise, of course, demonstrating recovery of a shot bird. As a spectacle it is always most exciting. Handler direction is minimal, sometimes absent altogether. One young Czech handler merely stood the whole time like a statue, no word, no whistle, not even a handwave. Maybe he had established thought transference with his dog. How could one fail to admire?

The Kleeman Trial of 1968, however, did not please the German judges. They complained about the quality of the males in the conformation examination that preceded the opening of this blue-ribbon, breed-search trial that has always sought out the producing stars to carry on the breed. The bitches were better, and it was possibly in keeping with the conformation assessment that next day of seven dogs that secured the coveted K. S. (Kleeman Sieger title) five were bitches, including the beautiful Cara v. Hohenfeld, an Axel v. Wasserschling daughter that had already won my attention at the Internationale the previous autumn.

There was sustained debate in Committee, even anxiety. Where was the breed heading, and why was quality so down? My best fortune was to make the acquaintance of the vice-president and breed master, Herr Richard Kölbl, representative of the new generation taking over now from the old. He verified my belief that there was concern and dissatisfaction at what had been seen at this famous shop window of the breed. He spoke of the great dogs of the 1930s, considered now to have been the *spitz* (apex) of breeder achievement.

"No upward trend can be counted on to continue into infinity," he said. "When a specific goal is reached, then reassessment has to be made. New goals must be set." Not only dog quality of conformation and performance was being modernly revised, but also trial conduct and rule that took note of changing social and environmental factors: "We here in Germany are no longer privileged to use large hunting estates. Expanded agricultural interests have taken over much of the land. Mechanization and artificial fertilizers have increased acreage under cultivation, so now we have to recognize a changing work pattern for our dogs."

Oh, everywhere, ran my thought. Everywhere in the world!

"So, now we make new rules for our trials. The greater part of a hunting dog's work becomes important *after* the shot, rather than as it used to be, *before*. There was a time with us also when work before the shot was the

280

Up and over barbed wire. Australian Ch. Heathman of Friuli, owned by Jack Thomson of Victoria.

Austrian dog on point, 1968. (The galleryite from the picture on Page vi)Austrian and Czech dogs are still strong in ticked color inheritance.—*C. Bede Maxwell.*

all-important, but now, while no reduction in the *quality* of search and pointing is made, a dog must also be able to cope in best style with post-shot requirements of location and recovery of downed game, land and water, and of course with us the tracking of touched deer or stag, or the recovery of portable fur or feather in stylish retrieving over long distances."

Trial rules were revised in 1968, adjustment to modern conditions. The change affects not only the assessment of performance, but strikes to the very core of producing a dog suited to the work: "Even the best heart and will do not take a dog to the top in performance if it suffers serious fault and bodily imbalance," Herr Kölbl pointed out. "We demand conformation qualities not merely in pursuit of some show ring ideals, but because we understand that Working Ability without Form is as useless as Form without Working Ability."

The German breeders are greatly concerned to rid their breed of a multiplicity of what I have always called Minnie-Mouse Shorthairs, the little boneless degenerates that proliferate also in the United States as field prospects. The Germans have been engaged in ridding themselves of such for quite a while, and the sad truth is that many have come over to America. A Shorthair that cannot gain a rating in conformation in Germany is not permitted to compete in the trials. So, what to do with it? In some cases when the choice has been between shooting it and selling it to the Americans, where would one guess it went? The pity of that is often that because it has in the United States the status of *imported,* many believe that is the type the Germans favor. It is not always understood that what the substanceless creature actually is, is a discard. Herr Kölbl had observations along those lines too: "In our tough requirements a dog may be asked to retrieve weights of from 10 to 20 lbs, and over long distances. Neither the undersized nor the oversized sluggish is suited. So, we make our plans for the future in clear understanding that without this utility-serving conformation there can be no outstanding performance. Too many of our best dogs are privately employed with hunters and foresters, and too many less well suited are being used for breeding. Recent competitive occasions here in Germany prove to us need for a change. We all aspire to the so-called 'fine-celled' elegant, medium-sized dog, but we have alas at present too many of a size approaching too closely the lower reaches of the permissible."

These the German breeders are screening out as fast as they can.

The modern German concern to rid a hunting dog breed of substanceless stock, bitches especially, is nothing new under the sun. Four hundred years ago already George Turberville was expounding a like advice which far too many modern breeders still merrily ignore, though the truth of it has been proved over and over since Turberville's time to this: "If you would have a faire Hound you must first have a faire Bitch, which is of a good kind, strong

Dramatic and unusual on-point! German Shorthaired Pointer, Ch. Wildburg's Point-riever. Owner, A. Hamilton Rowan, Jr., New York.

and well-proportioned in all parts, having her ribs and flanks great and large." (*The Noble Art of Venerie of Hunting*, London, 1576.)

The inadequate bitch represents the quicksand into which so many sporting breeds and strains have within this last century disappeared, leaving no trace.

Turberville, good dog man that he was, and of his time, was also of his time enough to be steeped in superstitions. If such included astrology we may indulge him for many moderns share his interest. Discussing the mechanics of breeding, he recommended the "concoction boiled of the flies called Cantharides to make her go proud and to the dog to make him go delirious; afterwards, when you feel your bitch goeth proud, attend the full of the moon till it be passed, and then cause her to be lyned, if it may be, under the signs of Gemini and Aquarius, a recommend to escape madness and get more dogs than bitches. Do not take her hunting when she begins to show because the forces used in hunting do marre and keep from prospering the little Whelpes when in theyre Bellies."

Herr Kölbl cautioned, "There should always be realistic assessment of breeding stock in one's own kennel, as well as acceptance of the truth that other owners have good dogs too. But the other extreme should be avoided— the belief that whatever is novel, or from the outside, is necessarily better."

That there is a warning for would-be importers in the foregoing is difficult to doubt. There is always, everywhere, a peril in buying dogs sight unseen— even from the next county, let along another country.

Herr Kölbl also examined the commonly-held American belief that the Germans will not sell their best dogs: "Such do not often leave the country because they are not a cheap commodity, even in their homeland being much less abundant than we could wish. Even among ourselves such dogs bring high prices. D.M. 4–5000 ($1000–$1250) is not at all uncommon."

There are however still Americans who hope best European dogs can be bought for pennies. Dr. Julius Duy, of Austria, who owns famous old K. S. Blitz v. Ovilava, Austrian Sieger of 1961, pictured p. 208 of my *New German Shorthaired Pointer* book, showed me in 1968 a letter he had received from a Midwestern Shorthair breeder who offered to buy old Blitz (then 10) for $200 and a percentage of the stud fees he would earn! This set me to wondering what manner of "deal" had been offered in hope to secure the famous Axel v. Wasserschling in *his* extreme old age, this time involving different breeder interests. That deal fortunately fell through, while Dr. Duy had of course ignored the rich proposition made him. Blitz is very much beloved, a personal dog. Nothing revolts a thoughtful person more than attempts to buy an old producing animal at the end of its days, usually on the cheap, and seldom for other than frank exploitation. Some years ago, after having shown my Australian champion Pointer bitch, aged 9, at San Francisco, Golden

Seydel's Vera working out the duck trail *on top of the water*. She finished that day (the Solms Field Trial of 1967) with a First. Owner, Frau Maria Seydel, Recklinghausen-Sud.—*C. Bede Maxwell*.

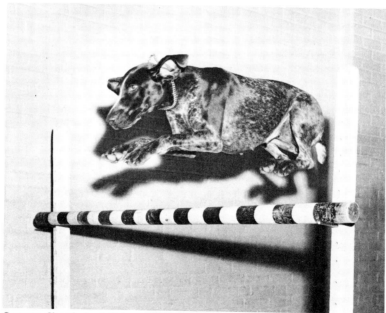

German Shorthaired Pointer, Can. and Am. Ch. Kaposia's Apache Maiden, U.D.; Can. C.D. Owners, Mr. and Mrs. Marvin Davis, Minnesota.

285

Gate show, merely for "kicks," a letter followed me home, a bid to buy her "to start a Pointer kennel" by a gentleman who wrote he "couldn't pay much for her, he was only on Social Security." As I was then living in Oregon he didn't expect me to recognize his name, that of a famed, wealthy, San Franciscan restauranteur. The letter is still in my file!

Herr Kölbl regrets no automatic control operates in dogs as in domestic livestock, where unworthy stock goes to the butcher. I too once made this observation to a friend who sighed: "But a bull doesn't sleep on the foot of your bed!" "For us remains only the harder way of resolute continued selection, using only our best," said the German breed master in conclusion. But, of course, selective control *is* exercised in Germany through the trials. A dog lacking a good trial record has slight hope at stud. If he cannot first pass in conformation he is not permitted to run in trials.

Axel v. Wasserschling's influence as a stud has been so overwhelming the past decade in Germany that breeders now must seek what *Axel-frei* (free of Axel) blood they can find. Americans with modern imports boasting Axel blood might reflect that this is the easiest blood of all to acquire. What of value and performance that is *not* Axel is now at a premium in that country, of highest value because of its scarcity.

That the 1969 National Shorthair Champion in America, Fld. Ch. Blick v. Shinbeck, combines Axel blood with that of the prepotent Austrian import, American Fld. Ch. Greif v. Hundsheimerkogl, is very interesting. He is by an Axel imported son ex a Greif granddaughter. Greif's influence, prepotency exerted still more than a decade after his death, justifies his continued place of honor in the frontispiece of my breed book. His blood has strong mortgage on the National. 1965/67/68 National champions were all his grandget, through his son, Fld Ch. Von Thalberg's Fritz II. Others of the family (Von Bess) have filled placings in that event. The 1969 National Field Champion, by imported Esser's Chick, an Axel son, is out of the same line, through a dam who was ex Patti v. Greif, a daughter of old Fritz and that famous first Can. Am. Dual Ch. Gretchen v. Greif that has topped the bitch producing records in the breed.

It pleases me to know personally all these dogs. Esser's Chick has shown under me. Axel v. Wasserschling has posed and visited with me at his home in Germany. Old Greif hunted for me in California, to show me how good he still was at age 12. My color slides of him, taken on the day, are historically unique. His son, Fld. Ch. Von. Thalberg's Fritz II, has oozed charm while panhandling chocolate doughnuts from me for years. Patti v. Greif liked to sleep, head in my lap, when I visited the Ralph Park home in Seattle. Dual Ch. Gretchen was "Sandy" we all loved, and rounding Hundsheimerkogl association, Blitz v. Ovilava being age 12 in 1968, worked for me in Austria,

Puppy appeal.—*Photo, P. Carl Tuttle, Virginia.*

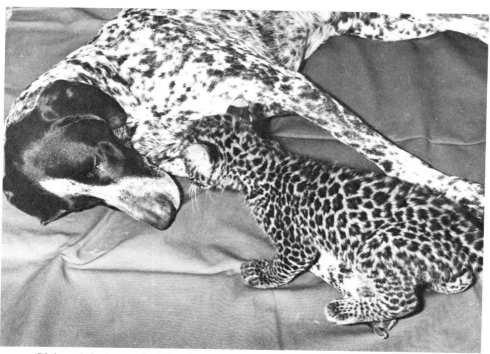

Pixie and the Leopard cublet. Owner, Dr. Charles Gandal, New York.—*V. Martine.*

An all-time record, not only in German Shorthairs, but in any breed! Ch. Gretchenhof Cinnabar, C.D.X. (litter sister to famous Ch. Gretchenhof Moonshine), extreme right, musters her children: (l. to r.) Jillian of Klarbruk, U.D.T., has field points (spayed, not eligible to show); Dual Ch. Frei of Klarbruk, U.D.T.; Ch. Heide of Klarbruk, U.D.T., has field points; and Ch. Neckar v.d. Klarbruk, U.D.T. (Absent from the muster, Ch. Moonshine Sally of Runnymede.) Ch. Neckar's sire was a son of imported K.S. Ulk v.d. Radbach. The other four are littermates, sired by Dual Ch. Kay v.d. Wildburg, also a German import. Owners, Julia and Joe France, of Maryland.

lakeside and in the woods, every imaginable exercise from water-retrieving to the difficult-to-teach *Todverbeller* (baying the dead.)

Reading is fine. Pictures are better. Personal contact is best of all.

Czech influence is strong in Austrian Shorthairs, and this may well be the strength in the Hundsheimerkogl inheritance; old Greif had a Czech sire, and Blitz v. Ovilava comes through the same Hundsheimerkogl strain. Very recently, Dr. F. Byhain, of Nuremberg, the pleasant president of Klub Kurzhaar, returned from a Czech visit, and praised again the Shorthairs he saw, remarking how free were the Czechs of the lack-substance rubbish currently plaguing the Germans.

It should not be held that Shorthairs in Germany are all Axel, even if most of them seem to be. There are other good dogs. To name just a few, Herr Kölbl draws his Donaria strain from K. S. Arco v. Niestetal blood. The dog that made most appeal to me in Germany, Caesar v. Bomberg, 1085, I/59, D. I.; S. I.; m.s. saw his get virtually dominate Solms competition in 1969. He stems from the same K.S. Kobold Mauderode-Westerholt family that provided so much good blood to American lines in the peak period of the breed in Germany, the 1930s.

It may well be that the time will come when breeders here have to be as realistic in assessing the productive worth of their dogs as the Germans must be. If the shrinkage of terrain and increasing urbanization impose changes, as who will dare predict they may not; if American rules should swap over to emphasis on post-shot instead of as now on pre-shot performance, revision will have to be drastic. This could revolutionize not only training practice but also breeding practice. The dog that is scared to stop long enough to search cover could become an anachronism, and judges be spared the need to climb down from the saddle complaining that dogs could find only the birds they fell over. Such prevailing state of affairs that disgraces so many trials was defined by an experienced American judge: "In an Open All Age Stake, which is about the easiest to win, a dog needs only to find a bird and handle it properly. More All-Age placements seem to be withheld in my (Midwest) area than any other." (*Kurzhaar Punkte,* the publication of the German Shorthaired Pointer Club of America, 1969).

To scan the reports of the trials in *Purebred Dogs, The American Kennel Gazette,* official AKC publication, is to be regularly shocked by the multiplicity of placings withheld. Either the dogs fail to match Stake requirements or Stakes are unsuitably geared to the instincts of the dogs. Either alternative calls for thoughtful, practical breeder and governing body concern. American Kennel Club thoughts steadily crystallize. An official there has written me that: "The special requirements for certain breeds invariably raise the question of the quality or extent of performance required for a Field Championship in these breeds. We believe the new policy should remove the tempta-

English Sh. Ch. Patrick of Malahide, a beautiful specimen, made German Shorthair history in England. Following Crufts BOB wins in successive years, he took the Group at that famous show in 1968. Owner, Miss A. M. Ward, Warwickshire.—*Sally Anne Thompson.*

Hie-On Clyde, Scottish owned, is a successful trial competitor, and regularly shot over for grouse, pheasant, and wild duck. When this picture was taken he was starting his fifth shooting season. The British, of course, like the Germans, use the German Shorthaired Pointer extensively in water work. Owner, George Richmond.—Photo, *Cheshire Life.*

Eng. Field Ch. Littlestat Barker, first Shorthair to gain the field title in England. Owner, Geoffrey Sterne, Cumberland. Breeder, Brian Mottram.—*By courtesy of Cheshire Life.*

tion to produce dogs of a particular breed that will perform in a manner for which the breed was not intended."

There are of course many American trainers who understand thoroughly the Shorthair abilities and who can turn out practical hunting dogs that would please the most carping critic. It was a comfort to me, returned from Europe, to be able to go out on the hill slopes with Dick Johns, in Pennsylvania, watching his dogs work wild unshackled game released from his "return pens," free-flying as against the sickening artificiality of too many trials and training procedures of dizzied, half-dead miseries, poked under straw with their legs shackled so they cannot run. Dick stirs out perhaps a dozen birds from a pen, and leaves a dozen behind to call the free ones home later in the day. The dogs work these under completely natural conditions. Dick says his pen-reareds get smart after a while. "Then I take them up the mountain and let them go to rear me wilder ones, and put fresh batches in the pens."

Many (the best!) trainers follow a like procedure, but then come the trials in which they are stuck to work on the dizzied miseries under those heaps of straw in the bird field. A wise dog can come to take little interest in such. Reminds me of a fine practical hunting Wirehaired Pointing Griffon, sent in a trial to retrieve a duck that had been shackled and had its beak taped shut. He'd had a hundred ducks naturally shot over him. He swam out, looked at the taped number and just turned round and swam again. Some like assessment may motivate some Shorthairs set down to work on planted game.

It is also the height of owner folly to believe a Shorthair can be bred or flogged into matching Big-Circuit Pointer pace. Even cross-breeding won't do it. Cross the Kentucky Derby winner with a best Morgan mare and you'll never see the rose-wreath draped around the neck of their produce. Dozens of Shorthair owners have boasted to me that their dogs "have run against and beaten the Pointers." It has to be asked what quality of Pointers? No Shorthair born could live with a magnificent top-ranking American Big-Circuit Pointer star nor should it be asked to try. One doubts that the infusion of Pointer blood in trial stock in Shorthairs could produce dogs that could run a three-hour course, either. Many moderns fold in less than an hour!

If show folk feel that they have been neglected in this discussion, please accept my assurance that no neglect is intended. Merely space pressure within a book examining so many breeds enforces emphasis on subjects not usually aired elsewhere. Show dogs have much space in my breed book, where credit is given to the many greats in the breed that followed the winning of their show titles by going out in middle life and gaining the field points to become Duals. The likely envious, unable to duplicate the honor, tend to harp on the matter of points won only in Gundog Stakes. So? The Shorthair *is* a

"And now Asta will know better than to trouble a swan again!"—Dr. Julius Duy, Wels, Austria, 1968.—*C. Bede Maxwell.*

Gundog. It is what he was blue-printed to become as from the first, and it is what he remains wherever his purebred status is preserved. Hybrid vigor has carried some bastardized strains to temporary fame, but cross-breeding historically runs out of steam in a few generations. That is the oldest story in field trial breeding in America—and not only in Shorthairs.

Rudolf Freis (*Unsere Jagdhunde,* Germany, 1960) writes: "After every cross-breeding to alien blood follows a long hard selection, often in no relation to the benefit, for it costs much in time, work, money" (p. 83).

Those who over the years launched themselves recklessly into "selective breeding" have invariably bowed out when it became a matter of time, work, money. They left better-motivated breeders to try to cope with the mess inherited. American breeders of German Shorthairs will be screening out those little substanceless nothings yet for many a year to come.

The "hunting dog" book writers and journalists that spend so much type sniping at the show dogs have much to learn—if they cared to look. Apart from well-proportioned, true-type show dogs that can go out and take training and secure their Dual titles, there comes to mind the results of the work and enterprise of two remarkable people of Maryland, Julia and Joseph France. Elsewhere in this work is pictured their distinguished show-bred Shorthair with her remarkably performed progeny that stem also from the best of imported German studs. Joe and Julie bred their dogs, trained, showed, handled them all in show, field, obedience. Four U.D.T.s, all but one a show champion, and all but one with Field points, and one even a Dual!

The Shorthair is a dog with which an owner can expect to have *sport.* The ingrained versatility is remarkable. What an owner requires of his dog it is genetically endowed to provide. The trouble arises when some owners, with or without the approval of their trainers, dedicate themselves to forcing the breed to work in ways towards which its instincts do not direct it. A Shorthair is a good water dog, but not specifically a good *coursing-run* dog. His nature is cautious and his instincts are to *find* game, not to race it by on his way to the next county. When pressure is put upon him to go against his instincts it comes into collision with yet another deeply ingrained instinct—to please the wishes of his master.

As one surveys at times sadly the American competitive scene that has always been content to barter all else for the historically-proved destroying ideal of mere run, one cannot avoid reflecting again the example provided by the subsequent fortunes of the Irish and the Llewellin Setters. For the promotion of personal comfort and faith in belief that the Shorthair will long endure *as a breed* one remembers that when the Irish Setter was discarded by field trial interests for lack of pace and the "show people" inherited him, these latter preserved to the world what has to be recognized as a consistently approved public favorite. Moving about the country—including among other

The most famous German Shorthaired Pointer stud in modern German breeding, Axel v. Wasserschling. Photographed in his 10th year, at his home kennel, Dortmund, Germany, 1968.—*C. Bede Maxwell*.

A classic Shorthair head from the photofiles of Frau Maria Seydel (Germany).

294

opportunities the personal judging of (to date) five Specialties in this breed—
it is clear that breeders of Shorthairs *are* preserving the elegant, intelligent,
true-type. There will, one feels confident, always *be* Shorthairs when the last
off-type horizon-runner has joined the Llewellin Setters in a turned-down
page of history.

Never know who you might find watching the judging of GSHPs! At Pebble Beach, California.
—*C. Bede Maxwell.*

"Been duckhunting, I see, boss. When do I get to go?" Four-months-old WHP puppy, owned by Robert Knutson, Wisconsin.

German Wirehaired Pointer puppy at play.

The German Wirehaired Pointer

THE German Wirehaired Pointer was the last formed of the Germanic sporting utility breeds. His type in his homeland is still considerably in state of flux. That one sees perhaps a greater type consistency in some other countries may be consequent on the fact that in such countries numbers are smaller, and often represent the produce of a far narrower breed pool, built perhaps on a comparatively few founding imports. In Germany, where the numerical strength tops that of all the other popular sporting breeds, type is most widely variant. It has been said that the Scandinavian countries produce a greater uniformity, and indeed there are those to claim that the Wirehaired Pointers of this part of the world are the best there are. It may however still be true that uniformity aim is helped by lesser numbers to deal with.

The Germans have for a long time measured their Deutsch-Draathaar by the classic application, Through Performance to Type. They concede the differences in the appearances of their dogs, but point to the uniformity of a magnificent work pattern.

In first delving into the interest for this book, type diversity seen right here in the United States really bothered me. Thus it was possible to find even in some single kennels dogs differing as from hairy Griffon-like types to smooth-coateds with Shorthair suggestion and long narrow, pointed heads. So, as is my regular habit when important questions are for asking, the way taken was right to the top. My good friend, Herr Richard Kölbl, put me in touch with the breed master of the Deutsch-Draathaar Klub, Germany—Herr George Greller, of Veitsbron.

"It is not naturally true that our Deutsch-Draathaar are purebreds," wrote Herr Greller. "Nor do we claim that type has been preserved as from some ancient time. Breeder aim has always been concerned primarily with the production of a good utility hunting dog, a first-class performer, land or water. Our dog has also to be sharp. It has to be a good tracker enough to lead an owner to wounded game so the miseries of creatures can be relieved. It has to be able and strong to carry anything of a size a dog could possibly carry.

"Within reason, no one will expect to find spontaneously all such characteristics in a one breed. Many breeds had to be drawn upon to make our Draathaar. It is further clear that such characteristics will differ in respect of local emphasis. Thus, in one area, waterwork is the main consideration. In another it is birdwork. A breeder makes his plans, mates his dogs, to serve his own requirements. This may produce different appearances in the dog, performance being the first consideration."

This must read as reasonable in America. It is what the field trial people have held for decades. The difference however lies in the circumstance that while the European breeder breeds for performance, he never dodges the fact that the essentials of size and soundness must also be preserved. The American field trialler too often announces: "I don't care what he looks like, as long as he runs!" And in the long haul pays the penalty . . .

Herr Greller insists that while appearance can vary, basic type in terms of soundness and size is never lost sight of: "As a breed organization we promote trials and conformation assessments. We check carefully for minimum requirements of body and coat, and dogs not conforming are not permitted breeding privileges. Basic type is thus preserved while we continue to pursue the aim towards the ideal."

The breed Standard in Germany has been revised as of February 1969, and the Klub feels it provides a base sufficiently broad. Herr Greller suggests Herr Mersmann's dog, Cent v.d. Eifalhöhe, DD 59543, wh. 1965, represents the type sought: "However, recognition of an ideal does not debar reappearance of factors within the inheritance drawn from the differing breeds of the original formation. We do not hold this a tragedy. Merely, we exclude nonconforming dogs from our breeding program. We feel that in using the best blood available to us, retaining our ideal of Through Performance to Type, we provide our Draathaar with sound conformation and good coat, the indispensable utility needs" (*Letter to me*, May 20, 1969).

It is no secret to American breeders of the Wirehaired Pointer that type can vary. Mrs. Louis Faestal of the Haar Baron strain of Wisconsin writes: "When we have used German studs, if there were 8 puppies, all would look as if they had come from different litters. Always they were good, sound, healthy, strong, but color range could be from roan to tick to liver. Coat

German Wirehaired Pointer, Cent v.d. Eifalhöhe (Germany) D.D. 59543, wh. 1965. Club opinion in Germany describes this dog as the model toward which the breed modernly aspires. Photo sent by Herr Udo Mersmann, Birkenfeld/ Nahe.

German Wirehaired Pointer, Fieldways Peder, by Int. Dual Ch. Karr (Sweden) ex Ch. Fieldway Magdalena. Breeder, J. Farnstrom. Owner, James Koeniger, New Jersey.

German Wirehaired Pointer, Ch. Jennum's Riss, a Scandinavian import, pictured at 8 months. Took First in Group from puppy class at a California show. The win was disallowed as she should have been shown in Open, but there it *was!* A magnificent bitch. Owner, Robert Cockcroft, California.—*C. Bede Maxwell.*

texture could be from long to short (as in a Shorthair) and lack whisker," Mrs. Faestal added that her theory had always been that it was because the females had not been of comparable line. Breed type variation represents a fresh thought!

Variation in litter types disturbs knowledgeable breeders in any breed. That Haar Baron has had this problem matches with the remarks of Herr Greller. Haar Baron has produced dogs that do not always look alike, but that have honored the strain with several magnificently-performed Dual Champions, all homebred. Whatever his specific type, a well-bred Wirehaired Pointer can be usually counted as a sound, capable hunting dog, and it is not seldom one comes upon such with a construction much to be admired.

The indispensable characteristic is the coat. A Wirehair is a *Wirehair!* "Breed as you like, *but breed Wirehairs!*" wrote another German authority, (Gorny: *Ein Hundebuch*) not so long ago. It might also here be mentioned that coat in this breed is not necessarily to be judged in terms of glamor, overdressed presentation. It is at least possible that some judicial leanings shown for some Wirehaired Pointers with coats coaxed and barbered to shapings and luxuriances way out of normal for the breed has contributed to the discouragement of other would-be exhibitors with dogs equally as good, as sound, but not blessed with the extra endowment that is, in any case, not required.

Mrs. Bengt Farnstrom, of New Jersey, with wide experience in the breed, tells me she believes the Scandinavians have the best Wirehaired Pointers, a circumstance it has not been possible for me to check in those countries. But beyond doubt, the best dog in this breed ever to come under my notice was a Scandinavian import, first seen as an 8-months pup on the bench at Oakland, California a few years ago. This was (later) Ch. Jennum's Riss, perhaps the best-engineered Sporting dog of my experience. The picture she posed that day is still one I use to depict for lecture audiences the epitome of front-end excellence. That this is not my lonely opinion is emphasized by the fact that a little later, from Puppy Class, she took a Group I in California. The win was subsequently disallowed as her entry should have been in Open, as an import. The lapse from legality took away her win, but not the proud circumstance that a widely experienced judge sent her up to the honor. Riss was a hunting dog, seldom shown, sparsely bred. I am acquainted with a daughter of hers every whit as worthy that had been spayed in puppyhood, a family dog. Riss could have been improved by a darker eye but quibbling had to stop right there.

The German Klub was formed as late as 1902, with an original Stud Book entry of four. By 1966 it had become Germany's strongest hunting dog organization with a membership of 3500. Stud Book control aims towards standardization, limiting entry to dogs with desired coat texture, color, and with work abilities and character. Height is strictly regulated, dogs not to be under 58 cm (approximately 23″), bitches not under 56 cm (approximately 22″). As with the Shorthair Klub in Germany, the Wirehair folk also realize that changing modes of life impose changing fashions in hunting. They too now have moved the emphasis from work *before* to work *after* the shot (See Shorthair Chapter).

The rule that limits the use of a stud to no more than six bitches a year will surely astonish some ownerships here. The intention is to guard against breed-swamping by any single dog, a problem acutely troubling Shorthair interests in Germany of late years, and in many breeds not unknown here.

Differences as between the 1969 German Standard and the 1959 American are minimal. A major difference is that Germany allows black-ticked (as also in the Shorthair). It asks for oval feet while the American asks for round, and there is no mention of webbing. Much emphasis is placed on tail character, to be "set-on in line with the back, straight carriage, or *very slightly* raised, never straight up; of substance not too thick, and docked in the interest of work." An interesting comparison is that the American Standard concerns itself only with length of dockage (two-thirds) and omits all reference to carriage. Handlers of Wirehaired Pointers however do in the main pose dogs with straight-out tails, correctly.

Coat, Characteristics, and Head get most Germanic attention. Coat shall be hard and wiry, close and thick, thickly under-jacketed, with good eyebrows and a hard-textured beard. Outline must not be hidden by hair. Characteristics are desired in terms of temperament, cheerful, energetic, an intelligent expression. Heads are described as in the American apart from ear, which the Germans ask for as broad, the Americans as "not too broad." Colors are from dark to mid-brown, light-ticked, black-ticked, with or without patches. That the Germans allow black-tick suggests that an American breeding from German import stock may possibly be surprised by such a pup in a litter, a meeting of recessives. Same in Shorthairs. The Shorthair breeder, however, runs the greater risk in proportion to how much under-the-counter American Pointer blood may be in the background of his stock. The Wirehair is doubtless protected from this risk as Pointer incross would play havoc visibly in more ways than one with a Wirehair! Movement is defined in the German (but not the American) Standard, asked to be strong, reachy, fluid, balanced, qualities one should be able to take for granted in a good Sporting dog in any case.

American Kennel Club recognition was given this breed only in 1959. Dispersal is wide, numbers still modest. 1970, 420 were registered. The ownership appears to have an appreciation of the worth of the utility qualities. A 95% vote was returned recently in favor of including a Water Test to

Cliff and Louise Faestal of Wisconsin handling, respectively, Haar Baron's Gremlin Too and Haar Baron's Big Ben, WB and WD at a German Wirehaired Pointer Specialty. The breed is heavily indebted to the energy and enterprise of these owners.—*Frank*.

Ch. Rusty v. Schnellberg, German Wirehaired Pointer of striking breed quality and proper presentation of unexaggerated, tough-textured jacket. Third of the breed to win a Best in Show, and compiling an exciting record, multiple BIS and Group placings. Judge, C. Y. Smith. Owners: David and Patsy Hillstead, Michigan. —*Ritter*.

303

make a Field Champion under AKC rule. Dual Champions counted to seven at this time of compilation, most of them descended from Dual Ch. Haar Baron's Gremlin owned by the Faestals, "Gremmie" their beloved, whelped 1952. Her matings to Herr Schmardt v. Fox River was a matter of propinquity but led directly to Dual Ch. Strauss' Melody; Dual & National Ch. Haar Baron's Tina, C.D.; Dual Ch. Haar Baron's Hans. Dual Ch. Haar Baron's Gretchen was by a Danish import, Zep of Odensee, but also ex Gremmie. Dual Ch. Herr Schmardt's Boy Yancy (finished 1969) is by Fld. Ch. Haar Baron's Mike (Herr Schmardt/Gremmie). The Dual outside this pattern is a German import, Dual Ch. Quandu v. Elbmarsch (Barry v. Annanhof ex Lassi v.d. Elbmarsch).

Haar Baron's Mike was another good dog whose leg injury kept him from the show ring and the Dual, but on "three legs" he won the National German Pointing Dog Championship of 1959, and *Sports Afield* honored him in 1960, the first of his breed to receive the distinction.

The show champion list as kindly provided for me by the generously co-operative club officers is so long as to astonish one, considering how recent is AKC recognition and how seldom one seems to see Wirehaired Pointers in the rings. It is impossible to name them, it taking all the leverage one can exert to squeeze in the Duals. This, however, is not intended to be an owner-identifying work; such statistics are proper to the breed definitive books. One ownership name does however leap at me by name, that of Mr. Erik Bergishagen (Jagersbo) of Michigan, a strain name famous in English Setter history by way of great dogs imported by Erik's father, all from Scandinavia.

Other lands seem as yet unaware of the virtues of a good Wirehair. The English Kennel Club recognizes the breed, but none appeared within my sight there, nor in Australasia.

Front end exposure. Amazingly, all of these fronts belong to dogs with big winning records!

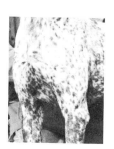

305

The Pudelpointer

W HEN Altmeister v. Zedlitz formed the aim to make an experimental crossing of Poodle with Pointer, Kaiser Friedrich II lent his best English Pointer, Tell, for use with the black poodle, Molly, owned by a forester, Walter zu Wolfsburg bei Goldberg. The cross was not as radical as might modernly seem, for Poodles and Pointers share a very similar body proportioning and anatomical construction. The first litter included many wild ones and wide color differences. By 1897, however, with von Zedlitz president of the new-formed Pudelpointer Club, breed control was instituted. More Pointer was needed, and was added until the Pudelpointer stood at about three-quarter Pointer to one of Poodle. No further Poodle was ever introduced after that first cross. More Pointer could be added only by club permission, and then followed a three-generation wait before the eventual stock could be registered, and even then only when the parents, having been first approved, produced stock that could qualify in working trials.

Such careful control must read as a very slow-poke progression, waiting out the generations, to dedicates of "selective" experimental field trial breedings conducted with joyous freedom and elasticity of conscience in respect to what goes on the papers for registration. In such light-hearted experimentation, as we and those who went before us have seen, the way forward is in terms of downs rather than ups, and accounts for the disappearance of strains, of breeds even.

Pudelpointers are not numerous in Germany but are exceptionally good as careful control of a strong club ensures. They are medium-sized, squarish built, favor Pointer outline, but carry a hard-textured black or dark-brown

306

coat. Eyebrows are important, giving breed character. Ears, medium-sized, must be fine, well-covered, pointed not round, thereby emphasizing absence of hound influence in the breed. A loose eyelid denies a dog to the Stud Book. Registration is postponed until hair quality can be assessed, that is at three months old. A breeder delaying to register his Pudelpointer until age four months has to pay double. No compromise operates in respect of temperament which is lively but balanced—no kooks! Strength in one respect is not allowed to balance weakness in another: "This only drives undesirable characteristics underground to the hurt of future generations. Only he who uses the best stock need expect success. He who uses faulty stock disgraces his breed, ruins what earlier breeders have handed down to him" (*Pudelpointer Verein Breed Book,* 1960) .

If one could only sell that direction as widely as need be!

Kleinermünsterländer, Fee vom Westfalanland, ZB
21474, DGStb 13445. Breeder-owner-handler, Helmut
Chilla, Dorsten.

Kleinermünsterländer, Frey vom Westfalenland, wh. 1963, ZB 21469, DGStb–
14007. Owner, G. Ries, Kirchhellen.

The Longhaired German Sporting Utility Breeds

VIRTUALLY unknown outside their German homeland, four interesting sporting utility breeds must have mention here. Two suggest Setter type, but are not Setters—the *Deutsch-Langhaar* (German Longhair) and the *Grosser Schwarzweisser Münsterländer* (the Big Black-White Münsterländer). Two suggest Spaniels but are not Spaniels, the *Kleiner Münsterländer* and the *Wachtelhund*. The former may suggest to casual observers an English Springer with too light a foreface and an uncut tail. He is NOT a Springer. The Wachtelhund may suggest a Cocker Spaniel in an unusual brown color. He is not a Cocker Spaniel, likely owes most to inheritance from hound.

The German Longhair and the little Münsterländer are recognized by the English Kennel Club, although without the privilege of Challenge Certificates, a classification loosely to compare with the AKC Miscellaneous.

Brittany historians have always been interested in the two smaller breeds and feel there could have been linkage with the Little Münsterländer especially. Maybe—for the area (*Westfalen*) where this breed developed was at one time subject to France, ruled over by Jerome Napoleon—"hunt happy King Lustig," as he was locally called. The "Frenchiness" may be best expressed in the characteristic head (somewhat wedge-shaped, light-muzzled, ski-slope stop), they all seem to have.

The Longhair is tall and elegant, has the short high (French) ear and also such a lightish foreface as one sees in the representations of medieval

Grosser Schwarzweisser Münsterländer (large black-white Münsterländer), Westmark's Ulex, owned by Dr. Pelz, Marl-Ruls. If this dog doesn't look right by English Setter standards, that's how it should be—he isn't an English Setter. His background is predominantly hound, as a breed, and his skill in water work is considerable. His debt is likeliest most strongly to the blue Gascon hound of France.

Grosser Schwarzweisser Münsterländer. Herr A. E. Westmark, of Recklinghausen (Westf.) is a noted breeder of this distinctively German breed.

310

falconers' dogs. He is a very ancient breed, a hound by suggestion of surviving documentation. The Big Black-White will not please Setter fans that see it for the first time, for they will likely consider it merely an off-type Setter. In fact, the blue-tick-patch (beltonish) pattern seems to have reached it via the spectacular blue-ticked hounds of France. It is just one more of the several dog breeds of this world that merit assessment by what they are rather than by careless cramming within a frame of reference that does not apply to them (as Belgian Sheepdogs, sometimes faulted in the United States by German Shepherd Dog standards, are by no means the only example). It is versatile in performance, a good tracker, and proud of a magnificent hound voice. My luck was that the current best of the breed in Germany lived handily to my then-hostess, Frau Maria Seydel, at Recklinghausen-Süd, an interesting city where tourists don't seem to penetrate. The breeder, Herr Westmark, had a long association and success with his Black-Whites.

The Little Münsterländer, of the four, most consistently increases his popularity. His flat, handsome brown-white (our liver-white) jacketing is preferred free of ticking, which is held throwback to Longhair cross. The undocked tail is a handsome plume on so small a dog.

Rudolf Freis concedes cross-breeding in this breed, adds: "these things do not matter in making new breeds provided they are properly and honorably done." Germany can make provision for honorable, but not for furtive, boostings when needed.

A beautiful Little Münsterländer, with his owner, Herr Helmut Chilla, attended the private duck hunt Frau Maria Seydel promoted on her private preserve for my instruction in 1967. He worked very well in water, getting up ducks out of the reeds, retrieving the downed in competition with the many Shorthairs. Most people would like the breed, but how to establish it here where it would be confused with Springers, as the Black-White would be confused with Setters, and both would be penalized for not matching Standards that are in any case alien to their own?

The Wachtelhund continued to elude me, though one or two were met with on leads in cities. Freis describes this as the ideal dog for the owner who wishes to keep a hunting dog but has neither space nor food for a big one. He classifies it as a *Stöberhund*, which translates near enough to "flushing dog." All the German long-haired sporting breeds, large or small, can however fulfill all hunting chores, just as can their opposite numbers in other breeds, this being the universal European requirement.

Ch. Debreceny Dezso (Herzog Schloss Loosdorf ex Ch. Bess v. Debretsin), Vizsla Club of America National Specialty winner, 1968. Owner, Gary Carpenter, California.—*Ludwig.*

Vizsla, Ch. Akil v. Debretsin, owned by Mrs. W. Crawford, California.—*C. Bede Maxwell.*

Ch. Bolen's Geza Bell (Fld. Ch. Ripp Barat ex Bolen's Athena), Best of Opposite Sex at Vizsla Club of America National Specialty, 1968. Owner, Mrs. Connie Johnson, Nevada.

312

The Vizsla

INTENTION to examine the background of the beautiful golden Pointer of Hungary, the Vizsla, founders on the rocks that wait for researchers—The Passage of Time, Language, Geography, Political Considerations, Hazards of War and Occupation, Inaccessibility of Records, Lack of Mention in Literature or Depicting in Art. Even the Hungarian-born have their troubles. Bela Hadik, Hungarian-born American Vizsla breeder writes: "No one knows for certain how the breed developed."

Perhaps the color is that of Canis Aureus, the Golden Jackal. The Yellow Turkish Hunting dog, often mentioned in Vizsla history, must have stemmed from mid-East influences. Certainly yellow-reds are linked with many breeds anciently out of this area. Rudolf Freis (*Unsere Jagdhunde,* 1960) who sees the Hungarian Pointer as influenced by the Turkish, finds himself unable to establish what the Turkish may have been. Did it cross Asia after the fall of the ancient Chinese empire, the dog to serve the falcons carried out of the east by migratory tribesmen?

Some breed authorities mention the existence of hunting dogs in pictures in the National Museum in Budapest (Hungary). These are described as white, but what's unique about white hunting dogs?——they cavort across every tapestry in Europe. Yellow dogs are hard to find. Only two have come under my notice in art till now—a white-colored one tearing at a deer in a French canvas, and a portly, sleek Puggish one on a Dutch work exhibited in the magnificent "Age of Rembrandt" collection exhibited in the United States a few years ago.

One modern American hunting-breeds writer feels that the Magyar tribesmen could not have owned elegant hunting dogs, only coarse sheepherding sorts. Conceding that the Vizsla as now we recognize it is a modern production, that is yet no proof that the tribesmen necessarily lacked swift elegant non-herding sorts to work for the falcon. These people valued fine horse stock, nationally still do. A man who appreciates a good horse appreciates a good and elegant dog. The thought was in the forefront of my mind one day, standing in a square in Budapest, where a remarkable group of statuary portrayed Arpad and his Chieftains of a thousand years ago, mounted on superb horses with manes billowing to their fetlocks and deer-horn sets for tack. What manner of dogs went with such men in their hunting?

The development, or say the fate, of national dog breeds is linked with the fortune of the nations that sponsor them. Thus the yellow dog of Hungary appears to have endured yo-yo periods of peace and war, surviving the sweep of invaders and the results of his people taking the wrong side when great nations quarreled. It was stabilized as a breed in the 19th century with the help of professional gamekeepers introduced to Hungary by aristocratic patrons. These brought with them their dogs out of several countries, Pointers, Irish Setters, and such. The miseries of the World War I period virtually wiped out the gains. Postwar, the aristocratic patrons sponsored a revival, founded a Stud Book on three bitches and a dog to which, from time to time, approved recruits were added. A second wrong-guess as to which side to take led to the over-running of Hungary by the Russians in 1944. A few refugees managed to clear away ahead of the occupying force, taking their Vizslas. Some authorities now say that the dogs so taken were the nation's best.

Some few came later into the hands of various Military Commissions in Hungary. Austria and Czechoslovakia also received quite a few good ones, both of these being good dog-fostering lands likely to improve, not downgrade stock that reached them. Infiltration into Germany came still later. Rudolf Freis dates the increase of German interest in the Magyar Vizsla as becoming noticeable in the 1950s. From there, the way seems to have led into the Lowlands, where the Hongaarse Staande Hound has also established a beachhead. There are Vizslas, Kennel Club–recognized in England too, now in numbers sufficient to compete for Challenge Certificates.

America seemed to have received a first specimen when Joseph Pulitzer brought his sister a gift in 1938. It would be long thereafter before numbers and interest built up sufficiently to justify official AKC recognition, given in 1960. Club establishment was sponsored by the late Colonel Jeno Dus, bringing two favorite dogs to the United States after World War II, having until then kept Vizsla pedigrees safely for the Hungarian club while on active service.

From a very small beginning in Kansas City the Vizsla Club of America expanded into national interest. The Parent Club Specialty has for years been held in the Midwest which sponsored this, as well as so many other good Sporting breeds during their difficult introductory years.

The Vizsla has great eye-appeal. It seldom goes unnoticed when galleries watch Group judging. "What is that golden dog?" is a common question asked by the attending public. It has also had the good fortune to escape so far the attention of commercial breeders. Just as well. This is no breed for mass production. A kennel-confined, unsocialized Vizsla is as sad a dog as one could see. The breed instincts are backed by a record of aristocratic household associations, as also in the case of the Weimaraner. These need to be people-dogs. Ownerships in Vizslas range by way of a Prince of Monaco as from Pope Pius XII to Zsa Zsa Gabor.

The Vizsla shares also with the Weimaraner and the German Wirehaired Pointer the boon of inbuilt protection against "improvement" by "selective breeding." It would be impossible, surely, to justify the acceptance of a white-patterned Vizsla, a white-and-liver Weimaraner, a smooth-hound-jacketed Wirehaired. For this reason, maybe, these breeds remain their own dogs, retain the versatile working skills infused by those that formed them into breeds. This does not render them very desirable in the eyes of those meshed in the Bird Dog fantasy of performance, which, likely enough, is their Good Luck. Tell the truth, none of them, Vizsla included, do startlingly well in a form of trial competition to which the priority values of their entire inheritances and their physical and mental endowments are opposed. Owners, however, tend to be quiet about the fact that their breed is best suited to forms of trial competition outside the Pointer/Setter sphere, wishing to do their breed's reputation no harm. My thought is that they should yell it forth at the top of their voices! As matters rest they have to play by the prevailing rule or stay home. If they stay home they run the risk of having their breed contemptuously dubbed "show." A successful American Vizsla owner-breeder spells it out: "Even a good hunting dog leaves field trial people cold. No wins or placings in Trials? Forget that dog! Show people are left with the responsibility of keeping breeds looking the way they should. After all, the only true safeguard any sporting breed has is through the fostering of Dual Champions."

True. But the odds are heavy against such as the Vizsla for he is not geared to run a Pointer course, not even a cross-bred Pointer course. His utility and versatility are however well-proven. Under tough German trial judgment he does very well. The German judges approve his "good field manners, enduring search, liking for waterwork and retrieving, his color attractive for field work, and with versatile skills to bring joy to the heart of a hunter" (Freis, p. 134).

Few of these qualities will take him far in American trial competition, especially as his work pattern tends to be close, 150 feet being fairly general.

Climatic conditions don't bother him much. He will work duck in all but the iciest environment, and like his far-back relative the Pointer, he can go long periods without water.

As mentioned in the Hungarian Standard, the breed is "intelligent, docile, quiet, with a type of vivacious temper . . . affectionate. It bears well any guiding. It is obedient but susceptible to bad treatment. It is a many-sided hunting dog." (*Standard for Magyar Fajtak* (Hungarian Breeds), Budapest, 1966).

The Vizsla shares also with the English Setter an inability to support harshness. Bullwhips are not for this one, nor electronic jolts.

It was my privilege in 1968 to see, within a few months, two representative entries of Vizsla competition, at Budapest, Hungary in May; at Ravenna, Ohio, in August. Both were Specialties, with entries in each case around the hundred, but contrasts were considerable. Though the Vizsla is what the Germans describe in a dog as *finesellig* (fine-celled, elegant) there is a point at which this quality can become the over-light, the shelly (as the Germans also concede in assessing agonizing problems of modern Shorthair drift). Breed appeal did not lack in Budapest, but anatomical substance and essential soundness was to question. My camera picked up too many bowed fronts and poor rears, lack of depth, maybe matters linked with nutrition. The American entry was far more impressive for quality, and it is my belief that breeders have now nothing to gain from imports out of the land of origin. Breeders have done very well with the Vizsla in America. If it has been necessary for me continually to complain of decades-long American mis-use of European sporting utility breeds in terms of separate field trial employment and classification denied, there is no manner of charge to level against the show folk who really have established the Vizsla here on the soundest of footings. This is not unusual. Many breeds here—Silky Terriers outstandingly one—have gone ahead in quality as compared with the stock to be found now in the lands of origin; one reason advanced is that countries tend to export their best stock for dollar gain.

Interesting to see in Budapest was the entry of Drotszoru Magyar Vizslas, the Wirehaired Vizsla which so far has not reached the United States. The book of Standards given me by the Hungarian Kennel Club explains the variety as having "originated in the 1930s, a spontaneous mutation coming into being in the Hungarian Pointer as a result of crossing with the German Wirehaired Harrier." As one or two of the exhibits seen had patched-color heads of broken hair it seems likely that the "Harrier" was the Wirehaired Pointer. The variety has as yet no international recognition but Hungarian sportsmen "greatly value it for its work on moist ground" (*Standard,* above).

At time of writing there are more than a hundred show champions finished in America, and Bela Hadik set the sights high with his Futaki Darocz, the

Judging Vizsla bitch class in Budapest, Hungary, 1968.—*C. Bede Maxwell.*

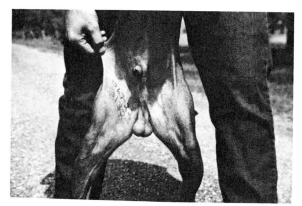

This is a Vizsla, but the application is general. A tattoo protection that protects—the owner's Social Security number on the inside of the thigh. Not so good, perhaps, for coated breeds.—*C. Bede Maxwell.*

317

Am. and Can. Ch. Count Jonish Mignotte, Vizsla Club of America National Specialty winner, 1967. Owner, Elizabeth N. Minotte, Ontario, Canada.

Vizsla litter sisters, Ch. Magyar's Zem Biro and Magyar's Kimyal Zem Biro. Photographed, New Jersey, 1968. Owners, Mr. and Mrs. T. Del Giudice, New York.—*C. Bede Maxwell.*

318

first Vizsla to reach Dual Championship honors. Strains have been established and fine production records already honor many good dogs, waiting out the appearance of a breed definitive work that can compile statistics for which we have no space here. The approved Standard is a very good one, AKC-approved 1963. It includes only one disqualification, penalizing *"deviation in height of more than 2 inches from standard either way,"* a liberal allowance. The size is given as males to 22–24″; females 21–23″.

Examination of the quaintly translated Hungarian standard helps establish what original breeders valued. Heads—"gaunt and noble . . . vigorously sinewy, along the middle-line somewhat stitched; in state of rest the forehead is smooth. The eye-arches are medium developed. The stopline shows a moderate curvature. The frontal part of the muzzle ends bluntly in every direction and it does not get pointed."

Loose lips and deep-set, pop eyes are disapproved but tight eyelids are mandatory. Eye color is "always of a hue darker than the hair," and "hawk, fish, or black eyes" disallowed. The Hungarian makes no mention of nose color. The American does, reminding a judge that this must be brown, never black or slate-grey. Both Standards ask for thin ears (important!) silky, proportionately long, rounded at the ends.

Body is in harmony with breed type, never heavy or over-fleshy, and in running gear "too much angulation at the hocks (is) as faulty as too little." There have always been judges who fall for over-angulation in many breeds.

Feet are cat, that is rounded rather than spoon (hare) shaped. Both Standards emphasize close toes, thick pads, and object to dewclaws, which in the Hungarian are identified as "bastard fingers." Bastard thumbs might be even more accurate. The dog possesses only in rudimentary form the wonderful tool that made civilization possible. Also worth mentioning, the AKC has some concern presently that Standards shall be more explicit in references made to dewclaws, pro or con.

The Hungarian description of the Vizsla tail sent me to Webster: "The tail is attached a bit low and is of moderate thickness. It is cut off; only two-thirds are left. So it reaches the popliteal space . . ." Webster defines popliteal as "of or pertaining to the ham or back part of the leg behind the knee joint." There is also the advice that "while moving the tail it is kept horizontally." Many Vizslas are ring-posed with Boxer-pegged tails but one notes such drop to proper position in gaiting. It is one of the several troubles for handlers that while American field trial fashion wants tails up, the natural construction of purebreds favors the straight or the down, as per the breed standards. The latent danger can be illustrated with examples from the German Shorthair rings these days, where many dogs are appearing with tails as naturally high-set-and-carried as in any terrier ring. Remembering Arkwright's famous dictum: "for the certificate of blue blood, apply at the

319

other end" (tail end!), my hope is that Vizslas, with that inbuilt protection against "selective breeding," may escape any alteration in the anatomical construction of their hinderparts. My own practice in the rings is to ask the handler to correctly position the tail of any mishandled dog that seems likely to interest me to place.

That this is no mere personal idiosyncrasy is established by the Vizsla Standard: *"Tail: Set just below the level of the back, thicker at the root, and docked one third off."*

Coat is to be smooth and dense, lacking undercoat, and of color range from rusty-gold to dark sandy yellow. One feels it unlikely that the Vizsla will ever lapse into the dubious pale creams that (in England especially) have become so noticeable in "Golden" Retrievers. Any tendency should be firmly scotched by the parent club.

Though the fortunes of the Golden Pointer of Hungary have been at times precarious, one feels that in his present world-wide dispersal and increasing popularity his future is safeguarded. He is in good hands.

A puppy is BORN with correct construction. If he doesn't have it at this age, exercise won't develop it, nor prayer produce it. A Vizsla baby.—*photo by the late C. Y. Smith.*

320

Vizslas love to play—land or water. L. to r.: Twiggy, Jinks, and Trixie, or to give them their full names: Twiggy, Behi Neves Hanos, and Ch. Behi's Csinos Csiny, C.D. Owners: Mr. and Mrs. B. C. Boggs, Springfield, Ohio.

You could call it seduction! Vizsla, Ch. Glen Cottage D'hadur.

Am. and Can. Ch. Gourmet's Sardar. This superb dog compiled a remarkable show record including several BIS honors, rarely falling to Weimaraners. His sound, balanced construction, adequate body length to facilitate good movement, his breed-true head qualities, contributed to his success also as a sire. His stud record includes 14 champion get. Owner, Mrs. Emma Muster, Illinois.

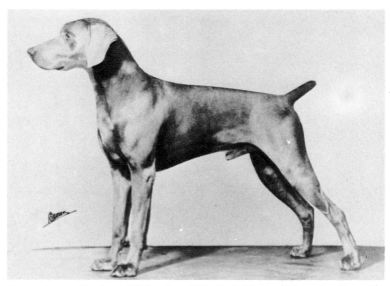

Am. and Can. Ch. Ann's Rickey Boy, C.D. (Int. Ch. Deal's Sporting True Aim II ex Int. Ch. Ann's Sidney Sue). Best in Show winning Weimaraner. Breeder-Owner, Mrs. Ann Kepler, Pennsylvania.—*Brown.*

The Weimaraner

OF all the introduced European sporting utility breeds, the Weimaraner may have had it hardest in America, not least because his early promotion had such a disastrous effect upon his eventual acceptance. The need to outlive the "Wonder Dog" tag made his way difficult, even painful.

Of European utility breeds now recognized this is chronologically the oldest. He was known long before the time the Germans call the *kynological,* that rich dog-productive last quarter of the 19th century. He differs radically from all the others in that he is the only one that has nothing of English Pointer infusion in his makeup, as from his origins anyway. He was around for centuries, the Grey One, before Prinz zu Solms-Brauenfels sponsored the fashionable if brief interest in English Pointers in Germany. He differs further from those breeds fashioned in the 19th century in that he is wholly a hound and managed to retain the status. Like all early-time German hounds he could and still can use his good nose on birds, and do modest bird work whenever such is required of him, but anciently and modernly he was most used as a tracking hound, as were and are the *Schweisshunde* with whom his original kinship is so close, and his color, in mutation, derived.

In Germany he is not particularly numerous. Wherever owned, however, he earns his keep in the same versatile employment as other breeds, including water work at which he is so good. That he does better in some work than in others is not to hold against him. He does all manner of hunting chores but is not required to shine or even to aspire to specialist eminence in any. No one in Europe would expect him to run a Big Circuit Pointer course, or even the approximation of such, but he outshines any Pointer as a *Verlorenbringer* (retriever-tracker) or a *Todverbeller* (finding and baying the dead) .

His name must have been drawn from the city of Goethe and Schiller but no one claims he actually originated there. Merely, it was a focal gathering place for princes and nobles interested in pageantry of sport, and he was there treasured for the rarity of his color, silver or mouse-grey sprung as mutations from the Schweisshund inheritance which is firmly within the red-yellow range. It is important to remember this, for there are still those who believe his grey is dilute black—which it is not. Many of him still demonstrate in the form of sheen, the illusive suggestion of the brown (red) color that is his birthright in a spectacular, changed form.

Just how old in time his breed may be is difficult to establish. Of course there is the famous Van Dyke picture of young Prinz Rupprecht v.d. Pfalz, now housed in the Hofmuseum, Vienna, Austria. My reproduction of this shows the tall grey dog as recognizably Weimaraner type, though one would reject him nowadays in the breed ring with his needle nose, high round skull, pigeon breast and the front that put his forefeet together like shoes outside a hotel-room door.

From centuries of cherishing in princely houses, in the 19th century he filtered down to lesser men, maybe as his numbers somewhat increased. A Weimaraner Club, in Thuringia was formed in 1897. It denied ownership to non-members, forbade promotion and publicity, restricted breeding to maintaining current numbers, ordered drastic litter culling, forbade export. Stud Book entry was difficult to achieve. A first brace, brought to America by Mr. Howard Knight proved to have been sterilized before export. Later, as war clouds gathered over Europe, Mr. Knight was luckier, securing fresh, uncut dogs, of which the bitch, Aura v. Gaiberg, proved to possess a pre-potency that endured down the generations, matched perhaps only by that of the great Shorthair import matron, Arta v. Hohreusch, that came to the United States about the same time.

Early Weimaraner sponsors (the Club was formed in 1941) faced the same problem as Dr. Thornton had faced earlier, seeking a proper slot for his Shorthairs in the late 1920s. No one in America knew how to classify correctly these imports in the several breeds, not even as late as the time of Weimaraner recognition. There just was no understanding of a Do-It-All breed of dog. We know now, in this our time, that Dr. Thornton was in sad error in battling AKC to secure recognition for his Shorthairs as "Pointers." His trouble, of course, was that under any lack of such designation he would not have been able to sell them, his being a time in which dog men were in general rather considerably less informed concerning dog character in general than the average wise guy is even nowadays. He could not reason-

324

ably accept the designation merely of "Shorthair" which AKC favored at the time. Yet all subsequent ills of mis-management and mis-classification of the European breeds stemmed likely from Dr. Thornton's success in getting his dogs classified as "Pointers." If nothing else, it helped to make cross-breeding appear to be reasonable as "merely in the family."

The Weimaraner was caught in the same wrong classification trap. Nowadays, however, his sponsors are in benefit from the first steps taken officially to compound with the results of the errors of the past. There comes to be hope of more suitable competitive classification—which inevitably will have to battle entrenched opposition, active and passive, from those with a stake in the status quo.

The Weimaraner Club of America sponsors most excellent Shooting Dog and Retrieving Dog Tests, much in the manner of the Working Certificate tests for Retrieving breeds—geared to demonstrate the natural working abilities of the individual dogs. These, called "rating tests" are open to all Weimaraners whose owners are members of the W.C.A. They are "for use in rating the hunting and field ability of individual Weimaraners on a common and equal basis. The Degrees awarded to qualifying dogs may be used as a permanent record for purposes of breeding, advertising, etc.

"The Ratings are divided into two separate classifications: one covering pointing and upland bird field work, and the other covering retrieving. The two classifications are completely independent from, and not related to each other. However, a dog showing outstanding ability by obtaining degrees in both classifications would be greatly desired."

Such Ratings provide the owner whose interests (and financial status) do not lean towards licensed Field Trial competition, with the opportunity to train his dog and have its abilities tested on an official basis. As in the Retrieving breeds, the Rating becomes part of the dog's official record.

The worst thing, however, to happen to the Weimaraner was that "Wonder Dog" promotion. It has taken time to mute the blowing of horns, the blaring of trumpets. When the "Grey Ghost" proved unable to match the Big-Going Pointer fantasy he suffered severely in repute. Registrations plummeted as original promoters sheared away from the breed on which they had wrought so much harm. It took longer for the news to filter down to backyard breeders and commercials who had hoped to reap a harvest that had been however already fully gathered. A columnist in the *American Kennel Gazette* spelled out the pitiful truth of whole litters of purebred Weimaraners sent into animal shelters for sheer inability to sell them.

As always, following exploitation, there appear those dedicates who work to stabilize the breeds. "Show people" maintained the Weimaraner as a breed just as Irish Setter "show people" maintained the red dog when the field interests discarded it (See Irish Setter chapter.) The Weimaraner folk carried a further burden in that not every Weimaraner is geared to show business. Mrs. Tony Gwinner, of California, than whom none modernly exhibit more successfully in the breed, has the professional's objective approach: "Good show ring temperament in a Weimaraner has to be *there*—an absolute must. If we could only convince every owner of that! This includes importantly high head carriage which, in turn, calls for denial of the ancient hound endowment that tends to drop heads down."

If a show dog has the instinct to drop the head, a gallows' show-lead won't necessarily persuade it to carry the head high. Who in the judging ring has not watched dogs gag and choke their distress in high-dragged handling? High-dragged handling often, in many breeds with instinct to carry the head down, has exactly the opposite effect to what is intended; the dog fights the lead even harder to get the head down and be free to breathe. Many the dog sent by me down the way again on "loose lead please" that moves out in a much better style, able to breathe, and able to get his legs under him to find his correct center of gravity.

A show Weimaraner must also look like the breed he is supposed to be, not like a grey Shorthair or Vizsla. Sometimes, when dog magazines print their black-and-white photos, one has to look at the caption to satisfy oneself what breed of dog is pictured. The Weimaraner should never be other than unmistakably what he is. He is not just a grey dog, he is a special kind of dog, different in shape and make—including underline. He has heavier bone, should not be Americanized into an elegance that, while it may please some judicial eyes, is not correct for him. He should never be stacked like an Irish Setter, and he should not have low-slung ears, though one does find dogs with such off-type characteristics preserved in photographs of some very successful winners in times not so far past.

He is a big dog—legitimately 25–27″ for males; 23–25″ for females, with leeway of an inch below or above, beyond which tolerance a disqualification clause operates. This, by the way, is a fairly recent introduction, added to the revised Standard approved in 1965. Amusingly, some few months after this revision appeared, a Shorthair owner who is rabid on the subject of size and dedicated to the hope of corsetting the Shorthair inside restrictions told me solemnly how beneficial the Weimaraner disqualification clause had already proved to be to that breed. Within six months!

Weimaraner heads are wrinkle-free, devoid of exaggeration, somewhat pronounced of occiput. Noses are grey, pink undesirable, but turned back lips may show pink. Black inside the mouth and lips is a serious fault. Muzzles are required to be strong and neat, snipiness objectionable as a hindrance to retrieving. Long, high-set folded ears represent the ideal.

Many dislike the Weimaraner eye, condemn the breed because of it. It is not possible in this breed to have coat color without the linked eye color.

A Weimaraner's best tool is his excellent nose. This fine fellow, owned by Mr. and Mrs. John Guzevich, Las Cruces, New Mexico, employed at tracing fallen missile parts on the White Sands Testing Range. That missile parts are treated with shark oil helped in the search success.—*Photo, Photographic Section, White Sands Missile Range, N.M. Especial thanks to the Measurements Division (U.S. Army) for permission to use.*

Longcoated Weimaraners, infrequently seen, crop up in litters from time to time.

Standards (English and American) say the Weimaraner eye darkens under excitement. Pupil dilation? The reason is not known to me nor has the phenomenon so far come to my own attention. If for excitement one should read anger then my aim is not even to have it come to my attention.

Temperament is very important (as in all breeds) and to be fostered by good management. This is no breed to be allowed to get out of hand.

Color is acceptable from mouse to silver grey, with the small white chest spot permitted as in most breeds—this ancient dog endowment that defies all breeders' efforts in virtually all breeds to defeat it. The German Standard emphasizes the need to repudiate any red or yellow in the coat, but a long coat, here a disqualification, is allowed in Germany in a dog with four registered Weimaraner generations behind it. It is not known to me if such a dog is also eligible to show or whether the situation is as that applicable to the Gordon Setter, where in both England and America a red whelp from registered parents is registerable but not eligible to show. The German philosophy in respect of the long Weimaraner's coat it "it is not likely to happen very often."

Feet are to be strong, high-arched toes, webbed, strong-nailed, and dew-claws are for removal—with this Standard also lacking the specific direction AKC would prefer—front legs? Back legs? Both?

If dewclaws are to be removed, the time is in the nest, a few days after birth. If delayed a few months, surgery becomes major. My Cattle Dog came over from Australia with front dewclaws so long and sharp it became a case of her dewclaws or my arms to the elbows, all her loving, scoring pats! She came home with 5 stitches up each leg (at age 6 months) and the citronella on the bandages to stop her chewing them off practically moved me out of the house! In the nest the removal is an affair of a minute or so.

Tail: The Weimaraner appears by common consent to have higher tail carriage than the other breeds as none of his Standards make specific demand, as do the Standards of the other breeds, for low set-on or carriage in line with, or below the back. The possibility is that this remains one of his basic hound endowments and so higher carriage is proper. The direction is that *"it should be carried in a manner expressing confidence and sound temperament,"* but its positioning may have as much to do with anatomical hound construction proper to the breed. It is of course always docked.

Gait asks that topline be strong and level, which likely translates as taut. The English Standard includes the interesting observation that the walk of the Weimaraner is "rather awkward." Many breeds of big dogs go awkwardly at the walk which, in truth, is not a natural gait for the canine race which in slow motion favors the trot or lope. It has always seemed to me, especially in the restrictive indoor judgings, reasonable to query mentally the rightness of judicial direction to "take him again, and slowly this time, please." Most

328

English-bred Weimaraner quality, in best specimens, is very high. Eng. Sh. Ch. Ragstone Remus was BOB at Crufts, 1967–68. This beautiful dog is now yielding the fray to his young son . . . Owners, Gwillian and Tony Burgoin, Peterborough, England.—*Cooke*.

Ragstone Ritter, the son of Sh. Ch. Remus, does not yet have his title, but already has a BIS. I judged him as a lively, spring-heeled puppy: one to remember. Owners, Gwillian and Tony Burgoin, Peterborough, England.—*Pearce*.

big breeds fall justifiably apart. As has been said already, an awful lot of nonsense tends to be talked around in respect of dog gait, and the greatest triumph, especially in galleryites, tends too often to be in terms of "I don't like the way he goes behind." There are so many imponderables in the assessment of a dog's gait in show ring restriction, indoor especially, that it has never seemed reasonable to me to damn a good dog only in terms of what he happens to do with his back legs in the artificiality of the ring. My assessment of a dog's soundness and muscle tone is made with my hands *before* he moves. Frank Longmore, to whose memory this work is dedicated, taught me that so many years ago the number entirely escapes me. My approval is never for a judge who operates as did one who wrote in his English critique his reason for dumping a famous dog: "I caught him standing wrong!" So he did, damn his poor judgment! The same applies to those who might have "caught him moving wrong!" in some awkward and restricted environment.

English breeders currently do well by the Weimaraner. Introduced only in 1952, the breed had to weather insular prejudice, of course. The first litter was registered in 1953, but in 1968, walking along the benching at Crufts, my thought was in terms of doubt whether it would be possible to see as many good ones in a long straight line of benching at home. Several fully-qualified (i.e., work qualified) champions have been made, and several show champions as well—and any form of championship has to be fought for there.

In work, the Weimaraner is a very good water dog, and in countries or such American states as permit dog work on deer, can show his inherited qualities, being strong, able, willing to pull down a buck in or out of water. He can however also double as a family dog, proud and protective. He is not for kennel confinement either, nor for harsh treatment. He does not wilt like the Vizsla and one would expect complications if a bullwhip were taken to him, and more power to his pride and his teeth because of it! He has suffered in reputation as a trial dog under the criticism of those who can measure sporting breed worth and performance only with a single vernier. Now that the granting of the requirement to qualify in water work as a prelude to making a Weimaraner field champion operates under AKC rule, there may be hope for eventual re-classification that will spin off all these breeds from Pointer/Setter competition as elsewhere in the world.

The Weimaraner is not necessarily an "easy" breed but undoubtedly a satisfactory one for those who foster it. There is reward for the breeder who undertakes the task realistically, avoids the trap of starting with poor stock. Life isn't long enough to grade up dog breeds—just to screen out any single fault, any breed, can count up to a matter of multiple generations.

Recently, a first Best in Show award fell to Ch. Gwinner's Sportswheel, for the past few years the top-winning dog in the breed as, in an earlier time, his sire, Ch. Gwinner's Pinwheel, was before him. Mrs. Gwinner wrote how

Am. Ch. Gwinner's Pinwheel (Am. & Can. Ch. Johnson's Arco v.d. Auger ex Ch. Cati v.d. Gretchenhof), top Weimaraner for 1963–64. Owners: Mr. and Mrs. Tony Gwinner, California.—*Francis.*

Am. and Can. Ch. Gwinner's Sportswheel followed his sire's example, and even improved upon it. Top Winning Weimaraner (Phillips System) for 1966–67–68, and in 1969 added a BIS to his laurels. Owners, Tony and Beatrice Gwinner, California.—*Bennett Associates.*

proud she is "that two Weimaraner champions live with her." She notes that: "Proud is defined in Webster as 'pleased or satisfied, something regarded as highly honorable and creditable to oneself.' All these years I have tried so hard to add something very honorable to the breed I dearly love . . . so I am proud!"

The label of "Wonder Dog" long since outworn, the Grey Ghost stands now four-square on his merits wherever he is kept in the world. May he always be in the care of those who have the intention, "highly honorable and creditable," to do the best they can for him.

Ch. Kris-Miss Shadow, C.D., Weimaraner. An excellent show bitch that is credited with an ever-lengthening list of titles and pointed offspring. Owners: Karla and Martin South, California.

Epilogue

MORE than three years later; more than many thousands of miles travelled in a roster of countries in both hemispheres; acres of print, ancient and modern, studied; who knows how many typewriter ribbons worn out . . . this that went before in these pages is the distillation of it all. No writer can ever guess what will be the verdict passed in respect of work done, however faithfully, but maybe Mrs. Gwinner will permit me to borrow and to say that I too have tried very hard to add something honorable and creditable towards the better understanding of the Sporting breeds that I hold so dear.

C. BEDE MAXWELL

Bibliography

AMERICAN KENNEL CLUB, *The Complete Dog Book*, Garden City, N.Y., Garden City Books, 1968.

ARKWRIGHT, WILLIAM, *The Pointer and His Predecessors*, Humphreys, 1902.

A'WOOD, ANTHONY, *Athenae Oxoniensis*.

BEILBY, WALTER, *The Dog in Australia*, Melbourne, Geo. Robertson, 1897.

BERJEAU, CHARLES, *Varieties of Dogs, as Found in Old Sculptures, Pictures, Engravings, Books*, London, 1866.

BERNERS, DAME JULIANA, *Boke of St. Albans*, 1496.

BEWICK, THOMAS, *A General History of Quadrupeds*, England, 1792.

BOWTELL, KEVIN (Editor), *The Labrador Retriever in Australia*, 1961.

BRITISH GORDON SETTER CLUB, *Handbook*, 1958.

BROWN, CAPTAIN THOMAS, *Biographical Sketches and Authentic Anecdotes of Dogs*, Edinburgh, 1829.

CAIUS, JOHANNES, *Of English Dogges* (English translation, 1576, of Latin original, 1550).

CANADIAN KENNEL CLUB, *Book of Breed Standards*, 1962.

CARTWRIGHT, GEORGE, Esq., *Journal of Transactions & Events during Residence of Nearly 16 years on the Coast of Labrador*, Newark (England), 1792. 3 vols. (Also in reprint, 1911.)

COMPTON, HERBERT, *The Twentieth Century Dog*, Sporting Sec. Vol. II, London, Grant Richards, 1904.

COX, NICHOLAS, *The Gentleman's Recreation*,

DALZIEL, HUGH, *British Dogs*, 1888 et sel., Upcott Gill.

DANIEL, REV. WILLIAM B., *Daniel's Rural Sports*, England, Bunny & Gold, 1802–3.

DE BYLANDT, COUNT HENRI, *Dogs of All Nations*, Kegan Paul, Trench, Trubner & Co., 1905.

DE FOIX, GASTON, *Livre de Chase*, English translation, Edward, 2nd Duke of York, 1406–1413. (Modern translation, Chatto and Windus, 1909.)

DENLINGER, MILO G., *The Complete Cocker Spaniel*, Denlinger, 1946.

DE TOURNES, JEAN, *Sketch Book,* Pub. Lyons, France, 1556.

DOBSON, WILLIAM, *Kunopaedia,* London, 1814.

EARL, MAUD, *The Power of the Dog,* London, Hodder & Stoughton, 1912.

EDWARDS, SYDENHAM, *Cynographia Britannica,* London, 1800–5.

FIENNES, RICHARD and ALICE, *The Natural History of Dogs,* New York, Natural History Press, 1970.

FREVILLE, *Les Chiens Celebres,* Paris, 1796.

FRIESS, RUDOLF, *Unsere Jagdhunde,* BLV Verlagsgesellschaft, 1960.

GAYOT, EUG., *Le Chien Histoire Naturelle,* Paris, 1867.

GERMAN SHORTHAIRED POINTER CLUB OF AMERICA, *Year Books.*

GILL, JOAN, *Golden Retrievers,* London, W. & G. Foyle, 1962.

GLEIG, GEORGE ROBERT, *A Narrative of the Campaigns of the British Army at Washington and New Orleans, in the Years 1814–15.* London, Murray, 1821.

GOODALL, CHARLES S., *The Complete English Springer Spaniel,* New York, Howell Book House, 1951.

GOETZ, THEODOR, *Hunde Gallerie oder Nature Getreue Darstellung des Hundes,* Weimar, 1838.

GOLDEN RETRIEVER CLUB OF AMERICA, *Year Books.*

GORDON SETTER CLUB OF AMERICA, *Year Books,* 1939–1968.

GORNY, *Ein Hundebuch,* Germany, circa 1940.

GRAHAM, JOSEPH, *The Sporting Dog,* London, The Macmillan Co., 1904.

HAMILTON-SMITH, LT. COL. CHARLES, *Mammalia,* Vol. II, Edinburgh, 1843.

HERBERT, HENRY WILLIAM ("Frank Forester"), *Field Sports of the U.S.,* 2 vols., Woodward, N.Y., 1859.

HILL, FRANK WARNER, *The Labrador Retriever,* London, W. & G. Foyle, 1960.

HOCHWALD, ALBERT FREDERICK, *Bird Dogs, Their History and Achievements,* Cincinnati, Sportsman's Digest, 1922.

————, *Makers of Bird Dog History,* pub. author, 1927.

HOOPER, MRS. MORLAND, *The English Springer Spaniel.*

HUNGARIAN KENNEL CLUB, *Book of Breed Standards* (1966) and *Show Catalog,* 1968.

HUSBERG, C. and McCARTHY, D., *Leo Wilson on Dogs,* London, Robert Hale, 1969.

HUTCHINSON, WALTER (Editor), *Hutchinson's Dog Encyclopaedia,* London, Hutchinson & Co., 1935 (circa).

JESSE, GEORGE R., *Researches into the History of the British Dog,* London, 1866.

KELLER, GEORG, *Pointer und Setter,* Otto Meissners Verlag, 1964.

KENNEL CLUB, THE (England), *Stud Books, Crufts' Catalogs.*

LAUGHTON, DR. NANCY, *A Review of the Flatcoated Retriever,* 1968.

LITTLE, CLARENCE C., Sc. D., *The Inheritance of Coat Color in Dogs,* New York, Howell Book House, 1967.

LYON, MCDOWELL, *The Dog in Action,* New York, Howell Book House, 1963.

MACDONALD DALY, LOLA, *The Pointer as a Show Dog,* Manchester, "Our Dogs" Publishing Co., circa 1940.

MARR, HERR WALDEMAR, *Pointers and Setters.*

MARKHAM, GERVASE, *Hunger's Prevention, or The Whole Art of Fowling,* London, 1621.

MARPLES, THEO., *"Our Dogs" publications,* England.

MATHEWS, V. A. H., *The Cocker Spaniel,* Oxford University Press, 1949.

MAXWELL, *Field Book of Sports and Pastimes in the United Kingdom,* London, 1833.

MEYER, MR. and MRS. R. WILTON, *How to Raise and Train A Clumber Spaniel*, New Jersey, T.F.H. Publications, 1965.

MILLER, C. O. and GILBERT, E. N., *The Complete Afghan Hound*, New York, Howell Book House, 1965.

MOFFIT, ELLA B., *The Cocker Spaniel*, New York, Orange-Judd Publishing Co., 1947.

NATIONAL GEOGRAPHIC SOCIETY, *The Book of Dogs*, Washington, D.C., 1919.

———, *Greece and Rome*, 1969.

PEARCE, REV. THOMAS ("Idstone") , *The Dog*, Cassell, Petter and Galpin, 1872.

PHILLIPS, C. A. and CANE, R. CLAUDE, *The Sporting Spaniel*, "Our Dogs" Publishing Co., 1920.

REDLICH, ANNA, *Dogs of Ireland*, Dundalk, Dundalgan Press, 1949.

REVOIL, BENEDICT HENRI, *Histoire Physiologique et Anecdotique des Chiens*, preface par Alexandre Dumas, Paris, 1867.

RICHARDSON, V., *The Curly-Coated Retriever in Australia*, 1968.

RIEDEL, J. F., *Icones Animalum*.

ROSLIN-WILLIAMS, MARY, *The Dual Purpose Labrador*, London, Pelham Books, 1969.

RUTHERFORD, CONSTANCE, *How to Raise and Train an American Water Spaniel*, New Jersey, T.F.H. Publications, 1968.

SCHILBRED, LT. COL. CORNELIUS, *Irish Setter History*, Maryland, Denlingers, 1949.

SCOTT, MARY, *The English Springer Spaniel*, London, Nicholson and Watson, 1960.

SEIGER and DEWITZ-COLPIN, *The Complete German Shorthaired Pointer*, Maryland, Denlinger, 1951.

SHAW, VERO, *Illustrated Book of the Dog*, London, Cassell, 1890.

SOCIETE ROYALE SAINT-HUBERT, *Catalog Brussels Show*, 1968.

SOLARO, GIUSEPPI, *Il Pointer*, 2nd Edition, Italy, Nicolosi, 1954.

SPERLING, HEINRICH, *Feine Nasen, Sketches, Feld und Wild*, Germany, 1889.

SURFLEET, RICHARD, *Maison Rustique, or The Country Farm*. French publication translated by Surfleet, a "practitioner in physicke," London, 1606.

TAPLIN, WILLIAM, *Sportsmen's Cabinet, or a Correct Delineation of the Canine Race*, 2 vols., 1803–4.

THOMPSON, WILLIAM C., *The New Irish Setter*, New York, Howell Book House, 1968. Also earlier editions.

TOPSELL, *Historie of the Four-Footed Beasts*, 1607.

TUCK, DAVIS H., *The Complete English Setter*, New York, Howell Book House Inc.

TURBERVILLE, GEORGE Esq., *The Noble Art of Venerie or Hunting*, London, 1576.

VERBAND FÜR KLEINE MÜNSTERLÄNDER, Kleine Münsterländer Vorstehhunde, 1962.

VEREIN PUDELPOINTER, *Der Pudelpointer*, 1965.

VICTORIA and ALBERT MUSEUM, *Bulletin, July 1966*, Vol. II, No. I. London.

WALSH, JOHN HENRY, M.D., ("Stonehenge") , Various editions. First edition, pub. Cox, 1867.

WARWICK, HELEN, *The Complete Labrador Retriever*, New York, Howell Book House, 1964.

WINGE, DR. OJVIND, *Inheritance in Dogs, with Special Ref. to Hunting Breeds*, Trans. Roberts, Comstock Publishing Co., 1950.

WHITE, FRED Z., *The Brittany in America*, 1965.

YOUATT, WILLIAM, *The Dog*, London, 1838.

H22 057 273 9

A CHARGE
IS MADE FOR
REMOVED OR
DAMAGED
LABELS.

Richmond 31163 (imp.)

Mena II.

Sir Simon 24501

Belle of Furness 19516

Royal Albert 20307

Sir Alister 10165

Rock 4280

Meg (Cockerton's)

Sir Alister 10165

Novelty 12567

Royal IV. 7175

Tam o' Shanter 6118

Daisy 6130

Lill (Pilkington's) 8313

Dash II. (Laver-ack's)

Countess

Rall

Tam o' Shanter 6118

Daisy 6130

Novel 9163

Rum 1555

Rock 4280

Old Kate (Arm-strong's)

Blue Prince 4269

Belle (Laver-ack's)

Rock (Laver-ack's)

Cora II.

Daisy 1486

Dash 1342

Bess (Lort's)

Fred II. 1372

Rock 4280 •
Rum 1555 •

Blue Prince 4269 •
Old Kate •

Flame (Cockerton's)

Blue Prince II. 6097

Dash 1342 •

Flame 4290

Belle

Bess

{ Rall •
Countess •

{ Cora †

Blue Prince 4269 •

Carrie 1703

Rock

{ Bess
{ Pure Laverack dog †
{ Nell †

{ Bob 1700

{ Quall

{ Ranger †
{ Nell †

{ Judy
{ Rover †
{ Flonnce †

{ Dash (Geoff's) †
{ Fan †

Nellie 1833

Pride of the Bor-der 4376

Belle (Laver-ack's)
Cora (Blair's)

Rock (Laver-ack's)

Cora I.

Fred I. 1841

Sting (Laver-ack's)

Cora (Blair's)

Rock II.

Jet 1885

Duchess (Walker's)

Dash II. 1341 •
Pilkington's Lill 8213 •

Dash II. 1341
Moll III.

Fred I. 1871

Belle II.

{ Dash II. (Laverack's) 1341 •
{ Lill (Pilkington's) 8313 •

{ Dash II. (Laverack's) 1341 •
{ Kate (Armstrong's) †

{ Dash II. (Laverack's) 1341 •
{ Moll III. (Laverack's)

{ Dash II. 1341
{ Belle II.

{ Dash II. 1341
{ Moll III. (Laverack's)

{ Fred I. 1871 •
{ Cora (Blair's) •

{ Fred I. 1841 •
{ Cora I.

{ Cora (Blair's)
{ Jet I.

{ Jet I.
{ Regent

{ Fred I. 1871 •
{ Belle II.

{ Sting •
{ Cora II. •

{ Cora I. •
{ Belle I. •

{ Dash I. •
{ Belle I. •

{ Moll II.

{ Pilot •

{ Regent •

{ Pilot
{ Moll II.

{ Dash I.
{ Belle I.

{ Pilot
{ Moll II.

{ Dash I. •
{ Belle I. •

{ Ponto †
{ Old Moll †

{ Dash I. •
{ Belle I. •

{ Ponto †
{ Old Moll †